D1362014

SAY IT LIKE OBAMA

AND WIN!

THE POWER OF SPEAKING WITH PURPOSE AND VISION

SHEL LEANNE

Revised and Expanded
Third Edition

New York Chicago San Francisco Lisbon
London Madrid Mexico City
Milan New Delhi San Juan Seoul
Singapore Sydney Toronto

1 2 3 4 5 6 7 8 9 10   DOC/DOC   1 8 7 6 5 4 3 2

ISBN 978-0-07-180270-3
MHID 0-07-180270-3

e-ISBN 978-0-07-180271-0
e-MHID 0-07-180271-1

McGraw-Hill books are available at special quantity discounts to use as premiums and sales promotions or for use in corporate training programs. To contact a representative, please e-mail us at bulksales@mcgraw-hill.com.

This book is printed on acid-free paper.

CONTENTS

CHAPTER 8

FACING AND OVERCOMING CONTROVERSY

175

CHAPTER 9

MOTIVATING OTHERS TO ACTION AND LEAVING STRONG LAST IMPRESSIONS

192

ACKNOWLEDGMENTS

Over the years, I have greatly enjoyed teaching about leadership, focusing on leadership best practices and topics such as building high-performing teams, leading high-performing teams, and building a strong "personal brand." As I have taught or spoken on such topics in a wide variety of environments, leaders of all backgrounds and levels of achievement—from seasoned CEOs to young emerging leaders—have inquired about President Barack Obama. Regardless as to whether they support Obama's stances or not, they have universally viewed President Obama as a highly accomplished orator whose strength as a communicator has enabled him to gain the support of millions of people and helped him to make history. "What is President Obama doing?" they have asked. What best practices and techniques enable his success, and what can they learn? This book is intended to address these questions, providing a valuable glimpse into one of the most accomplished speakers in recent years.

Writing this book has been particularly fascinating for me given the depth of my work in South Africa. Since the 1990s, I have had the pleasure of meeting some of South Africa's greatest leaders—who are indeed among the world's most esteemed leaders—including President Nelson Mandela, Archbishop Desmond Tutu, Walter Sisulu, and Senator Govan Mbeki. I have greatly benefited from their examples and from our exchanges, and I have since enjoyed sharing some of the lessons I have learned from them through my leadership development work. Both in the United States and abroad, I have seen that some of the world's greatest leaders have been seeking the same goal—a world in which, as Martin Luther King Jr. put it, people would be judged not "by the color of their skin, but by the content of their character." In light of this background, it was intriguing for me to write this book assessing some of the factors that have helped make President Barack Obama one of the most distinguished communicators of recent times. It is clear that in many ways, Obama represents what many influential leaders of earlier generations had hoped to see.

I would like here to thank the many people who have supported me over the years. Thank you to my son, Joshua, for being the light of my life. A special thank-you to my parents, Barbara Geiger and the late Dr. David N. Geiger, and my siblings and their spouses. Thank you to Christine Baker and Aunt Mildred Geiger, who have provided such mentoring, love, and support. Thank you to my wonderful friends Ted Small, Audrey Gross-Stratford, Yvonne Chang, Ruby Lue Holloway, Jennifer Gonzalez, Cynthia Haines, Lorelee Dodge, and Bonnie St. John. A hearty thank-you must go also to my cousins, and to my aunts and uncles and their families, including William Geiger, Edward Geiger, Sr., Joyce Montgomery, Thomas and Eunice Holloway, Andrew Geiger, and Johnnie Scott. I also gratefully acknowledge the faculty and staff of St. Jeanne de Lestonnac School.

Very importantly, a huge thank-you to Mary Glenn, Zachary Gajewski, Janice Race, and Tania Loghmani of McGraw-Hill, and to Alice Peck.

"Absolutely masterful. He's a master of the craft."

Those words have described the oratorical strength of Barack Obama, who took the stage at the 2004 Democratic National Convention and electrified America with a rousing keynote address. His twenty-minute speech—less than 2,300 words—captured the imaginations of Americans and garnered praise from around the world. Obama successfully drove his points home, fused the best of rhetoric and substance, focused on a powerful message, and delivered it with great effectiveness. His words and vision inspired millions of viewers. The media instantly dubbed Obama a "Rising Star" and Obama's stirring keynote delivery greatly accelerated the trajectory of his career, transforming him overnight into a distinguished national political figure. Obama went on to successfully build one of the most diverse political movements in American history, shattering historic barriers and becoming the presumptive 2008 Democratic presidential nominee. Few things have helped fuel Obama's rapid political ascension more than his outstanding communication skills.

Say It Like Obama and Win! focuses on the communicative power of Barack Obama and the practices and techniques that have enabled him to take his place as one of the most notable orators of recent times. Obama's successes underscore a well-established fact: Leaders in all fields benefit when they develop outstanding communication skills, because the ability to convey vision, inspire confidence, persuade, and motivate others is key to effective leadership.

The words used to describe Obama's oratory style—*charismatic, magnetic, energizing*—speak to his strength as a communicator. So, too, do the adjectives invoked to characterize his speeches: *eloquent, inspiring, compelling*. Many observers consider Obama such an accomplished speaker that they compare him with the great communicators of our era—Martin Luther King Jr., John F. Kennedy, Robert Kennedy, Bill Clinton, and Ronald Reagan. Even overseas, Obama's talents and vision have generated excitement. In June 2008, the media widely noted that Europeans were deeply attracted to Obama's "mixture of Martin Luther King and John F. Kennedy." Populations abroad were described as "euphoric" in the aftermath of Obama's victory in the Democratic primary.[1] This enthusiasm was highly evident in July 2008, when Obama attracted an audience of 200,000 for a single speech in Berlin, Germany. Since assuming the presidency, Obama has continued to receive praise. Jonathan Freedland of the *The Guardian* wrote of Obama's "On a New Beginning" speech delivered in Cairo, Egypt, that President Obama "demonstrated not only his trademark eloquence but also the sheer ambition of his purpose—nothing less than bridging the divide between Islam and the west. . . . as [Obama] has proved, a major address can have a major impact—and there will be few more masterful speeches than this one."[2] President Obama has received equal praise for many other speeches, notable among them his acceptance address in 2008, his inaugural address, his 2011 Tucson speech following the tragic shooting of Congressional representative Gabrielle Giffords, his remarks on the resignation of General Stanley McChrystal, his remarks following the death of Osama bin Laden, and the remarks that allowed him to ease concerns following the Gulf oil spill of 2010.

What is President Obama doing? What communication practices have enabled him to move rapidly from obscurity, overcoming challenges that could have thwarted another candidate—his race, his youth, his "exotic" name—to become one of the most important figures in the Democratic Party and subsequently "leader of the free world"? What oratory skills account for his ability to bring such disparate segments of society together, "transcending" race, energizing millennials (generation Y voters), and inspiring newcomers—young and old—to participate in the electoral process? How does Obama manage to break down so many barriers? How does he connect so well with listeners, moving them on both an emotional and intellectual level as he translates his vision into the impulse to act? What can leaders in all arenas—business, politics, law, nonprofit, and academia—learn from him?

Regardless of what you think of his politics, Obama's achievements since the 2004 Democratic National Convention are striking. Four short years after his keynote address, the first-term junior U.S. Senator who ranked toward the very bottom in Senate seniority went up against the "Clinton machine" in an improbable quest for the Democratic presidential nomination. Obama stepped into a significant place in history when he passed the critical 2118 delegate threshold to become the presumptive Democratic presidential nominee, making him the first African American to ever become a major party nominee for U.S. president. It was a historic victory, a watershed moment that many people had believed unthinkable during their lifetimes. Significantly, Obama accepted the Democratic presidential nomination on August 28, 2008, only 45 years from the very day that Martin Luther King Jr. stood on the Lincoln Memorial and delivered his iconic "I Have a Dream" speech. As the late commentator Tim Russert aptly observed on June 3, 2008: "When you sit and reflect just for a . . . second about what we are witnessing—this young 46-year-old African American man, now the nominee of the Democratic Party. Just put that in the context of our nation and the whole issue of race—it's breathtaking."

Underpinning these notable achievements are Obama's communication abilities. His outstanding oration helped set in motion a so-called "phenomenon," with Obama's American rallies attracting audiences as large as 75,000.[3] Observers—noting Obama's accomplishment in expanding the electoral base in an unprecedented manner—called his effort more than a campaign; they deemed it a "movement." Given his popularity, Obama even affected popular parlance with newly minted words and phrases such as *Obama Mamas, Obamacans, Obamacize, Obamanomics, Obamamentum,* and *Obamamania.* With a donor base of nearly two million in 2008 and millions again in 2012, more individuals are believed to have contributed to Obama's campaigns than to any other presidential candidate in American history.

Many people credited Obama's astonishing campaign success in 2008 partly to his powerful messages of hope that transcended traditional divisions of party, economics, gender, religion, region, and race. Indeed, the themes of his 2008 campaign speeches appealed to significant numbers of people. Consider some of the themes: *Forging a New Future for America, A*

More Perfect Union, Keeping America's Promise, Reclaiming the American Dream, Our Moment Is Now, A New Beginning, Our Common Stake in America's Prosperity, Take Back America.

Given the strength of Obama's message, Governor Bill Richardson called Obama's candidacy a "once in a lifetime opportunity for our country" and referred to Obama as "a once in a lifetime leader." Caroline Kennedy concurred in her January 27, 2008, *New York Times* article entitled "A President Like My Father":

> Over the years, I've been deeply moved by the people who've told me they wished they could feel inspired and hopeful about America the way people did when my father was president. . . . All my life, people have told me that my father changed their lives, that they got involved in public service or politics because he asked them to. And the generation he inspired has passed that spirit on to its children. I meet young people who were born long after John F. Kennedy was president, yet who ask me how to live out his ideals.
>
> Sometimes it takes a while to recognize that someone has a special ability to get us to believe in ourselves, to tie that belief to our highest ideals and imagine that together we can do great things. In those rare moments, when such a person comes along, we need to put aside our plans and reach for what we know is possible.
>
> We have that kind of opportunity with President Obama.[4]

But there have been other advocates for the middle class and the poor. There have been other leaders with impressive personal stories. There have also been other leaders who have spoken words of unity and goodwill. What made Obama so compelling in 2008 and what has allowed his personal approval ratings to remain so relatively high while in office as U.S. president? It is more than the message: *it is also how the message is delivered.* This is acknowledged even from across the political aisle. As Louisiana's Republican Governor Bobby Jindal commented on August 10, 2008, "Senator Obama is one of the best speakers—one of the most inspiring speakers—I've seen in a political generation. You have to go back to President Ronald Reagan to really see somebody who's that articulate." Jindal noted that through excellent communication, Obama greatly inspires and motivates people.[5] And indeed, throughout the Republican primary contest of 2011–2012, many Republicans repeatedly voiced their concerns, insisting that in order to be competitive, the Republicans had to select as a presidential candidate someone strong enough to debate with President Obama. Oration, most observers agree, is one of Obama's key assets.

The sources of Obama's oratory strength are many. The natural resonance of his deep baritone is an asset. Buttressing this is his impressive ability to control his voice, which he wields like a fine-tuned instrument. Obama has shown he can alter the texture of his tone to become wistful, indignant, pulsing with optimism and determination—whatever the delivery requires. He has shown skill in quickening his cadence, slowing it down, amplifying the wind beneath his words, and allowing his voice to trail when it suits his needs. He has a keen awareness of when to employ pregnant pauses, metered just right—the intervals long enough to drive points home. He is excellent at creating dynamic images and moving people with effective gestures, sometimes with just one finger. Obama also knows how to draw on an impressive range of rhetoric, and he utilizes techniques such as repetition, backward loops, and symbolism to make his pronouncements influence and endure.

Obama knows it isn't enough to form a vision or set goals—success requires an ability to articulate vision and goals in a highly compelling manner. In accounting for Obama's oratorical strength, substance cannot be divorced from style of delivery. *Say It Like Obama and Win!* examines the lessons to be learned from the excellent communication practices that have helped bring about Obama's successes. It illuminates how leaders in all fields—business, politics, law, nonprofit, and academia—can draw from those best practices in order to develop excellent communication abilities.

Chapter 1 presents and annotates the full text of Barack Obama's 2004 Democratic Convention keynote address—the speech that started it all. An examination of this speech reveals many of the key practices Obama employs that give him such distinguished communicative power. Each subsequent chapter delves more deeply into the communication and leadership lessons that we can learn, exploring a variety of Obama's public pronouncements.

Chapter 2, "Earning Trust and Confidence," examines practices that have enabled Obama to inspire and motivate so many people so quickly, winning over many skeptics with his charisma. His success illustrates the importance of a strong first impression and how leveraging an excellent second impression helps foster trust and confidence. We'll look at how his exemplary use of nonverbal language as well as his ability to layer meaning beneath his words work together for striking results.

Chapter 3, "Breaking Down Barriers," explores Obama's exceptional skill in using oration to unify disparate groups. His forthrightness in acknowledging his unconventional background, combined with his skill in projecting this background as "quintessentially American" and his ability to establish common ground, are assets. Reinforcing this, Obama's ability to employ words that resonate has helped him build bridges, drawing out what brings people together rather than what sets them apart.

Chapter 4, "Winning Hearts and Minds," examines the best practices that have helped Barack Obama elicit reactions such as, "His words moved me," and "He understands." His speeches are far from mere recitations—he has demonstrated a remarkable ability to connect with listeners. Key has been his talent for knowing his audiences and identifying the issues they most care about. We'll discuss how he has been able to speak to those issues and how he has succeeded in communicating his empathy and personalizing his messages. What are the techniques behind his style that make the podium and lectern disappear, creating a sense of dinner table talk, as if you are speaking to him one-to-one? We will learn.

Chapter 5, "Conveying Vision," explores practices that have enabled Barack Obama to get his point across so effectively. It studies the lessons to be learned from his skill in using descriptive, multidimensional words, rich with corollary meaning. His ability to humanize ideas, themes, and emotions, to employ backward loops and to recount effective anecdotes distinguish him as a speaker, as do the ways he crystallizes his points so that they're remembered long after he has delivered a speech.

Chapter 6, "Driving Points Home," delves into techniques Obama employs to distill his main issues, making them dominant in the listener's mind. Despite significant time constraints—many of his speeches are only twenty minutes long—Obama speaks very effectively, employing an impressive range of rhetorical techniques to convey powerful messages. Among these techniques are conduplicatio, anaphora, epistrophe, mesodiplosis, alliteration, and tricolon. Fancy names, remarkable impact. We show how these techniques allow Obama to home in on key thematic ideas. We also explore how Obama communicates takeaways and slogans with such great effectiveness that many people can recite those slogans with ease.

Chapter 7, "Persuading," explores lessons to be learned about the practices Obama uses to bring others to his way of thinking. When seeking to do more than convey information, but also to impact opinion and encourage action, Obama pays particular attention to emphasizing a strong sense of logic, sequencing ideas, and addressing nonrhetorical questions. Particularly notable is his use of juxtaposition and the antithesis structure as hallmarks of his persuasion style, comparing and contrasting ideas excellently. Together, these techniques help him to elicit a "yes" response—the nod of affirmation of the persuaded listener.

Chapter 8, "Facing and Overcoming Controversy," takes a look at how Barack Obama uses his strong communication skills to weather and survive controversy, often defusing it and mitigating any damaging effects. Whether addressing a poor choice of words or dousing the fire set by the incendiary remarks of Reverend Jeremiah Wright, we see how Obama's communication practices have aided him in efforts to face and overcome controversies. His sincerity, as well as his tendency to address errors head-on and to accept responsibility while standing strong in his beliefs, offers many lessons.

Chapter 9, "Motivating Others to Action and Leaving Strong Last Impressions," explores the communication practices that have helped Obama motivate people to take action. It delves into the tools Obama uses to convey a sense of momentum and build a sense of urgency, while adopting a communication style that makes him seem more accessible to the audience, as if speaking one-to-one. It also explores how Barack Obama's communication style enables him to build to a crescendo, underscoring memorable takeaways and ending strong.

Chapter 10, "Speeches That Made History," includes historical speeches that Barack Obama gave both shortly before he assumed the office of the U.S. presidency and during his first four years in office as president of the United States. These speeches include Barack Obama's 2008 nomination acceptance speech, 2008 election night victory speech, 2009 presidential inaugural address, 2009 Middle East speech "On a New Beginning," 2009 remarks on financial reform, 2009 speech before the United Nations General Assembly, 2011 announcement of the death of Osama bin Laden, and 2012 State of the Union address. They illustrate some of Obama's hallmark communication techniques and practices. We have much to learn from these techniques and practices that, together, have helped make Barack Obama one of the most outstanding communicators.

CHAPTER 1

THE SPEECH THAT STARTED IT ALL

On a night of the 2004 Democratic National Convention, Barack Obama stepped onstage and electrified America with his keynote address. His discourse, widely hailed as inspiring and eloquent, provides a valuable snapshot of the excellent communication practices Obama employs as he harnesses the power of speaking with purpose and vision. Through his delivery, we learn how substance and style can work together to increase the effectiveness and impact of communication.

This chapter presents the 2004 keynote address in full. Obama's written words are annotated with references to some of the gestures, tone, and pacing techniques he employed in delivering his career-accelerating address. Let's look at what made the 2004 speech such a success.

⇥ 2004 DEMOCRATIC NATIONAL CONVENTION ⇤ KEYNOTE ADDRESS, JULY 27, 2004

In the minutes before Barack Obama takes to the stage, Illinois Senator Dick Durbin sings Obama's praises to the Boston audience and to millions of TV viewers. He refers to Barack Obama as a man whose "life celebrates the opportunity of America . . . family reflects the hope of an embracing nation . . . values rekindle our faith in a new generation. . . ." He praises Obama for having "the extraordinary gift to bring people together of all different backgrounds."

Barack Obama walks onto the stage with a brisk, purposeful, confident gait. He makes immediate visual contact with the audience, clapping his hands along with them—the first signs of connection. He stretches his arm toward the audience in an open-palmed wave and then greets Durbin with a warm embrace that signifies the deep respect of dear friends. With applause still ringing, Obama makes his way to the lectern, planting his feet firmly, shoulders squared. He touches each hand to the lectern, possessing it—a posture of confidence and authority. With chin lifted, he bows ever so slightly to the audience, his gesture of appreciation and gratitude. As the applause continues, Obama folds his hands neatly on the lectern and smiles humbly, seeming to gain strength from the crowd's enthusiasm.

As the applause subsides, Obama thanks Senator Durbin. He takes in a breath and the resonant baritone of his voice rolls as he begins his 2004 Democratic National Convention keynote address:

On behalf of the great state of Illinois, [*the crowd applauds, and Obama's eyes sparkle with pride at speaking the name of his home state*] crossroads of a nation [*pause*], Land of Lincoln, let me express my deepest gratitude for the privilege of addressing this convention. [*He reaches out to the audience with open hands, conveying his gratitude.*]

Tonight is a particular honor for me because, let's face it, my presence on this stage is pretty unlikely. [*Obama places his hand over his heart. His intonation underscores the irony of the circumstances.*] My father was a foreign student, born and raised in a small village in Kenya. He grew up herding goats, went to school in a tin-roof shack. His father, my grandfather, was a cook, a domestic servant to the British. [*He pinches the fingers of his right hand, underscoring his point.*]

But my grandfather had larger dreams for his son. [*Obama stretches his palms upward, as if measuring the enormity of the dreams.*] Through hard work and perseverance my father got a scholarship to study in a *magical* place: *America* [*italics added for emphasis*], that shone as a beacon of freedom and opportunity to so many who had come before. [*His inflection conveys patriotic pride and generates applause.*]

While studying here, my father met my mother. She was born in a town on the other side of the world, in Kansas. [*Obama gestures with a hand off in a direction, indicating far, far away. He flashes a bright smile toward the part of the crowd that cheers upon hearing "Kansas" and waves to them in a tender gesture.*] Her father worked on oil rigs and farms through most of the Depression. The day after Pearl Harbor my grandfather signed up for duty, joined Patton's army, marched across Europe. Back home, my grandmother raised a baby *and* [*emphasis*] went to work on a bomber assembly line. After the war, they studied on the GI Bill, bought a house through FHA, and later moved west, all the way to Hawaii, in search of opportunity.

And they, too, had big dreams for their daughter, a common dream, born of two continents. My parents shared not only an improbable love; they shared an *abiding* faith in the possibilities of this nation. [*Obama speaks the words with pride and reverence; his hand extended to the audience, signifying shared awe in all the United States has to give.*]

They would give me an African name, Barack, or "blessed," [*he touches his hand over his heart*] believing that in a *tolerant* [*emphasis*] America [*he pinches the fingers of his right hand*] your name is no barrier to success. [*Applause.*] They *imagined* me going to the best schools in the land, *even though they weren't rich*, because in a *generous* America you don't have to be rich [*he raises a palm to the crowd, a little stop sign, as if to halt any notion that richness is a precursor to success*] to achieve your potential. [*Applause.*] They are both passed away now. Yet, I know that, on this night, they look down on me with great pride.

I stand here today, grateful for the diversity of my heritage, aware that my parents' dreams live on in my two precious daughters. [*Sincerity rings in his tone.*] I stand here knowing that my story is part of the larger American story [*he stretches a hand to the audience, reaching out to them*], that I owe a debt to all of those who came before me, and that, in no other country on earth, is my story even possible. [*He pinches his fingers with those words, his voice bursting with pride. He pauses as some audience members rise in ovation.*]

Tonight, we gather to affirm the greatness of our nation, not because of the height of our skyscrapers, or the power of our military, or the size of our economy. Our pride is based on a very simple premise, summed up in a declaration made over two hundred years ago, "We hold these truths to be self-evident, [*he amplifies his voice slightly, speaking the patriotic words with care and curls his right fingers into a C, motioning in front of him as if setting the words on air*] that all men are created equal. [*Applause.*] That they are endowed by their Creator with certain inalienable rights. That among these are life, liberty, and the pursuit of happiness."

That [*emphasis*] is the true genius of America, [*applause*] a faith in simple dreams, an insistence on small miracles. That we can tuck in our children at night and know they are fed and clothed and safe from harm. That we can say what we think, write what we think, without hearing a sudden knock on the door. [*Obama knocks a balled fist on an imaginary door.*] That we can have an idea and start our own business without paying a bribe. That we can participate in the political process without fear of retribution, and that our votes will be counted—at least, most of the time. [*He allows his tone to fall flat, disapproving, signaling a wry reference to the disputed 2000 U.S. presidential election results. The audience responds with jeers, sharing his disapproval.*]

This year, in this election, we are called to reaffirm our values and our commitments, to hold them against a hard reality, and see how we are measuring up to the legacy of our forebearers and the promise of future generations. And fellow Americans—Democrats, Republicans, Independents—I say to you tonight: we have more work to do. [*Obama stresses the words, his tone issuing the statement as a challenge. More applause.*] More work to do for the workers I met in Galesburg, Illinois, who are losing their union jobs at the Maytag plant that's moving to Mexico, and now are having to compete with their own children for jobs that pay seven bucks an hour. [*His tone rings with disapproval.*] More to do for the father that I met who was losing his job and choking back the tears, wondering how he would pay $4,500 a month for the drugs his son needs without the health benefits that he counted on. [*His tone conveys great empathy.*] More to do for the young woman in East St. Louis, and thousands more like her, who *has the grades, has the drive, has the will,* [*he emphasizes the words and his slight pauses add power to the delivery*] but doesn't have the money to go to college.

Now, don't get me wrong. The people I meet in small towns and big cities, in diners and office parks, they don't expect government to solve all their problems. They know they have to work hard to get ahead, and *they want to.* [*Obama stresses the words as he pinches his fingers to further accentuate his statement.*] Go into the collar counties around Chicago, and people will tell you they don't want their tax money wasted by a welfare agency *or by the Pentagon.* [*His amplification of these last four words makes a negative reference to the Iraq War, drawing reaction from the audience.*] Go into any inner city neighborhood, and folks will tell you that government alone can't teach our kids to learn. They know that parents have to teach, that children can't achieve unless we raise their expectations [*he gestures upward as if raising a bar*], and turn off the television sets and eradicate the slander that says a black youth with a book is acting white. [*He wags his index finger, as if chastising someone for that belief.*] They know those things. [*Enthusiastic applause.*] People don't expect government to solve all their problems. [*He lifts a vertical palm to the audience, as if halting the very notion.*] But they sense, *deep in their bones,* [*he raises a soft fist and thumps it in air*] that with just a slight change in priorities, [*he moves his right fingers as if turning a knob slightly to adjust it*] we can make sure that every child in America has a decent shot at life, and that the doors of opportunity remain open to all. *They know,* [*he pinches his fingers, underscoring his emphasis of the words*] we can do better, [*a brief pause*] and they want that choice.

In this election, [*Obama raises his index finger in the air, raising it like a staff*] we offer that choice. Our party has chosen a man to lead us who embodies the best this country has to offer. [*Pride rings in his tone.*] And that man is John Kerry. [*His tone is firm and resolute. Applause.*] John Kerry understands the ideals of community, faith, and service, because they've defined his life. [*He pinches his fingers to give each word weight.*] From his heroic service in Vietnam to his years as prosecutor and lieutenant governor, through two decades in the United States Senate, he has devoted himself to this country. [*He turns both palms upward, as if presenting a gift or offering, underscoring his description of Kerry's devotion and service.*] Again and again, we've seen him make tough choices when easier ones were available. His values and his record affirm what is best in us. [*He varies his tone and amplifies his volume.*]

John Kerry believes in an America where hard work is rewarded. So instead of offering tax breaks to companies shipping jobs overseas, [*Obama motions his hand off dismissively to the right*] he offers them to companies creating jobs here at home. [*He moves both hands to the left as if moving an object to where it belongs, signifying how much more Kerry would give to the alternative of keeping jobs at home. Applause.*]

John Kerry believes in an America where *all* [*emphasis*] Americans can afford the same health coverage our politicians in Washington have for themselves. [*Applause.*] John Kerry believes in energy independence, so we aren't held hostage to the profits of oil companies [*Obama motions his hand like a stop sign*] or the sabotage of foreign oil fields. [*Applause.*] John Kerry believes in the constitutional freedoms that have made our country the envy of the world, and he will never sacrifice our basic liberties nor use faith as a wedge to divide us. [*Pause for applause.*] And John Kerry believes that in a dangerous world, war must be an option sometimes, [*he points his index finger in the air, signifying the importance*] but it should never be the *first* [*emphasis*] option. [*Applause.*]   Willy

A while back, I met a young man named Shamus in a VFW Hall in East Moline, Illinois. He was a good-looking kid, six-two, six-three, clear-eyed, with an easy smile [*the texture of Obama's tone is wistful, conveying admiration*]. He told me he'd joined the marines and was heading to Iraq the following week. As I listened to him explain why he'd enlisted, the absolute faith he had in our country and its leaders, his devotion to duty and service, I thought this young man was all that any of us might ever hope for in a child [*he speaks the words with tender affection*]. But then I asked myself: Are we serving Shamus as well as he's serving us? I thought of the 900 men and women, sons and daughters, husbands and wives, friends and neighbors, who won't be returning to their own hometowns. I thought of families I had met who were struggling to get by without a loved one's full income, or whose loved ones had returned with a limb missing or nerves shattered, but still lacked long-term health benefits because they were reservists. [*Disappointment rings in his voice. Applause.*] When we send our young men and women into harm's way, we have a solemn obligation, [*he rests his palm over his heart*] not to fudge the numbers [*he raises his hand in a stop sign*] or shade the truth about why they're going, to care for their families while they're gone, [*he points an index finger, emphasizing the importance*] to tend to the soldiers upon their return, and to *never* [*pause*] *ever* [*he amplifies his voice greatly*] go to war without enough troops to *win* the war, *secure* the peace, and *earn the respect of the world.* [*He stresses the words, amplifying each to build to a high. Audience members rise in ovation.*]

Now let me be clear. [*Obama motions his index finger up in the air.*] We have real enemies in the world. These enemies must be *found*. [*He pinches his fingers. A slight pause gives gravity to the words.*] They must be *pursued*, [*his hand gesture underscores the importance of "pursuing"*] and they must be *defeated*. [*He pinches his fingers at these words, highlighting their importance.*] John Kerry knows this. And just as *Lieutenant* [*emphasis*] Kerry did not hesitate to risk his life to protect the men who served with him in Vietnam, *President* [*emphasis*] Kerry will not hesitate *one moment* [*emphasis*] to use our military might to keep America safe and secure. John Kerry *believes* [*emphasis*] in America. And he knows that it's not enough for just some of us to prosper. [*He moves his index finger in the air.*] For alongside our famous individualism, there's another ingredient in the American saga. [*His tone conveys a challenge beneath his words.*]

A belief that <u>we're all connected as one people</u>. [*His tone is filled with wistful, patriotic pride.*] If there's a child on the south side of Chicago who can't read, that *matters to me,* [*he moves his hand to his chest, stressing the heartfelt words*] even if it's not my child. [*Obama speaks the words with sincerity and evokes applause.*] If there's a senior citizen somewhere who can't pay for their prescription drug and has to choose between medicine and the rent, that makes my life poorer, even if it's not my grandparent. [*He places his hand tenderly over his heart and draws more applause.*] If there's an Arab American family being rounded up without benefit of an attorney or due process, [*he amplifies his tone*] that threatens *my* [*emphasis*] civil liberties. [*He taps a closed fist at his chest, drawing loud cheers from the audience. He pauses as applause rings on.*] It is that fundamental belief—*I am my brother's keeper,* [*he raises his volume even more, and his voice rings with moral rightness as he slices a hand through the air*] *I am my sister's keeper* [*he cuts his hand through the air again, making eye contact with the other side of the audience*]—that makes this country work. [*Applause.*] It's what allows us to pursue our individual dreams, and yet still come together as one American family. [*His tone grows reflective.*] E pluribus unum. [*He enunciates each word carefully, curls his right fingers into a C and motions as if placing the words on air for the audience to see, and gives a dramatic pause.*] Out of many, one. [*He lowers his pitch to emphasize the translation and curls his left fingers into a C, motioning again as if placing the words on air.*]

Now, even as we speak, there are those who are preparing to divide us, the spin masters, the negative ad peddlers who embrace the politics of anything goes. Well, I say to them tonight, there is not a *liberal* [*emphasis*] America and a *conservative* America [*he amplifies his volume, his tone mocking the notions*]—there is the *United States of America.* [*Obama enunciates each word carefully— U-ni-ted-States-of-A-mer-i-ca—moving his fingers as if writing in cursive. Applause.*] There is not a *black America* [*emphasis*] and *white America* [*emphasis*] and Latino America and Asian America; there's the *United States of America.* [*He enunciates the words carefully again, giving them dramatic impact. Applause.*] The pundits like to slice and dice our country into red states and blue states. [*His tone mocks the practice.*] Red states for Republicans, blue states for Democrats. But I've got news for them, too. [*He raises his index finger, chastising the pundits.*] We worship an awesome God [*he stresses the words, raising his hands and amplifying his voice to signify God's greatness*] in the blue states, and we don't like federal agents poking around in our libraries in the red states. [*He increases his cadence dramatically, underscoring the point. Applause.*] We coach Little League in the blue states and yes we've got some gay friends in the red states. [*Applause.*] There are patriots who opposed the war in Iraq and there are patriots who supported the war in Iraq. We are *one* [*emphasis*] people, *all of us* [*emphasis*] pledging allegiance to the stars and stripes, *all of us* [*emphasis*] defending the [*pause*] *United States of America.* [*He punches the words—U-ni-ted-States-of-A-mer-i-ca—scrawling his fingers as if writing in cursive. Applause. The electrified audience starts chanting "Obama! Obama!"*]

In the end, that's what this election is about. Do we participate in a politics of cynicism [*his voice falls flat, signaling disapproval*] or do we participate in a politics of hope? [*Obama raises his pitch, sounding hopeful and expectant. The crowd shouts out, "Hope!" as if participating in a "call and response."*] John Kerry calls on us to hope. John Edwards calls on us to hope. I'm not talking about blind optimism here—the almost willful ignorance that thinks unemployment will go away if we just don't think about it, or the health care crisis will solve itself if we just ignore it. That's not what I'm talking about. I'm talking about something *more substantial.* [*Emphasis.*] It's *the hope* [*emphasis*] of slaves sitting around a fire singing freedom songs; *the hope* [*emphasis*] of immigrants setting out for distant shores; *the hope* [*emphasis*] of a young naval lieutenant bravely patrolling the Mekong Delta; *the hope* [*emphasis*] of a mill worker's son who dares to defy the odds; *the hope* [*emphasis*] of a *skinny kid* [*emphasis*] with a funny name [*he thumps his palm against his chest, indicating he is speaking of himself*] who believes that America has a place for him, too. [*He reaches open palms toward his listeners. The audience goes wild with adulation, the applause extending so long that Obama adds two sentences as the cheers continue.*] Hope [*emphasis*] in the face of difficulty. [*His amplified words signify his approval of the audience's reaction.*] Hope in the face of uncertainty. [*He keeps his volume powerful.*] The audacity of hope! [*His volume rises.*]

In the end, that is God's greatest gift to us, the *bedrock* [*emphasis*] of this nation; *a belief* [*emphasis*] in things not seen; *a belief* [*emphasis*] that there are better days ahead. [*Passion resonates in Obama's voice.*] I believe [*emphasis*] that we can give our middle class relief and provide working families with a road to opportunity. *I believe* [*emphasis*] we can provide jobs to the jobless, homes to the homeless, and reclaim young people in cities across America from violence and despair. *I believe* [*emphasis*] that we have a righteous wind in our backs and that as we stand on the crossroads of history, we can make the right choices and meet the challenges that face us. *America!* [*Emphasis.*] Tonight! [*The intensity of his tone rings like a challenge, reaching a crescendo.*]

If you feel the *same energy* [*emphasis*] that I do, if you feel the *same urgency* [*emphasis*] that I do, if you feel the *same passion* [*emphasis*] that I do, if you feel the *same hopefulness* [*emphasis*] that I do—if we do what we *must* do, then I have *no doubt* that all across the country, from Florida to Oregon, [*he slices a hand through the air*] from Washington to Maine, [*he slices a hand through air again, his inflections rising and falling to convey the breadth of the geography, from coast to coast*] the people will rise up in November, and John Kerry will be sworn in as president, and John Edwards will be sworn in as vice president, and this country will reclaim its promise, and out of this long political darkness a brighter day will come.

Thank you very much everybody. [*He stretches his arm high, waving good-bye.*] God bless you. [*The energized audience rises in full ovation, with some people chanting "Obama! Obama!"; emphases provided.*]

In this 2004 keynote address, we see many of the outstanding communication practices that have helped make Barack Obama one of the most compelling speakers of our time. Public and media praise for Obama's keynote address was immediate. "One of the best [addresses] we've heard in many, many years. . . . He's a rising star," Wolf Blitzer declared. "That's as good as they come. . . . This is a fellow who is talking beyond the Democratic base to the whole country. . . . It was terrific," political analyst Jeff Greenfield commented. In the days to come, the press continued to commend the address as a masterpiece of oration. Many of the outstanding communication techniques Obama employed during his keynote address are worth highlighting here.

⇥ EFFECTIVE USE OF BODY ⇤
LANGUAGE AND VOICE

In the delivery of his 2004 keynote address, Barack Obama demonstrated outstanding use of body language. His confident gait, squared shoulders, and commanding stance reached out to the audience, set the tone, and opened a positive dialogue with the viewing public. In short, Obama created a very strong first impression. The deep timbre of his voice, his natural asset, heightened the positive impression. The way he controlled his voice—amplifying it when appropriate, gliding up a half-octave when needed, or allowing it to fall flat to denote disapproval—gave power to his words and helped highlight his key themes. Varying the emotional texture of his tone—making it wistful at times, affectionate at others, and indignant when appropriate—also gave great depth to his words.

Obama's gestures were equally effective—knocking on an imaginary door with a balled fist, pinching his fingers, placing imaginary words on air, holding his palm like a stop sign. They all combined to drive points home. Similarly, placing his hand over his heart at key moments conveyed the sincerity of his words. Obama came across as authentic. His gestures served as masterful elements of delivery.

⇥ ESTABLISHING COMMON GROUND ⇤

In the keynote address, we also see how Barack Obama addressed the "elephant in the room"—his unconventional background, which he skillfully projected as a quintessentially American story of immigration, hard work, and the American Dream. Obama wove in references to his family and Pearl Harbor, Patton's army, a U.S. bomber assembly line, the GI Bill, and FHA mortgage funding, thereby connecting himself to historic "apple pie" American experiences. The mention of these American hallmarks became his credentials for asserting that, in spite of his "exotic" name, he was just like every American. Obama placed himself squarely in the progression of history, demonstrating that he was dreaming the same dreams as most Americans.

Obama's choice of words also helped establish common ground. *Generous America. Beacon of freedom and opportunity. Faith in the possibilities of this nation.* This language resonated with the audience, tapping into patriotic sentiment. In a masterful way, Obama also wove in references to bible verses: *Belief in things not seen . . . I am my brother's keeper. . . . I am my sister's keeper. . . .* He lauded these references as "simple truth." The biblical words and principles reached across divisions of race, class, and party, helping him to connect with the audience. Simultaneously, Obama demonstrated his talents as he effortlessly transitioned from discussing biblical truths and linking them to America, to relating these truths to what *he* believes, creating the sense of a strong continuum. With these techniques, Obama successfully broke down barriers and built bridges.

⊰ SPEAKING TO AUDIENCE CONCERNS: ⊱ WINNING HEARTS AND MINDS

Obama demonstrated his ability to tap into the prevailing mood, strengthening the impact of his words by providing details and personalizing his message. When he spoke about the prevailing mood of many Americans who were tired of old-style politicking, he said, "There's not a liberal America and a conservative America. There's a United States of America." Like leaders such as John F. Kennedy, Obama made a meaningful connection with his audience.

As Obama offered specific examples about Americans facing challenges—like a father who had lost his job and needed to pay for his son's medicine—he connected with the audience, demonstrating that he understood intimately the concerns of middle America and could relate to these challenges. Similarly, as he personalized his message, explaining his deeply held belief in helping the middle class and working families, he won people over by speaking to them directly, almost intimately, and illustrating that their concerns were his concerns too.

CONVEYING VISION THROUGH PERSONALIZATION AND WORDS THAT RESONATE

In his keynote address, Obama employed a wide range of techniques to convey his vision. Vivid language, symbolic words, and personalized ideas were among his tools. His language painted pictures in the minds of listeners: *Slice and dicing us . . . We are one people, all of us pledging allegiance to the Stars and Stripes.* He tied the notion of hope to the experiences of slaves and immigrants and personalized the issue of the Iraq War through references to one particular soldier—Shamus—whose "easy smile" we could visualize instantly. These all provided rich, multilayered communication, conveying vision and ideas excellently.

⇥ DRIVING POINTS HOME ⇤

Obama also employed an effective range of rhetorical techniques as he drove his central points home. Repetition was a primary tool. His repeated references to hope, with carefully constructed sentence structures, underscored the theme. Similarly, stating "John Kerry believes" five times in six sentences reinforced the image of Kerry that Obama sought to stress. Obama's skillful use of repetition focused attention on key themes, making them more memorable.

⇥ EXCELLENT PERSUASION TECHNIQUES ⇤

In the 2004 keynote address, we also saw one of Obama's hallmark practices for persuasion: the use of juxtaposition for comparison and contrast. For instance, juxtaposition helped him crystallize the importance of the country's founding principles:

> Tonight, we gather to affirm the greatness of our nation, not because of the height of our skyscrapers, or the power of our military, or the size of our economy. Our pride is based on a very simple premise, summed up in a declaration made over two hundred years ago, "We hold these truths to be self-evident, that all men are created equal. That they are endowed by their Creator with certain inalienable rights. That among these are life, liberty, and the pursuit of happiness."

His use of juxtaposition also crystallized the argument that Americans are one people and should move forward with unity:

"There's not a *liberal* America and a *conservative* America—there's the *United States of America*."

⇥ BUILDING TO A CRESCENDO AND LEAVING ⇤ A STRONG LAST IMPRESSION

Finally, few people can forget the outstanding ending to the moving 2004 keynote address. Obama skillfully varied the rhythm of his words, emphasizing words at key times and amplifying his voice progressively as he built toward a crescendo. He knew how to ride the wave of applause so as not to stall momentum. Once he reached his high point, he ended his address passionately, issuing a challenge, a call to action: "Tonight! If you feel the *same energy* that I do, if you feel the *same urgency* that I do, if you feel the *same passion* that I do, if you feel the *same hopefulness* that I do—if we do what we must do, then . . ."

This powerful ending further energized the audience, leaving them a strong last impression.

Together, these highly effective communication practices enabled Obama to deliver a masterful speech that greatly accelerated the trajectory of his political career and transformed him into an influential national political figure. Now, let's delve further into these practices that have made Barack Obama one of the most distinguished orators of recent times.

CHAPTER 2

EARNING TRUST AND CONFIDENCE

If you aspire to be a highly effective leader, people must trust your judgment and ethics and have confidence in your leadership abilities, believing that you are worthy of authority. In the absence of trust and confidence, nothing else follows. A first task of every aspiring leader, therefore, is to earn the trust and confidence of those they seek to lead. Barack Obama has done this with great success, gaining the trust and confidence of a broad array of people—everyday citizens, politicians, policy makers, businesspersons, financial supporters, and young people. Before his ascension to the U.S. presidency, he drew on this trust and confidence to capture key opportunities and expand his influence. Since assuming the presidency, the trust and confidence he has earned has allowed him to cultivate productive foreign relations and retain relatively high personal approval ratings in the United States, even during his most heavily criticized decision-making periods. Key communication practices have helped Obama to earn the trust and confidence of others. Using communication as a tool for gaining support, Obama has displayed great personal charisma. He takes steps to form a strong first impression and to leverage excellent second impressions. He also employs effective gestures, uses props skillfully, gets off to strong beginnings, and conveys admirable ethics. This chapter explores these practices, which have helped Obama to earn the trust and confidence of millions of supporters both at home and abroad.

⇥ CHARISMA OF A LEADER ⇤

Most people say they know charisma when they see it—that certain fire in the eyes, passion, and command. They point, for example, to political leaders such as Martin Luther King Jr., Ronald Reagan, John F. Kennedy, and Bhenazir Bhutto, and to popular leaders such as Oprah Winfrey. Dynamic leaders. Not the sort to give humdrum, droning speeches; far from the listless speaker who is unenthusiastic about their topic.

The words often invoked to describe Barack Obama— magnetic, electrifying, energizing, and inspiring—speak of his charisma as a leader. Obama has a presentation and style that enable him to earn the confidence of listeners, inspire them, and move them to action. He manages to captivate audiences. From the moment he steps in front of an audience with his confident gait, people see a blend of passion and authority. He conveys charisma through many nonverbal attributes—the broad smile; his resonant voice; and body movement suggesting authority. Part of Obama's charisma involves his ability to convey his enthusiasm and passion effectively. He usually appears closely wedded to the things he talks about, cares deeply about the subjects, and is eager to share. His enthusiasm energizes people young and old.

Perhaps as important as having charisma is the ability to use it to establish an excellent first impression. The well-worn saying is true: First impressions last. In rising as fast as he did, from obscurity to his historic 2008 presidential victory, Obama demonstrated and capitalized on a formidable ability to establish a strong first impression.

⇥ CREATING STRONG FIRST IMPRESSIONS— ⇤ IMAGE AND BODY LANGUAGE

A first impression is a critically defining moment. The instant one person first moves into the presence of another, an opinion is formed. Even before you utter any words, you open a dialogue and have spoken volumes through image and body language. The strong first impression that Barack Obama makes reminds us that body movement and image speak a language to the audience as potent as anything said out loud.

Indeed, a highly influential executive coach and author of the book, *CEO Material,* D.A. Benton, once asked a group of young leaders at McKinsey & Company to imagine what they would do if they wanted to make people around them believe they were blind, even though they were not. She prodded them to consider how they would try to look and act. Perhaps they would wear a pair of dark glasses, get a white cane, and use that cane to feel their way across the floor. They might walk slowly or haltingly, displaying a bit of uncertainty about the path ahead. They might even get a guide dog and allow it to steer them down the street. In short, they would dress the part, act the part, and gather the right props. She then asked the group to consider the implications if they were seeking instead to project themselves as leaders.

The exercise was useful. Persons seeking to present themselves as leaders should dress the part, act the part, and gather the right props around them. This is because—without uttering a word—through first impressions these actions begin a dialogue and can lay an important foundation for commanding authority, gaining trust, and exercising effective leadership.

Barack Obama is adept at establishing excellent first impressions. The purposeful walk. The visual contact he makes with audiences early on, stretching his arm to them in a confident wave, narrowing the physical distance between himself and the audience. These mark the beginnings of a two-way conversation of sorts—it elicits a sit-up-and-listen response from audience members.

Good eye contact also has been valuable to Obama. Like Bill Clinton, Obama is perceived as never hesitating to establish firm eye contact; he thrives on connecting with members of his audience and is energized, not drained, by them. As Obama talks, he looks to one side of the room, sometimes with a slight nod of acknowledgment in that direction, and then to the other side. He varies his gaze throughout his discussions; by doing so naturally and smoothly, he pulls listeners in to his talks and engages audience members more fully. Audiences perceive this as respectful—the behavior of a person welcoming them.

They also interpret the actions as trustworthy—the behavior of a person willing to look them in the eyes. Those good first impressions last.

The confidence displayed by Obama's pat-on-the-back greetings with some people who introduce him is also an early action that communicates his comfort. He is at ease. Standing before audiences, feet placed firmly and shoulders squared—the message is one of confidence and authority. Where there is a lectern, he often places his hands on each side of it, taking control. The lectern is clearly not a crutch, nor does Obama allow it to serve as an obstacle between him and the audience.

Imagine if, instead of displaying such confidence, Obama had walked onto the 2004 convention stage with his chin lowered, his gait hesitant, and he had offered only a sheepish wave. What a vastly different image that would have conveyed. By contrast, leaders who walk with a purposeful gait, stretch their arm and wave confidently establish a more commanding image and expand their presence. It is best to get off to a strong start and avoid situations in which you must work hard to reverse the damage of a poor first impression. Outstanding communicators take care to use image and body language in ways that wield a highly positive impact.

⇥ LEVERAGING SECOND IMPRESSIONS— ⇤ VOICE AND INTONATION

Another important means of earning trust and confidence can be seen through effective use of voice and intonation. After a leader comes out with a commanding, confident air, exuding the charisma of a leader, then what? Voice and intonation play a role here; both are important tools for increasing the effectiveness of communication.

Voice

One dimension of voice that creates an immediate impression is the *quality* of the voice—its natural pitch and resonance. For Barack Obama, his commanding baritone is a natural asset. It sounds pleasing to the ears and is very authoritative. For most speakers, natural tone quality can be improved and enhanced with practice and voice techniques.

Beyond natural tone quality, the precise way leaders use their voices becomes important to the impressions formed and how effective a speech ultimately is. There are multiple dimensions of the verbal communication beyond the words actually spoken. *How* the words are said can transform a bland recitation into a powerful speech. The tools of the skillful speaker include volume, voice texture, pitch, pace, and inflection. Effective voice and intonation can move people, make words more memorable, and make the communication more effective overall. Talks, delivered powerfully, can elicit responses such as, "Something tugged inside of me." Barack Obama achieves this sort of impact through skillful use of his voice and intonation, which reinforces the substance of his messages.

Amplification

Barack Obama has shown the power of amplifying the voice at key moments. He uses volume to increase excitement as an audience rallies to his opinions. He knows how to stress important words at the right times, giving them an emphatic feel. He increases his volume when reaching a crescendo, the point when he hits the climax of his talk and underscores a key message. Just as he puts power in his volume when rousing a crowd, he knows how to allow his voice to trail off when speaking of something of which he disapproves. Amplifying and washing away—Barack Obama uses volume to enhance the efficacy of his delivery.

Pacing and Pregnant Pauses

Obama's outstanding use of pacing also greatly enhances the effectiveness of his communication. With well-chosen pacing, he slows when enunciating important ideas he wants to settle into the psyches of the listeners. He adopts clipped sentences at the right times, which helps to drive points home. The increase and decrease of his cadence allows him to draw listeners' attention to his most significant points.

Obama is also adept at leveraging silence and employing pregnant pauses. With pregnant pauses, Obama focuses attention on his more important themes, making his remarks more notable. He is also skilled at knowing when to let the silence endure a bit—very dramatic pauses that often elicit reaction from the audience.

Pitch and Emotional Texture

When assessing what makes Barack Obama such a powerful orator, it is easy to observe that he avoids drab recitations. He skillfully employs his delivery techniques. He has made an art of varying his volume and vocal color. The range of the inflections he uses—changes in the pitch of his voice—is also one of his strengths. He varies how he vocalizes key words, drawing on a range of vocal pitch to deepen the impact of what he says in a manner that cannot be achieved by the written word alone. His voice rises and falls when needed. For example, Obama knows how to drop his pitch, pulling on his lower register, and slow his cadence when he wishes to focus on a point, like underlining key words on a chalkboard.

Obama is also a master of strengthening his communication with vocal color. He can make his voice wistful, hopeful, dismissive, and a host of other emotional textures, as circumstances require. His ability to alter the emotional texture of his voice, which he reinforces with effective gestures, increases the impact of his communication.

Taken together, voice and intonation—emphasizing words at the right time, quickening or slowing the cadence, varying the tonal color, varying the rhythm of words—can result in superior communication power. Speeches and remarks become dynamic and full of impact and thereby part of a successful leader's strategic tool set.

⇥ USING EFFECTIVE GESTURES ⇤

Obama breaks the rule suggesting that gestures should be used sparingly. Frequent gesturing is part of his communication style. This works well for him because the movements are fluid and extensions of his words, and they convey his enthusiasm. They work in tandem with modulations of his voice and tone, and they thereby animate his words, providing valuable dimension to his remarks.

Obama's power as an orator helps illustrate that gestures can improve the impact of communication in multiple ways. For one, when used well, gestures create an impression that a speaker is at ease and relating well with the audience. Barack Obama, in particular, employs gestures in ways that create the feel of a one-to-one conversation, as if he is standing next to you conversing, rather than standing on a podium addressing an audience. His gestures help narrow the distance. Whether this involves an out-stretched hand to the audience, pinched fingers at appropriate times, or a raised hand, his gestures transform his speeches into dialogues and establish a sense that you are standing near him enjoying an animated conversation.

The use of gestures can also create the sense that a speaker is deeply invested in a topic and earnest in his or her desire to get others to see his or her points. For example, a hand placed sincerely over the heart shows deeply felt emotion. Additionally, effective gestures make speech more lively, engaging, and memorable. Cupping fingers in a C, as if placing words on air. Waving an index finger side-to-side, chastising. Motioning fingers toward oneself, beckoning someone near. A "disdainful flick" of the hand, shooing someone away. A soft fist. A closed fist. A palm held out to the audience in a little stop sign. These and countless other gestures can breathe life into speech. As Obama has shown, the precision of certain gestures enhances the descriptive content of oration and underscores key ideas, increasing the potency of spoken words.

⇥ MAXIMIZING PROPS ⇤

The use of props can be another important way to create impressions as well as to reinforce key messages. Consider our earlier example: if you want to convince others you are blind, what props would you use? Sunglasses, a dog, a white cane? Now extend the example. If political candidates are attempting to look presidential, what props might they use? They might flank themselves with large national flags on each side of a lectern. If speakers are trying to look strong on foreign policy, what props might they use? They might choose to invite military leaders to stand behind them when they make their foreign policy pronouncements.

If a speaker is seeking to present themselves as a leader, what props are appropriate? While the answers will depend in part upon the circumstances—the type of audience and its mood, or the subject and goal of the talk, for instance—the role of props in creating impressions should not be overlooked. For the Democrat seeking to connect with Republicans, a red tie conveys a subtle message. For leaders seeking to demonstrate their religious values, they might choose to deliver a speech in a church, where the physical background frames their comments. Similarly, leaders seeking to project authority in a casual setting might choose to forgo the coat and tie, dressing only a tad bit more formally than the audience. They might also arrange the room in a way that will make the audience comfortable (perhaps a room with chairs formed in a circle and no podium, rather than a more formal setting of a podium and lectern). Props—what others call staging—are an important source of nonverbal messaging. Carefully choosing backgrounds for delivering talks or leading groups is important. The backdrop helps to frame remarks.

Barack Obama has shown considerable skill in using props and staging to reinforce his messages. When he first announced his bid for the White House on February 10, 2007, for instance, he delivered his remarks in Springfield, Illinois, which naturally evoked memories of the lauded U.S. president Abraham Lincoln. Obama fixed attention on the significance of the setting, stating:

> It was here, in Springfield, where north, south, east, and west come together that I was reminded of the essential decency of the American people—where I came to believe that through this decency, we can build a more hopeful America.
>
> And that is why, in the shadow of the Old State Capitol, where Lincoln once called on a divided house to stand together, where common hopes and common dreams still live, I stand before you today to announce my candidacy for president of the United States.
>
> I recognize there is a certain presumptuousness—a certain audacity—to this announcement. I know I haven't spent a lot of time learning the ways of Washington. But I've been there long enough to know that the ways of Washington must change.
>
> The genius of our founders is that they designed a system of government that can be changed. And we should take heart, because we've changed this country before. In the face of tyranny, a band of patriots brought an empire to its knees. In the face of secession, we unified a nation and set the captives free. In the face of Depression, we put people back to work and lifted millions out of poverty. We welcomed immigrants to our shores, we opened railroads to the west, we landed a man on the moon, and we

heard a King's call to let justice roll down like water, and righteousness like a mighty stream.

Each and every time, a new generation has risen up and done what's needed to be done. Today we are called once more—and it is time for our generation to answer that call.

For that is our unyielding faith—that in the face of impossible odds, people who love their country can change it.

That's what Abraham Lincoln understood. He had his doubts. He had his defeats. He had his setbacks. But through his will and his words, he moved a nation and helped free a people. It is because of the millions who rallied to his cause that we are no longer divided, North and South, slave and free. It is because men and women of every race, from every walk of life, continued to march for freedom long after Lincoln was laid to rest, that today we have the chance to face the challenges of this millennium together, as one people—as Americans.[1]

Similarly, when addressing the Reverend Jeremiah Wright controversy, Obama carefully considered the nonverbal messages he would be sending. Given his association with the controversial minister, Obama needed to address the incendiary words of Reverend Wright, which were perceived by many Americans to be racist and contrary to the values Obama espouses. Obama's association with Wright threatened the very foundation of his candidacy. Obama delivered his remarks from a lectern flanked by large American flags. While denouncing the divisive words of Reverend Wright, the large flags in back of Obama reinforced the notion that he is a loyal, patriotic American. The backdrop helped frame his remarks and sent a positive message.

⇥ BEGINNING STRONG ⇤

Another communication practice that helps Barack Obama earn trust and confidence is his ability to start "strong." By this, I mean he begins his talks in ways that tap into the prevailing mood, lighten any tensions, and focus attention. There are many ways to start strong—a moving quotation, a vivid anecdote, a lighthearted joke, a direct statement about the topic of the discussion, to name a few.

Given his consistency with strong starts, Obama seems keenly aware that if leaders begin their remarks in a weak manner, they will need to spend too much time recovering, trying to persuade people to give them another look. In practice, his motto could be characterized as, "Get off on the right foot the first time." Obama's achievements testify to the positive impact of catching attention early and steering audience focus to the most important themes. Consider, for example, Obama's win of the North Carolina primary. He used his beginning remarks to draw attention to the momentum of his campaign. He stated:

> You know, some were saying that North Carolina would be a game-changer in this election. But today, what North Carolina decided is that the only game that needs changing is the one in Washington, DC.

I want to start by congratulating Senator Clinton on her victory in the state of Indiana. And I want to thank the people of North Carolina for giving us a victory in a big state, a swing state, and a state where we will compete to win if I am the Democratic nominee for president of the United States.

When this campaign began, Washington didn't give us much of a chance. But because you came out in the bitter cold, and knocked on doors, and enlisted your friends and neighbors in this cause; because you stood up to the cynics and the doubters and the naysayers when we were up and when we were down; because you still believe that this is our moment, and our time, for change—tonight we stand less than two hundred delegates away from securing the Democratic nomination for president of the United States.[2]

Even in the light of defeat, Obama skillfully chooses opening words. Consider, for instance, his remarks following his loss of the Pennsylvania primary. He projected that loss as a "win-because-we-narrowed-the-margin" situation:

I want to start by congratulating Senator Clinton on her victory tonight, and I want to thank the hundreds of thousands of Pennsylvanians who stood with our campaign today.

There were a lot of folks who didn't think we could make this a close race when it started. But we worked hard, and we traveled across the state to big cities and small towns, to factory floors, and VFW halls. And now, six weeks later, we closed the gap. We rallied people of every age and race and background to our cause. And whether they were inspired for the first time or for the first time in a long time, we registered a record number of voters who will lead our party to victory in November.[3]

Obama is so aware of the importance of beginning strong that when put in awkward positions unexpectedly, he makes sure to reset the tone of the conversation before proceeding with his remarks. A notable example of this occurred in December 2006 when Barack Obama appeared before a group of 2,000 Christians at a conference on HIV/AIDS at Saddleback Church in southern California. Another politician speaking at the same event, Senator Sam Brownback, spoke minutes before Obama. Standing on the church podium, Senator Brownback began his remarks to the primarily Caucasian audience by mentioning that he and Senator Obama had both recently addressed the National Association for the Advancement of Colored People (NAACP) and that, "They were very polite to me, but I think they kind of wondered, 'Who's this guy from Kansas?'" Brownback complained that, by contrast, the NAACP and its audience had treated Obama like a rock star and Brownback seemed to imply that the difference was racial. He turned to Obama, seated behind him on the podium, and joked that he believed the tables were now turned, saying, "Welcome to *my* house."

Shock registered throughout the audience. Barack Obama is a Christian, and they were sitting in a church! Brownback's comment seemed, rightly or wrongly, racially charged; it suggested that even though Obama was Christian, the church was not his house because the majority of people in the audience were white. It is very possible to argue that Brownback did not, in fact, intend this meaning and only referred to the audience's conservative bent, or that he misspoke, but the words were highly insulting and placed Senator Obama in a very awkward position.

When Brownback finished his speech minutes later and Obama moved to the lectern, many audience members seemed to hold their breaths, wondering if Obama would address the insult. Obama began by offering greetings from his church, underscoring quite intentionally that he was Christian. He then proceeded to offer Brownback compliments and more compliments. He spoke about how it was an honor to work with Senator Brownback on so many important issues and he praised Brownback's leadership. He went on at some length— a truly gracious beginning in light of the insult he had just received.

Then Obama did something quite brilliant. Before he proceeded to start his speech, he took the opportunity—having placed himself on the moral high ground by refusing to come out swinging—to turn to Senator Brownback who was seated at the back of the church podium. Obama smiled and said, "There is one thing I've got to say, Sam. This is my house, too! This is *God's* house."

The crowd erupted in applause. "I just wanted to be clear!" Obama said, riding the wave of support. Obama set the record straight. Had he not, he would have started "weak" and proceeded forward in a highly compromised position, which could have undercut his speech. Instead, he successfully recast the dialogue and proceeded with a well-received talk.

⇥ Conveying Admirable Ethics— ⇤
Developing Teflon

Finally, making certain to convey admirable ethics is an important way to earn trust and confidence. When a leader succeeds in conveying strong ethics and substantiates those ethics consistently through subsequent deeds, people begin to have great faith in that leader's character and choices. Conveying strong ethics has the added benefit of helping to "develop Teflon"—that is, a leader can build such an excellent ethical reputation that accusations and controversy "bounce off" of that leader rather than stick. When controversy arises, there is a greater likelihood that people will respond by thinking, "No, that is not who I have seen all this time." They are more likely to await an explanation and give a leader a chance.

In his public pronouncements, Barack Obama takes opportunities to convey his high ethical standards and commitment to principled values. Consider his remarks during his 2007 announcement for president in Springfield, Illinois:

> [L]et me tell you how I came to be here. As most of you know, I am not a native of this great state. I moved to Illinois over two decades ago. I was a young man then, just a year out of college; I knew no one in Chicago, was without money or family connections. But a group of churches had offered me a job as a community organizer for $13,000 a year. And I accepted the job, sight unseen, motivated then by a single, simple, powerful idea—that I might play a small part in building a better America.

My work took me to some of Chicago's poorest neighborhoods. I joined with pastors and laypeople to deal with communities that had been ravaged by plant closings. I saw that the problems people faced weren't simply local in nature—that the decision to close a steel mill was made by distant executives; that the lack of textbooks and computers in schools could be traced to the skewed priorities of politicians a thousand miles away; and that when a child turns to violence, there's a hole in his heart no government alone can fill.

It was in these neighborhoods that I received the best education I ever had and where I learned the true meaning of my Christian faith.

After three years of this work, I went to law school because I wanted to understand how the law should work for those in need. I became a civil rights lawyer and taught constitutional law, and after a time, I came to understand that our cherished rights of liberty and equality depend on the active participation of an awakened electorate. It was with these ideas in mind that I arrived in this capital city as a state senator.

It was here, in Springfield, where I saw all that is America converge—farmers and teachers, businessmen and laborers, all of them with a story to tell, all of them seeking a seat at the table, all of them clamoring to be heard. I made lasting friendships here—friends that I see in the audience today.

It was here we learned to disagree without being disagreeable—that it's possible to compromise so long as you know those principles that can never be compromised;

and that so long as we're willing to listen to each other, we can assume the best in people instead of the worst.[4]

In offering this short summary of his life choices, Obama underscored his principled values, morality, and commitment to community.

Similarly, Obama conveys admirable ethics by taking care in how he criticizes his opponents. When criticizing presidential candidate John McCain in 2008, he usually took care to first affirm McCain's service to the United States. This helped him avoid an image of mudslinging. For instance, Obama said:

> In just a few short months, the Republican party will arrive in St. Paul with a very different agenda. They will come here to nominate John McCain, a man who has served this country heroically. I honor that service, and I respect his many accomplishments, even if he chooses to deny mine. My differences with him are not personal; they are with the policies he has proposed in this campaign.[5]

Obama's care in conveying strong ethics helped him to weather storms and missteps during both his presidential bid and his time as U.S. president.

❧ WHAT WE'VE LEARNED — PRACTICES ❧ FOR EARNING TRUST AND CONFIDENCE

Leaders can learn from the way Obama uses excellent communication practices to earn the trust and confidence of others.

We have seen that charisma plays a role in earning trust and confidence. People know charisma when they see it—that certain fire in the eye, passion, and command. Charisma helps leaders energize and motivate others. Image and body language are also important for forming strong first impressions. Adept leaders capitalize on that first defining moment. Through skillful use of body movement and image, they start a two-way dialogue of sorts, making excellent impressions that last. This helps establish a firm foundation for commanding authority and wielding leadership.

Notable second impressions can reinforce strong first impressions. Through voice, intonation, and skillful use of gestures, effective communicators underscore their confidence, self-assuredness, and worthiness as leaders. Effective communicators also bear in mind that how they say their words can give great potency to their remarks. They leverage excellent use of voice and intonation. Similarly, gestures serve as their tools, becoming fluid extensions of their spoken words, animating their dialogue and bringing greater impact to their pronouncements.

Strong communicators remember the importance of props and staging in sending submessages that reinforce key themes. They make efforts to "start strong" with their remarks, tapping into the prevailing mood and ensuring they begin their dialogues on favorable footing. Additionally, exceptional communicators take opportunities to convey their strong ethics, deepening a basis for trust and confidence that can bring benefits well into the future.

CHAPTER 3

BREAKING DOWN BARRIERS

Back in 2004, the notion of a 2008 Obama quest for the U.S. presidency would have been termed *improbable* at best. Many Americans would have scoffed, "He'll never get past his name!" The last name that sounds like "Osama;" that middle name, Hussein. Not to mention his race. Yet by 2008, Barack Obama was widely hailed as "a world-transforming, redemptive figure"[1] with a strong bid for the White House, whose victory could help heal a world long split along white-black, North-South, and rich-poor divides. His 2008 presidential victory was indeed a milestone in U.S. history. How did Barack Obama manage to break down barriers that could have served as insurmountable obstacles for many other aspiring leaders? How did he manage to draw and unite millions of supporters from widely varying backgrounds during both his 2008 and 2012 presidential runs? What has allowed him to break down barriers and build bridges among leaders even in international arenas?

One of the answers lies in Obama's distinguished ability to use communication to bring people together despite their differences and to establish common ground. The ability to unite people, build camaraderie, and promote a sense of shared goals is vital for every highly successful leader. Obama's skill in this area is particularly deep, as manifested by the magnitude of his political achievements. His success in claiming the 2008 Democratic nomination for president ranks as exceptional by way of world history. In the U.S. context alone, it remains remarkable how Obama managed to unite during 2008 and 2012 such a highly diverse political coalition, which has included white-collar workers, blue-collar workers, students, academics, soccer moms, policy makers and entrepreneurs of all races and ages. Obama put forth the message many times that "this election is not between regions or religions or genders. It's not about rich versus poor; young versus old; and it is not about black versus white. It is about the past versus the future."[2] But how has he been able to cast aside divisions? This chapter explores the specific communication practices that have enabled Barack Obama to successfully tear down barriers and forge ties to many disparate groups.

⊰ ACHIEVING TRANSCENDENCE ⊱

Barack Obama's highly effective communication practices have allowed him to achieve a high level of "transcendence." Obama has alluded to this himself, as he has insisted on many occasions that once people get to know him, they usually "come around." And how do people "get to know him"? Oration. Speeches. Public remarks. Because Obama's communication is so highly effective, he has been able over the years to grow his support exponentially.

Several specific communication practices help account for Obama's success in inspiring a diverse set of people to band together, focusing not on their differences but on their commonalities. There are valuable lessons to be learned as we examine how Obama acknowledges differences but focuses on shared values, dreams, histories, and experiences and the way he peppers his remarks with words that resonate, pulling from a powerful lexicon of political rhetoric, shared principles, biblical truths, and words of celebrated icons. These techniques have allowed him a pave many paths to success both in the United States and abroad. Below, we explore Obama's effective communication techniques.

⊰ ACKNOWLEDGING THE ELEPHANT IN THE ROOM ⊱

Barack Obama has achieved tremendous success in shattering conventional wisdom and breaking historic barriers. In a 2004 interview, Obama pointed to several sources of his success, explaining why many people considered him an attractive Democratic candidate and convention speaker. He noted the way he had won the Illinois U.S. Senate primary election months earlier. "We defied conventional wisdom about where votes come from because the assumption is, whites won't vote for blacks, or suburban folks won't vote for city people, or downstate won't vote for upstate. . . . We were able to put together a coalition that said, you know, people are willing to give anybody a shot if they're speaking to them in a way that makes sense."[3] Obama also reiterated subsequently that people "are more interested in the message than the color of the messenger."[4]

But many leaders have failed in efforts to build such broad coalitions in the past. Obama's success in such efforts involved more than good luck. He employs specific communication practices that have helped him to tear down obstacles and forge ties. One such practice: Obama openly acknowledges sources of potential discomfort early on. When he begins his public remarks, he often seems to act according to the principle, "If there's an elephant in the room, acknowledge it."

During his 2008 presidential bid, when many Americans were first learning about him, the elephants in the room often included his race, his "funny name," and the fact that his father came from a developing part of the world and once lived in a hut. Given the history of race in the United States, this background might have presented an insurmountable obstacle for leaders less skilled than Obama.

Rather than ignoring such issues of potential discomfort, Obama is adept at acknowledging them head-on, often with touches of humor. For instance, when campaigning for the U.S. presidency, Obama joked that all too often people found his name confusing and accidentally called him by other, more familiar names like "Alabama" or "Yo mama."[5] Obama also referred to himself as "a skinny kid with a funny name." As he acknowledged earlier at the 2004 convention, "Let's face it, my presence on this stage is pretty unlikely." Obama's comfort in acknowledging the elephants in a room eases the comfort of those to whom he speaks. This, in turn, sets him free to redirect attention skillfully to areas of common ground.

Just as this served him well earlier in his political career, after assuming the office of U.S. president, this same approach helped Obama move toward designated goals. During his historic 2009 speech about U.S. relations with countries in the Middle East, for instance, Obama acknowledged candidly the grievances that plagued those relationships, yet he also set forth a challenge to open a new chapter in these relationships. The speech was well received throughout the Middle East. Obama shows that as a public speaker, it is useful to try to acknowledge sources of potential discomfort early on and in a forthright manner. Doing so can aid a quest to move beyond issues that divide in order to build ties and foster greater unity.

⇥ STRESSING COMMON DREAMS AND VALUES ⇤

As Obama adeptly recasts the dialogue to stress commonalities rather than differences, he focuses on key aspects such as shared dreams and values. Consider this example:

> [I] finally took my first trip to his tiny village in Kenya and asked my grandmother if there was anything left from [*my father*]. She opened a trunk and took out a stack of letters, which she handed to me.
>
> There were more than thirty of them, all handwritten by my father, all addressed to colleges and universities across America, all filled with *the hope of a young man who dreamed of more for his life.* And his *prayer was answered*

when he was brought over to study in this country [6] [*Emphases provided.*]

In these remarks, Obama focuses our attention on <u>the hope of a young man and the prayers that were answered</u>—things to which average Americans can relate. The aspects of his father's experience that would serve to separate Obama from many Americans—the hut and Kenya—fade in our mind as Obama steers our attention to the areas of commonality. Aspiring leaders can learn much from this. When preparing remarks, consider this: What common ground elements can you bring to the fore to establish strong ties to your audience? How can you skillfully direct attention to areas of common ground rather than keep the audience focused on elements that divide?

We can also learn much from Obama's skill in establishing common ground among diverse sets of people as we observe how he focuses away from traditional societal divisions—class, race, ethnicity, region, and religion—and focuses toward shared values and dreams. On March 18, 2004, the *New York Times* quoted Obama as saying, "I have an unusual name and an exotic background, but <u>my values are essentially American values.</u>"[7] Obama promotes this theme vigorously and <u>uses shared values—such as strong work ethic, belief in the American dream, and desire for education</u>—as the basis for relating to a broad array of the American public. Consider his remarks at the Associated Press annual luncheon in Washington, DC, in April 2008:

It doesn't matter if they're Democrats or Republicans; whether they're from the smallest towns or the biggest cities; whether they hunt or they don't; whether they go to church, or temple, or mosque, or not. We may come from different places and have different stories, but we share common hopes and one very American dream.

That is the dream I am running to help restore in this election. If I get the chance, that is what I'll be talking about from now until November. That is the choice that I'll offer the American people—four more years of what we had for the last eight, or fundamental change in Washington.

People may be bitter about their leaders and the state of our politics, but beneath that they are hopeful about what's possible in America. That's why they leave their homes on their day off, or their jobs after a long day of work, and travel—sometimes for miles, sometimes in the bitter cold—to attend a rally or a town hall meeting held by Senator Clinton, or Senator McCain, or myself. Because they believe that we can change things. Because they believe in that dream.

I know something about that dream. I wasn't born into a lot of money. I was raised by a single mother with the help of my grandparents, who grew up in small-town Kansas, went to school on the GI Bill, and bought their home through an FHA loan. My mother had to use food stamps at one point, but she still made sure that, through scholarships, I got a chance to go to some of the best schools around, which helped me get into some of the best colleges around, which gave me loans that Michelle and I just finished paying not all that many years ago.

In other words, my story is a quintessentially American story. It's the same story that has made this country a beacon for the world—a story of struggle and sacrifice on the part of my forebearers and a story of overcoming great odds. I carry that story with me each and every day. It's why I wake up every day and do this, and it's why I continue to hold such hope for the future of a country where the dreams of its people have always been possible.[8]

In his remarks above, Obama again joins himself firmly to the diverse audience he is addressing as he draws attention to their shared American dream. Similarly, in the example below, Obama solidifies his ties to a diverse set of Americans as he describes his family's pursuit of the American dream and their commitment to commendable values—hard work and dedication:

This is the country that gave my grandfather a chance to go to college on the GI Bill when he came home from World War II; a country that gave him and my grandmother the chance to buy their first home with a loan from the government.

This is the country that made it possible for my mother—a single parent who had to go on food stamps at one point—to send my sister and me to the best schools in the country on scholarships.

This is the country that allowed my father-in-law—a city worker at a South Side water filtration plant—to provide for his wife and two children on a single salary. This is a man who was diagnosed at age thirty with multiple sclerosis—who relied on a walker to get himself to work. And yet, every day he went, and he labored, and he sent my wife and her brother to one of the best colleges in the nation. It was a job that didn't just give him a paycheck, but a sense of dignity and self-worth. It was an America that didn't just reward wealth, but the work and the workers who created it.[9]

As political commentator Jamal Simmons noted on June 3, 2008, Obama has succeeded in presenting his life story as a "uniquely American story. . . . Like Bill Clinton's story, Ronald Reagan's story, Harry Truman's story. . . ."[10] The *New York Times* concurred on July 28, 2004, indicating that Obama tells "a classic American story of immigration, hope, striving, and opportunity." Given his excellent communication practices, Obama has portrayed his life's tale as that of an American with humble beginnings making his way to extraordinary success. This has helped him connect with audiences; his life story is viewed as a classic story and it has endeared Obama to millions of Americans.

As U.S. president, during times of great importance or challenge when he has needed to reassure the American people, rally the American people, or mark an important moment in national history, Obama has made certain to stress the shared values and ideals of the American people. When issuing public comments in 2011 following the American military effort that led to the death of Osama bin Laden, for example, President Obama stated:

> . . . today's achievement is a testament to the greatness of our country and the determination of the American people.

The cause of securing our country is not complete. But tonight, we are once again reminded that America can do whatever we set our mind to. That is the story of our history, whether it's the pursuit of prosperity for our people, or the struggle for equality for all our citizens; our commitment to stand up for our values abroad, and our sacrifices to make the world a safer place.

Let us remember that we can do these things not just because of wealth or power, but because of who we are: one nation, under God, indivisible, with liberty and justice for all.

Thank you. May God bless you. And may God bless the United States of America.[11]

⇥ DRAWING ATTENTION TO SHARED HISTORY ⇤

When possible, Obama also stresses shared history as a way of relating to audiences. In his 2008 speech titled "A More Perfect Union," for example, he stated:

I am the son of a black man from Kenya and a white woman from Kansas. I was raised with the help of a white grandfather who survived a *Depression* to serve in *Patton's army during World War II* and a white grandmother who worked on a *bomber assembly line at Fort Leavenworth* while he was overseas. I've gone to some of the best schools in America and lived in one of the world's poorest nations. I am married to a black American who carries within her the *blood of slaves* and *slave owners*—an inheritance we pass on to our two precious daughters. I have brothers, sisters, nieces, nephews, uncles, and cousins of every race and every hue, scattered across three continents, and for as long as I live, I will never forget that in no other country on Earth is my story even possible.

It's a story that hasn't made me the most conventional candidate. But it is a story that has seared into my genetic makeup the idea that this nation is more than the sum of its parts—*that out of many, we are truly one.*[12] [*Emphases provided.*]

While Obama acknowledges that his father was a Kenyan, he casts his father's story as a typical American immigrant story characterized by great hope for a better future, education, hard work, and the attainment of the American dream. Obama's references to shared history—the Depression, Patton's army and World War II, and the bomber assembly line at Fort Leavenworth—help him do this convincingly. These familiar historical references help Obama establish himself as being "just like any other American." He successfully directs the conversation away from his "funny" name and unorthodox upbringing to the many ties that bind. In doing so, Obama projects himself as firmly a part of the "we," part of the same team as most Americans, striving for the same goals.

Consider another example, in which the specific details Obama provides help form connections with a diverse audience:

[W]hat I learned much later is that part of what made it possible for [my father to come to the United States] was an effort by the young senator from Massachusetts at the time, John F. Kennedy, and by a grant from the Kennedy

Foundation to help Kenyan students pay for travel. So it is partly because of their generosity that my father came to this country, and because he did, I stand before you today—inspired by America's past, filled with hope for America's future, and determined to do my part in writing our next great chapter.[13]

In these comments, Obama uses an outstanding choice of detail to tie himself firmly to the American audience: He refers to one of the most famous American political families, taps into patriotic sentiments as he refers to the "generosity" of an American, and projects himself as "inspired by America's past" while also representing its future.

Similarly, Obama drew attention to shared history as a means of building links to an audience at the Kennedy endorsement event in Washington, DC, in January 2008. He commented:

Today isn't just about politics for me. It's personal. I was too young to remember John Kennedy, and I was just a child when Robert Kennedy ran for president. But in the stories I heard growing up, I saw how my grandparents and mother spoke about them and about that period in our nation's life—as a time of great hope and achievement. And I think my own sense of what's possible in this country comes in part from what they said America was like in the days of John and Robert Kennedy.

I believe that's true for millions of Americans. I've seen it in offices in this city where portraits of John and Robert hang on office walls or collections of their speeches sit on bookshelves. And I've seen it in my travels all across this country. Because no matter where I go or who I talk to, one thing I can say for certain is *that the dream has never died.*

The dream lives on in the older folks I meet who remember what America once was and know what America can be once again. It lives on in the young people who've only seen John or Robert Kennedy on TV, but are ready to answer their call.

It lives on in those Americans who refuse to be deterred by the scale of the challenges we face, who know, as President Kennedy said at this university, that "no problem of human destiny is beyond human beings."

And it lives on in those Americans—young and old, rich and poor, black and white, Latino and Asian—who are tired of a politics that divide us and want to recapture the sense of common purpose that we had when John Kennedy was president.

That is the dream *we hold in our hearts.* That is the kind of leadership we need in this country. And that is the kind of leadership I intend to offer as president.[14] [*Emphases provided.*]

In Obama's 2011 State of the Union address, when underscoring his belief that the United States could strengthen its position as a world leader, he employed references to history to connect with listeners. He said:

Half a century ago, when the Soviets beat us into space with the launch of a satellite called Sputnik, we had no idea how we would beat them to the moon. The science wasn't even there yet. NASA didn't exist. But after investing in better research and education, we didn't just surpass the Soviets; we unleashed a wave of innovation that created new industries and millions of new jobs.

This is our generation's Sputnik moment.[15]

Obama drew attention to shared history very effectively once again during his 2012 State of the Union address. He remarked:

Think about the America within our reach: A country that leads the world in educating its people. An America that attracts a new generation of high-tech manufacturing and high-paying jobs. A future where we're in control of our own energy, and our security and prosperity aren't so tied to unstable parts of the world. An economy built to last, where hard work pays off, and responsibility is rewarded.

We can do this. I know we can, because we've done it before. At the end of World War II, when another generation of heroes returned home from combat, they built the strongest economy and middle class the world has ever known. My grandfather, a veteran of Patton's Army, got the chance to go to college on the GI Bill. My grandmother, who worked on a bomber assembly line, was part of a workforce that turned out the best products on Earth.

The two of them shared the optimism of a nation that had triumphed over a depression and fascism. They understood they were part of something larger; that they were contributing to a story of success that every American had a chance to share—the basic American promise that if you worked hard, you could do well enough to raise a family, own a home, send your kids to college, and put a little away for retirement.

The defining issue of our time is how to keep that promise alive. . . .

These familiar themes have enabled Obama to break down barriers and nurture bonds. He casts aside traditional divisions and lays in their places other bases for uniting—shared values and shared history.

Notably, since assuming the role of U.S. president, Obama has succeeded in using this technique in international arenas. When seeking to help establish a new era in U.S. relations with Middle Eastern countries in 2009, President Obama helped cultivate fertile ground by drawing attention to Muslim contributions to America and how the histories of Muslims and Americans have been intertwined. He stated:

. . . That is what I will try to do today—to speak the truth as best I can, humbled by the task before us, and firm in my belief that the interests we share as human beings are far more powerful than the forces that drive us apart.

Now part of this conviction is rooted in my own experience. I'm a Christian, but my father came from a Kenyan family that includes generations of Muslims. As a boy, I spent several years in Indonesia and heard the call of the Azaan at the break of dawn and at the fall of dusk. As a young man, I worked in Chicago communities where many found dignity and peace in their Muslim faith.

As a student of history, I also know civilization's debt to Islam. . . .

I also know that Islam has always been a part of America's story. The first nation to recognize my country was Morocco.... And since our founding, American Muslims have enriched the United States. They have fought in our wars, they have served in our government, they have stood for civil rights, they have started businesses, they have taught at our universities, they've excelled in our sports arenas, they've won Nobel Prizes, built our tallest building, and lit the Olympic Torch. And when the first Muslim American was recently elected to Congress, he took the oath to defend our Constitution using the same Holy Koran that one of our Founding Fathers—Thomas Jefferson—kept in his personal library.[16]

Obama used references to history equally effectively when he spoke before the Joint Session of the Indian Parliament in 2010. He underscored a sense of shared history as he noted:

For me and Michelle, this visit has, therefore, held special meaning. See, throughout my life, including my work as a young man on behalf of the urban poor, I've always found inspiration in the life of [Gandhi] and his simple and profound lesson to be the change we seek in the world. And just as he summoned Indians to seek their destiny, he influenced champions of equality in my own country, including a young preacher named Martin Luther King. After making his pilgrimage to India a half-century ago, Dr. King called Gandhi's philosophy of non-violent resistance "the only logical and moral approach" in the struggle for justice and progress.[17]

⇥ ILLUMINATING SHARED EXPERIENCES ⇤

Another important lesson of Obama's outstanding communication style is how he leverages shared experiences to build rapport and a strong sense of camaraderie. As we have seen, when addressing an audience, Obama searches out the common ground and deliberately directs attention to this. At times, this common ground may be limited to tangential experiences. But Obama manages to leverage even tangential experiences, using them to forge a foundation upon which to relate to an audience. Consider the example below, when Obama spoke before a group of working women. Clearly, Obama is not a working woman! But he took time to consider how he could relate to the group. The relevant questions he seemed to consider beforehand included: What is the basis of our common experiences? How can I elaborate on those common experiences—even if they are only tangential—in establishing a firm connection to the audience? Obama creates a firm connection magnificently as he uses his experience as the son of a working woman and as the husband of a working woman to illuminate common ground. He remarked:

> It's great to be back in New Mexico and to have this opportunity to discuss some of the challenges that working women are facing. Because I would not be standing before you today as a candidate for president of the United States if it weren't for working women.
>
> I am here because of my mother, a single mom who put herself through school, followed her passion for helping others, and raised my sister and me to believe that in

America there are no barriers to success if you're willing to work for it.

I am here because of my grandmother, who helped raised me. She worked during World War II on a bomber assembly line—she was Rosie the Riveter. Then, even though she never got more than a high school diploma, she worked her way up from her start as a secretary at a bank and ended up being the financial rock for our entire family when I was growing up.

And I am here because of my wife, Michelle, the rock of the Obama family, who worked her way up from modest roots on the South Side of Chicago, and who has juggled jobs and parenting with more skill and grace than anyone I know. Now Michelle and I want our two daughters to grow up in an America where they have the freedom and opportunity to live their dreams and raise their own families.[18]

In another example, Obama gave a speech before a metropolitan group in Florida. He calculated again how he could relate to the audience. What sorts of experiences or histories did he and the audience members share? How could he elaborate in a way that would create a lucid picture of himself as a candidate who understood their situations, challenges, and needs? Although the group was based in Miami, Florida, Obama pulled effectively from his prior experience as an organizer in Chicago, Illinois, establishing common ground:

This is something of a homecoming for me. Because while I stand here today as a candidate for president of the

United States, I will never forget that the most important experience in my life came when I was doing what you do each day—working at the local level to bring about change in our communities.

As some of you may know, after college I went to work with a group of churches as a community organizer in Chicago so I could help lift up neighborhoods that were struggling after the local steel plants closed. And it taught me a fundamental truth that I carry with me to this day— that in this country, change comes not from the top down, but from the bottom up.[19]

For leaders aspiring to diminish perceived areas of division and to expand common ground, Obama's successes demonstrate the value of taking time to identify the many bases that might serve as common ground areas. Do your listeners share common histories? Common values? Common experiences? Common goals? Shine a light on the areas of commonalities in order to build bridges and unite disparate groups of people.

✒ EMPLOYING WORDS THAT RESONATE: THE ☚ HISTORICAL AND POLITICAL LEXICON

We have seen above how Obama skillfully creates a sense of "we-ness," making himself and the audience a part of the "we" as he elaborates on common values, dreams, histories, and experiences. Buttressing this, Obama peppers his remarks with words that resonate with his audiences. Sometimes when addressing American audiences, he pulls those appropriate words from relevant political lexicons, drawing on cherished sociopolitical values. Sometimes when speaking in countries abroad, he draws on language with significance in those settings. At times, he draws on valued principles, biblical truths, and proverbial wisdom. At other times, he refers to the words of iconic figures in order to underscore his message.

Consider this example from his March 18, 2008, "A More Perfect Union" speech, when Obama responded to fiery and divisive comments of Reverend Jeremiah Wright, which threatened to undercut Obama's assertions that he stood for a united America. Obama chose to draw on America's rich history of political rhetoric, using words from the Declaration of Independence that resonated with the audience. Referring to the Declaration of Independence was akin to pouring buckets full of water on a fire, quenching its flames. In the single opening sentence below, Obama affirmed his patriotism and communicated his unwavering support of the ideals of unity:

"We the people, in order to form a more perfect union."

Two hundred and twenty-one years ago, in a hall that still stands across the street, a group of men gathered and, with these simple words, launched America's improbable experiment in democracy. Farmers and scholars, statesmen and patriots who had traveled across an ocean to escape tyranny and persecution finally made real their declaration of independence at a Philadelphia convention that lasted through the spring of 1787.

The document they produced was eventually signed but ultimately unfinished. It was stained by this nation's original sin of slavery, a question that divided the colonies and brought the convention to a stalemate until the founders chose to allow the slave trade to continue for at least twenty more years and to leave any final resolution to future generations.

Of course, the answer to the slavery question was already embedded within our Constitution—a constitution that had at its very core the ideal of equal citizenship under the law; a constitution that promised its people liberty, and justice, and a union that could be and should be perfected over time.

And yet words on a parchment would not be enough to deliver slaves from bondage or provide men and women of every color and creed their full rights and obligations as citizens of the United States. What would be needed were Americans in successive generations who were willing to do their part—through protests and struggle, on the streets and in the courts, through a civil war and civil disobedience and always at great risk—to narrow that gap between the promise of our ideals and the reality of their time.

This was one of the tasks we set forth at the beginning of this campaign—to continue the long march of those who came before us, a march for a more just, more equal, more free, more caring, and more prosperous America. I chose to run for the presidency at this moment in history because I believe deeply that we cannot solve the challenges of our time unless we solve them together—unless we perfect our union by understanding that we may have different stories, but we hold common hopes; that we may not look the same and we may not have come from the same place, but we all want to move in the same direction—towards a better future for our children and our grandchildren.

This belief comes from my unyielding faith in the decency and generosity of the American people. [*Emphases added.*]

In this speech, Obama rooted himself firmly as a part of the "we." He directed attention to treasured historic principles that have guided the United States in the past and affirmed his desire to help ensure that these same principles would lead the United States into a secure future. The success of speeches like this helped build his winning momentum.

When speaking abroad, Obama has shown great skill in using words that resonate with specific foreign audiences, even down to the smallest of phrases. During his historic 2009 "On a New Beginning" speech in Cairo, Egypt, for example, he began with a simple greeting that went far in creating a positive atmosphere. He said:

I'm grateful for your hospitality, and the hospitality of the people of Egypt. And I'm also proud to carry with me the goodwill of the American people, and a greeting of peace from Muslim communities in my country: *Assalaamu alaykum.* [*Applause.*][20]

A simple gesture—his use of these indigenous words—resonated excellently, were received as a sign of great respect and created goodwill.

⇥ USING WORDS THAT RESONATE— ⇤ BIBLICAL TRUTHS

Another practice that allows Obama to shatter barriers and construct ties effectively is his practice of referencing biblical wisdom. Obama, a Christian whose faith is dear to him, often sprinkles his public remarks with words that evoke positive feelings among other Christians: *faith in things not seen; I am my brother's keeper.* Many people cherish these biblical truths and principles. The verses are familiar to their ears and resonate in their hearts. In many settings, therefore, Obama's choice to refer to biblical verses helps him to build bridges and to establish a high level of connectedness. Just consider this excerpt from Obama's 2004 Democratic Convention keynote address:

> For alongside our famous individualism, there's another ingredient in the American saga.
>
> A belief that we are connected as one people. If there's a child on the South Side of Chicago who can't read, that matters to me, even if it's not my child. If there's a senior citizen somewhere who can't pay for her prescription and has to choose between medicine and the rent, that makes my life poorer, even if it's not my grandmother. If there's an Arab American family being rounded up without benefit of an attorney or due process, that threatens my civil liberties. It's that fundamental belief—*I am my brother's keeper, I am my sister's keeper*—that makes this country work. It's what allows us to pursue our individual dreams, yet still come together as a single American family. "E pluribus unum." Out of many, one.[21] [*Emphases provided.*]

Similarly, in his seminal "A More Perfect Union" speech in Philadelphia in March 2008, Obama's biblical references served him well:

In the end, then, what is called for is nothing more and nothing less than what all the world's great religions demand—*that we do unto others as we would have them do unto us. Let us be our brother's keeper, Scripture tells us. Let us be our sister's keeper.* Let us find that common stake we all have in one another, and let our politics reflect that spirit as well."[22] [*Emphases provided.*]

During his inaugural address in 2009, President Obama also used biblical truth to set a positive tone and connect with the American audience. He stated:

We remain a young nation. But in the words of Scripture, the time has come to set aside childish things. The time has come to reaffirm our enduring spirit; to choose our better history; to carry forward that precious gift, that noble idea passed on from generation to generation: the God-given promise that all are equal, all are free, and all deserve a chance to pursue their full measure of happiness. [*Applause.*]

⇥ LEVERAGING OTHER PEOPLE'S WORDS ⇤

Drawing on the words of lauded icons has also helped Obama establish linkages to audiences. The icons he chooses are often well known to audiences, and their words are sometimes familiar. Referring to the words of carefully chosen icons or leaders helps establish an emotional connection to the audience. Here is an excerpt from Obama's January 2008 speech:

[O]n the eve of the bus boycotts in Montgomery, at a time when many were still doubtful about the possibilities of change, a time when those in the black community mistrusted themselves, and at times mistrusted each other, King inspired with words not of anger, but of an urgency that still speaks to us today:

"Unity is the great need of the hour" is what King said. Unity is how we shall overcome.

What Dr. King understood is that if just one person chose to walk instead of ride the bus, those walls of oppression would not be moved. But maybe if a few more walked, the foundation might start to shake. If a few more women were willing to do what Rosa Parks had done, maybe the cracks would start to show. If teenagers took freedom rides from North to South, maybe a few bricks would come loose. Maybe if white folks marched because they had come to understand that their freedom too was at stake in the impending battle, the wall would begin to sway. And if enough Americans were awakened to the injustice; if they joined together, North and South, rich and poor, Christian and Jew, then perhaps that wall would come tumbling down, and justice would flow like water, and righteousness like a mighty stream.

Unity is the great need of the hour—the great need of this hour.[23]

The poetry of King's words, along with his iconic stature, helps to bring an emotional impact among many listeners. By drawing on such words, Obama has on many occasions related to audiences with greater effectiveness. In another example, Obama references, with great effect, Martin Luther King Jr.'s eloquent words, "the arc of the moral universe is long but it bends toward justice":

Through his faith, courage, and wisdom, Dr. Martin Luther King, Jr., moved an entire nation. He preached the gospel of brotherhood; of equality and justice. That's the cause for which he lived—and for which he died forty years ago today . . .

[I] think it's worth reflecting on what Dr. King was doing in Memphis, when he stepped onto that motel balcony on his way out for dinner. . . .

And what he was doing was standing up for struggling sanitation workers. For years, these workers had served their city without complaint, picking up other people's trash for little pay and even less respect. Passersby would call them "walking buzzards," and, in the segregated South, most were forced to use separate drinking fountains and bathrooms.

. . . [O]n the eve of his death, Dr. King gave a sermon in Memphis about what the movement there meant to him and to America. And in tones that would prove eerily prophetic, Dr. King said that despite the threats he'd received, he didn't fear any man, because he had been there when Birmingham aroused the conscience of this nation. And he'd been there to see the students stand up for freedom by sitting in at lunch counters. And he'd been there in Memphis when it was dark enough to see the stars, to see the community coming together around a common purpose. So Dr. King had been to the mountaintop. He had seen the Promised Land. And while he knew somewhere deep in his bones that he would not get there with us, he knew that we would get there.

He knew it because he had seen that Americans have "the capacity," as he said that night, "to project the 'I' into the 'thou.'" To recognize that no matter what the color of our skin, no matter what faith we practice, no matter how much money we have, no matter whether we are sanitation workers or United States senators, we all have a stake in one another, we are our brother's keeper, we are our sister's keeper, and "either we go up together, or we go down together."

And when he was killed the following day, it left a wound on the soul of our nation that has yet to fully heal. . . . That is why the great need of this hour is much the same as it was when Dr. King delivered his sermon in Memphis. We have to recognize that while we each have a different past, we all share the same hopes for the future—that we'll be able to find a job that pays a decent wage, that there will be affordable health care when we get sick, that we'll be able to send our kids to college, and that after a lifetime of hard work we'll be able to retire with security. They're common hopes, modest dreams. And they're at the heart of the struggle for freedom, dignity, and humanity that Dr. King began and that it is our task to complete.

You know, Dr. King once said that the arc of the moral universe is long, but that it bends toward justice. But what he also knew was that it doesn't bend on its own. It bends because each of us puts our hands on that arc and bends it in the direction of justice.

So on this day of all days *let's each do our part to bend that arc.*
Let's bend that arc toward justice.
Let's bend that arc toward opportunity.
Let's bend that arc toward prosperity for all.

And if we can do that and march together—as one nation and one people—then we won't just be keeping faith with what Dr. King lived and died for. We'll be making real the words of Amos that he invoked so often and "let justice roll down like water and righteousness like a mighty stream."[24] [*Emphases provided.*]

In his 2008 acceptance speech following his election as U.S. president, Obama drew upon the statements of President Lincoln to reach out with powerful words to those who had not voted for him, pledging to work as U.S. president on their behalf also. He remarked:

As Lincoln said to a nation far more divided than ours, "We are not enemies, but friends . . . though passion may have strained it must not break our bonds of affection." And to those Americans whose support I have yet to earn—I may not have won your vote, but I hear your voices, I need your help, and I will be your President, too.

In his 2011 State of the Union address, Obama was able to connect more deeply with listeners as he employed the words of Robert Kennedy. He stated:

The future is ours to win. But to get there, we can't just stand still. As Robert Kennedy told us, "The future is not a gift. It is an achievement." Sustaining the American Dream has never been about standing pat. It has required each generation to sacrifice, and struggle, and meet the demands of a new age.

And now it's our turn. We know what it takes to compete for the jobs and industries of our time. We need to out-innovate, out-educate, and out-build the rest of the world. We have to make America the best place on Earth to do business. We need to take responsibility for our deficit and reform our government. That's how our people will prosper. That's how we'll win the future.[25]

For leaders aspiring to steer attention away from factors that divide listeners toward factors that unite them, Obama demonstrates that employing words that resonate—reflecting common values, principles, beliefs, tradition, and history—can be used to build a greater sense of unity.

➤ WHAT WE'VE LEARNED—PRACTICES FOR ⬅ BREAKING DOWN BARRIERS

Leaders have much to learn from the way Barack Obama breaks down barriers and establishes common ground among diverse sets of people. Obama has shown he can transcend traditional divisions of race, ethnicity, age, gender, religion, and region. He is adept at uniting disparate people, building camaraderie, and establishing a sense of shared goals. To do this, we have seen the importance of acknowledging "elephants in the room." Acknowledging potential issues of discomfort helps to ease tensions and enables leaders to refocus attention on areas of common ground. Leaders should seek to be forthright in acknowledging areas of potential discomfort early on and should proceed to focus away from sources of division and toward commonalities. They should steer attention in ways that promote a sense that listeners are on the same team, striving for the same aims.

When illuminating common ground, it is helpful to reference common histories, values, and experiences. It is also a best practice to employ words that resonate—well-chosen words reflecting time-tested principles, sociopolitical values, biblical truth, or words from a cherished lexicon. Effective use of "other people's words" can also play a role. Leaders can focus when needed on iconic figures, those we all admire, incorporating references to their words wisely and using those references to create a connection, a sense of "we-ness." In establishing common ground, referring to details about shared experiences can also prove useful. When preparing remarks, effective leaders should assess the basis of their shared experiences with their audiences, identifying ways to guide attention to those commonalities in order to enhance the power of their words.

CHAPTER 4

WINNING HEARTS AND MINDS

When fully harnessing the power of speaking with purpose and vision, outstanding orators can win hearts and minds, eliciting responses such as "That was a powerful speech." "He understands." "She addressed all of my concerns."

Barack Obama has shown a notable ability to sway the hearts and minds of audiences. He knows how to wield communicative power in ways that move people and motivate them to consider his ideas and follow his lead. He inspired young generations of Americans and reinvigorated older generations, spurring a historic grassroots campaign in 2008 that trumped political wisdom about traditional divisions of race, class, gender, and religion. His ability to sway broad swaths of the American public spurred new self-named cadres: Obama

Mamas, Obamacans, adherents of Obamanomics. What has allowed Barack Obama to connect so well with his audiences even amid periods of criticism during his tenure as president of the United States?

It is possible to glean important lessons from Obama's keen ability to adapt his remarks to the audience and topic at hand. He makes sure to know his audience, recognize their prevailing mood, and speak meaningfully to them about issues they most care about. Several other notable practices underlie Obama's skill in swaying hearts and minds. He acts according to the principle "Keep things personal," employing details effectively. He creates the feel of one-to-one conversation, making ample references to his personal experiences and leveraging the "I," "you," and "we" connection with skillful use of personal pronouns. The net effect: when Barack Obama speaks, the podium seems to disappear; Obama creates a two-way dialogue of sorts, as if he is standing near, speaking directly to listeners. Obama sways listeners as he speaks about issues of paramount importance to them and as he demonstrates understanding and empathy. He builds rapport. Given his communication style and substance, his audiences respond, feeling that with Obama they are a part of a "we," part of the same team, striving for the same goals.

⇥ KNOWING YOUR AUDIENCE ⇤

In order to win hearts and minds, it is necessary to know your audience and understand the circumstances its members face. Effective leaders not only know this information, but they also *convey* their understanding to the audience. They use language that captures the mood and addresses the audience's key concerns, grievances, and desires. Barack Obama has demonstrated an outstanding ability to connect with his audiences in this way. He acknowledges and addresses their prevailing moods and sentiments. The issues may vary—the economy, health care, education, the Iraq War. But in his comments, Obama shows skill in communicating to his audiences that he understands their perspectives and intends to address their concerns. Consider when Obama addressed the lack of optimism (some would say, outright cynicism) that some Americans felt in 2008 toward government and government officials:

> I chose to run because I believed that the size of these challenges had outgrown the capacity of our broken and divided politics to solve them; because I believed that Americans of every political stripe were hungry for a new kind of politics, a politics that focused not just on how to win but why we should, a politics that focused on those values and ideals that we held in common as Americans; a politics that favored common sense over ideology, straight talk over spin.
>
> Most of all, I believed in the power of the American people to be the real agents of change in this country because we are not as divided as our politics suggests; because we are a decent, generous people willing to work hard and sacrifice for future generations; and I was certain that if we could just mobilize our voices to challenge the special interests that dominate Washington and challenge ourselves to reach for something better, there was no problem we couldn't solve—no destiny we couldn't fulfill.

Ten months later, Iowa, you have vindicated that faith. You've come out in the blistering heat and the bitter cold not just to cheer, but to challenge—to ask the tough questions; to lift the hood and kick the tires; to serve as one place in America where someone who hasn't spent their life in the Washington spotlight can get a fair hearing.

You've earned the role you play in our democracy because no one takes it more seriously. And I believe that's true this year more than ever because, like me, you feel that same sense of urgency.[1]

In capturing the prevailing mood, Obama succeeded in connecting with his audience and advanced his goal of swaying hearts and minds. His remarks hit home. For leaders seeking to use excellent communication to win hearts and minds, take time to know your audiences and to understand what they most want to hear about. Find ways to tap into the prevailing mood and speak meaningfully to the audiences about the things they most care about.

⇥ KNOWING WHEN NOT TO ENUMERATE ⇤

When seeking to win hearts and minds—pursuing the aims of inspiring and motivating people—it is important to know when not to enumerate remarks. Strikingly, orators seeking to establish a strong emotional connection to listeners rarely enumerate their points. Numbering points, ideas, or themes can be an emotion-dampener. Imagine the impression a speaker makes when beginning a discussion by saying, "Let me elaborate on four key components of my vision. First. . . ." The talk will be perceived as formal, businesslike, distant, void of deep emotion, and less extemporaneous.

Certainly, enumeration has its place. It can be highly effective in business settings, when seeking to project a strong sense of leadership, or in relatively formal settings such as church services. Many a professor, for example, has been heard saying, "Let me elaborate on the three things that. . . ." Obama himself has enumerated much more frequently when addressing important matters or crisis situations as U.S. president. But for the broader aim of capturing hearts and minds, enumeration provides a stifling format. When seeking to sway hearts and minds, it is often best to provide structure to remarks without the formality of enumeration.

Barack Obama adheres to this strain of thought. During his 2008 campaign speeches, for example, he rarely delivered speeches to public audiences in which enumeration found a notable place. This is not to say that Obama offered speeches or remarks that are void of effective structure. Quite the opposite. Obama adopted multiple techniques for providing great structure to his remarks without enumeration, preserving his ability to make a strong visceral connection to his audiences. Consider this example:

So this will not be easy. Make no mistake about what we're up against.

We are up against the belief that it's ok for lobbyists to dominate our government—that they are just part of the system in Washington. But we know that the undue influence of lobbyists is part of the problem, and this election is our chance to say that we're not going to let them stand in our way anymore.

We are up against the conventional thinking that says your ability to lead as president comes from longevity in Washington or proximity to the White House. But we know that real leadership is about candor, and judgment and the ability to rally Americans from all walks of life around a common purpose—a higher purpose.

We are up against decades of bitter partisanship that causes politicians to demonize their opponents instead of coming together to make college affordable or energy cleaner; it's the kind of partisanship where you're not even allowed to say that a Republican had an idea, even if it's one you never agreed with. That kind of politics is bad for our party, it's bad for our country, and this is our chance to end it once and for all.

We are up against the idea that it's acceptable to say anything and do anything to win an election. We know that this is exactly what's wrong with our politics; this is why people don't believe what their leaders say anymore; this is why they tune out. And this election is our chance to give the American people a reason to believe again.

And what we've seen in these last weeks is that we're also up against forces that are not the fault of any one campaign, but feed the habits that prevent us from being who we want to be as a nation. It's the politics that uses religion as a wedge and patriotism as a bludgeon. A politics that tells us that we have to think, act, and even vote within the confines of the categories that supposedly define us. The assumption that young people are apathetic. The assumption that Republicans won't cross over. The assumption that the wealthy care nothing for the poor and that the poor don't vote. The assumption that African Americans can't support the white candidate; whites can't support the African American candidate; blacks and Latinos can't come together.

But we are here tonight to say that this is not the America we believe in. I did not travel around this state over the last year and see a white South Carolina or a black South Carolina. I saw South Carolina. I saw crumbling schools that are stealing the future of black children and white children. I saw shuttered mills and homes for sale that once belonged to Americans from all walks of life, and men and women of every color and creed who serve together, and fight together, and bleed together under the same proud flag. I saw what America is, and I believe in what this country can be.

That is the country I see. That is the country you see. But now it is up to us to help the entire nation embrace this vision. Because in the end, we are not just up against the ingrained and destructive habits of Washington; we are also struggling against our own doubts, our own fears, and our own cynicism. The change we seek has always required great struggle and sacrifice. And so this is a battle in our own hearts and minds about what kind of country we want and how hard we're willing to work for it.[2]

In this example, Obama demonstrates that a message can have a personal feel without sacrificing structure. The way Obama frames his paragraphs—repeating, "We are up against"—serves as a source of structure, no enumeration needed.

For leaders aspiring to employ effective communication, think about whether enumeration will help you achieve the goal of your speech or hinder your efforts to achieve the goal of your speech. Consider the purpose of your talk and the venue, and choose to use or avoid enumeration as appropriate.

⇥ EMPLOYING DETAILS EFFECTIVELY ⇤

Another way to capture hearts and minds is to speak meaningfully to the needs of listeners. Details matter. Important to listeners are the three Rs—recognizes, remembers, responsive. Listeners want assurance that the speaker *recognizes* the circumstances they are facing, *remembers* the details of those circumstances enough to reference them, and will be *responsive* to those issues. In providing details, a speaker helps to answer questions that are often in the minds of audience members, such as "What do you *really* know about my life and my challenges? Do you care?" Details provide evidence of awareness and empathy.

In countless cases, Barack Obama has shown excellence in communicating to audiences that he is aware of their circumstances, understands those challenges, and is preparing to do something about them. In a practice he has refined over time, Obama often provides sufficient details to convey, "I offer this evidence that I understand your concerns and that I care." Consider this example:

All across this state, you've shared with me your stories. And all too often they've been stories of struggle and hardship.

I've heard from seniors who were betrayed by CEOs who dumped their pensions while pocketing bonuses and from those who still can't afford their prescriptions because Congress refused to negotiate with the drug companies for the cheapest available price.

I've met Maytag workers who labored all their lives only to see their jobs shipped overseas; who now compete with their teenagers for $7-an-hour jobs at Walmart.

I've spoken with teachers who are working at doughnut shops after school just to make ends meet; who are still digging into their own pockets to pay for school supplies.

Just two weeks ago, I heard a young woman in Cedar Rapids who told me she only gets three hours of sleep because she works the night shift after a full day of college and still can't afford health care for a sister with cerebral palsy. She spoke not with self-pity but with determination and wonders why the government isn't doing more to help her afford the education that will allow her to live out her dreams.

I've spoken to veterans who talk with pride about what they've accomplished in Afghanistan and Iraq, but who nevertheless think of those they've left behind and question the wisdom of our mission in Iraq; the mothers weeping in my arms over the memories of their sons; the disabled or homeless vets who wonder why their service has been forgotten.

And I've spoken to Americans in every corner of the state, patriots all, who wonder why we have allowed our standing in the world to decline so badly, so quickly. They know this has not made us safer. They know that we must never negotiate out of fear but that we must never fear to negotiate with our enemies as well as our friends. They are ashamed of Abu Ghraib and Guantanamo and warrantless wiretaps and ambiguity on torture. They love their country and want its cherished values and ideals restored.[3]

Imagine the difference, the flatness of the remarks, if Obama had simply stated, "I understand there are tough economic times right now. My new policy can help." There is more credibility and power to his words when he demonstrates a depth of knowledge through carefully chosen details. By adding more precise details—$7 an hour, a need to work after school—outstanding orators like Obama make greater strides toward winning hearts and minds.

For leaders aiming to strengthen their ability to use communication to win hearts and minds, take time to think about what detail can help you communicate to listeners that you recognize, remember, and will be responsive to the issues they most care about. Employing effective detail is a powerful tool in the communication process.

⇥ PERSONALIZING THE MESSAGE: ⇤ "I" AND EXPERIENCE

Through some of his very influential public remarks, Barack Obama demonstrates that another important way to win hearts and minds is to personalize a message with well-placed use of pronouns—the "I," "you," and "we" connection. Tapping into a prevailing mood is important, yes. Providing effective details is important, also. But sometimes it is easy to overlook what you, the speaker, believe specifically and the experiences that underpin those beliefs. Personalizing a message and referring to your own relevant experience can help you personalize your message and establish credibility. Moreover, references to relevant experience, combined with skillful employment of "you," "I," and "we," help transmit the message that the speaker and the audience are part of the same team. It helps elicit the reaction, "He's been there; he knows." This, in turn, lays the foundation for swaying hearts and minds. Below, Obama demonstrates this practice:

> Finally, as *you and I* stand here today, know that there is a generation of children growing up on the mean streets and forgotten corners of this country who are slipping away from us as we speak. They walk down Corridors of Shame in rural South Carolina and sit in battered classrooms somewhere in East LA. They are overwhelmingly black and Latino and poor. And when they look around and see that no one has lifted a finger to fix their school since the nineteenth century; when they are pushed out the door at the sound of the last bell—some into a virtual war zone—is it any wonder they don't think their education is important? Is it any wonder that they are dropping out in rates we've never seen before?
>
> *I know* these children. *I know* their sense of hopelessness. *I began my career* over two decades ago as a

community organizer on the streets of Chicago's South Side. And I worked with parents and teachers and local leaders to fight for their future. We set up after-school programs, and we even protested outside government offices so that we could get those who had dropped out into alternative schools. And in time, we changed futures.

And so while I know hopelessness, I also know hope. *I know* that if we bring early education programs to these communities; if we stop waiting until high school to address the dropout rate and start in earlier grades; if we bring in new, qualified teachers; if we expand college outreach programs like GEAR UP and TRIO and fight to expand summer learning opportunities *like I've done* in the senate; if we do all this, we can make a difference in the lives of our children and the life of this country—not just in East LA or the South Side of Chicago, but here in Manchester, and suburban Boston, and rural Mississippi. *I know* we can. *I've seen* it happen. And *I will work* every day to do it again as your president.[4] [*Emphases provided.*]

Since assuming his role as U.S. president, Barack Obama has continued to use this technique very effectively and very frequently. When speaking in 2012 before the National Governors Association Meeting, for example, this practice helped him speak with great credibility about the need to keep access to higher education affordable. He stated:

Now, for students that are ready for college, we've got to make sure that college is affordable. Today, graduates who take out loans leave college owing an average of $25,000. That's a staggering amount for young people. Americans now owe more in student loan debt than they do in credit card debt. There's so many Americans out there with so much to offer who are saddled with debt before they even start out in life. And the very idea of owing that much money puts college out of reach for far too many families.

So this is a major problem that must be fixed. I addressed it at the State of the Union. We have a role to play here. My grandfather got a chance to go to college because Americans and Congress decided that every returning veteran from World War II should be able to afford it. My mother was able to raise two kids by herself while still going to college and getting an advanced degree because she was able to get grants and work-study while she was in school. Michelle and I are only here today because of scholarships and student loans that gave us a good shot at a great education. And it wasn't easy to pay off these loans, but it sure wasn't as hard as it is for a lot of kids today.[5]

⇥ CONNECTING ONE TO ONE: "YOU" AND "I" ⇤

Combining references to "I" with references to "you" also personalizes a message, creating a greater sense of closeness. The distance between the podium and the audience seems to narrow. Whatever physical barriers are present (a lectern, for instance) become lesser obstacles. The speaker's words strike closer to the heart. Consider this:

My father came from thousands of miles away, in Kenya, and went back there soon after I was born. *I spent* a childhood adrift. *I was raised* in Hawaii and Indonesia. *I lived* with my single mom and with my grandparents from Kansas. *Growing up, I wasn't* always sure who I was or where I was going.

Then, when I was about your age, I decided to become a community organizer. *I wrote* letters to every organization in the country that I could think of. And for a while, *I got no* response. Finally, this small group of churches on the South Side of Chicago wrote back and offered me a job to come help neighborhoods devastated by steel plant closings. My mother and grandparents wanted me to go to law school. My friends were applying to jobs on Wall Street. *I didn't know* a soul in Chicago, and the salary was about $12,000 a year, plus $2,000 to buy an old, beat-up car.

I still remember a conversation I had with an older man before I left. He looked and said, "Barack, I'll give you a bit of advice. Forget this community organizing business and do something that's gonna make you some money. You can't change the world, and people won't appreciate you trying. You've got a nice voice. What you should do is go into television broadcasting. I'm telling you, you've got a future."

Now, he may have had a point about the TV thing. *And to tell you the truth, I didn't have* a clear answer about what I was doing. *I wanted to* step into the currents of history and help people fight for their dreams but didn't know what my role would be. *I was inspired* by what people like Harris did in the civil rights movement, but when *I got to*

Chicago, there were no marches, no soaring speeches. In the shadow of an empty steel plant, there were just a lot of folks struggling. Day after day, *I heard* no a lot more than I heard yes. *I saw* plenty of empty chairs in those meetings we put together.

But even as *I discovered* that you can't bend history to your will, *I found* that you could do your part to see that, in the words of Dr. King, it "bends toward justice." In church basements and around kitchen tables, block by block, we brought the community together, registered new voters, fought for new jobs, and helped people live lives with some measure of dignity.[6] [*Emphases provided.*]

As Obama employed the strong use of pronouns, such as when he commented, "when *I* was about *your* age," he made the tone of this talk very personal. Combined with lighthearted humor and informal language such as, "To tell you the truth, I didn't have a clear answer," Obama succeeded in delivering an intimate address that hit close to the heart.

As president of the United States, Obama has continued to use this technique excellently. In 2012, as he challenged Americans to use their imagination, innovation, and strong skills to move America forward as it faced new challenges. For example, he related well with his audience as he stated:

And so when *I* see all the young people who are here today—or the young at heart—(laughter) —we need *you* guys to keep at it. This is *your* future at stake. We need *you* to work hard. We need *you* to dream big. We need *you* to summon the same spirit of unbridled optimism, that bold willingness to tackle tough problems that led previous generations to meet the challenges of their time—to power a nation from coast to coast, to touch the moon, to connect an entire world with our own science and imagination. That's what America is capable of doing.[7]

⇥ PERSONALIZING THE MESSAGE: ⇤ THE "WE" CONNECTION

Employing "we" has a similar effect to the "I-you" connection. It helps to send the message that the speaker and those listening are on the same team, in the same boat, facing the same fate. Consider this example from Obama's June 3, 2008, primary night speech in Minnesota:

> All of *you chose* to support a candidate you believe in deeply. But at the end of the day, we aren't the reason you came out and waited in lines that stretched block after block to make your voice heard. *You didn't do* that because of me or Senator Clinton or anyone else. *You did it* because *you know* in *your hearts* that at this moment—a moment that will define a generation—*we cannot* afford to keep doing what we've been doing. *We owe* our children a better future. *We owe* our country a better future. And for all those who dream of that future tonight, *I say, let u*s begin the work together. *Let us* unite in common effort to chart a new course for America.[8] [*Emphases provided.*]

Similarly, Obama used references to "I-you-we" very effectively during his December 27, 2007, "Our Moment Is Now" speech:

. . . *I know* that when the American people believe in something, it happens.

If you believe, then we can tell the lobbyists that their days of setting the agenda in Washington are over.

If you believe, then we can stop making promises to America's workers and start delivering—jobs that pay, health care that's affordable, pensions you can count on, and a tax cut for working Americans instead of the companies who send their jobs overseas.

If you believe, we can offer a world-class education to every child and pay our teachers more and make college dreams a reality for every American.

If you believe, we can save this planet and end our dependence on foreign oil.

If you believe, we can end this war, close Guantanamo, restore our standing, renew our diplomacy, and onceagain respect the Constitution of the United States of America. That's the future within *our reach*. . . .[9] [*Emphases provided.*]

For leaders aiming to sway and inspire listeners, consider how you can employ pronouns effectively—leveraging the "I," "you," "we" connection. Personalizing messages can add great power to communication.

⊰ WHAT WE'VE LEARNED—PRACTICES FOR ⊱ WINNING HEARTS AND MINDS

Obama's success demonstrates many best practices with regard to winning hearts and minds. When seeking to use communicative power to sway others, Obama adapts remarks to the audience, speaking meaningfully to audience members about the issues they most care about. He keeps things personal by leveraging personal pronouns—"I," "you," and "we"—to connect more closely with audience members, establishing a sense of one-to-one conversation. He talks about his own experiences to give power and authority to his words, so listeners understand, "He's been there; he knows." He uses details to demonstrate that he understands the experiences and perspectives of audience members. Empathy and action—these are things the audience seeks. Obama also uses details to show that he recognizes, remembers, and intends to be responsive to the needs and desires of the audience. For leaders seeking to use communication effectively, these best practices provide useful techniques to employ.

CHAPTER 5

CONVEYING VISION

During his career, Barack Obama has distinguished himself as a man of vision who has dared to pursue a dream of breaking historic barriers, moving past traditional divisions, and bringing about change. But it is not enough to form a vision and to believe in it profoundly. To achieve a vision, it is necessary to communicate that vision to others in an effective and compelling manner, enabling others first to understand the vision and inspiring them ultimately to embrace it.

For years, observers have noted Barack Obama's ability to communicate his vision with great success. In 2004, Senator John Kerry observed, "Barack is an optimistic voice for America" who "knows that together we can build an America that is stronger at home and respected in the world."[1] But there have been other activists working earnestly on behalf of the poor and the middle class. There have been other aspiring leaders with extraordinary personal stories of triumph and success against the odds. There have been others also who have sought to use their leadership to bring goodwill and hope. Yet Barack Obama's success has been extraordinary—more substantial than many people would have imagined a mere 45 years after Martin Luther King Jr.'s "I Have a Dream" speech. Why have so many people embraced Obama's vision both in the United States and abroad? What allows Obama to convey his vision so well? How does he use communication techniques as effectively as any visual aid when conveying his vision? How does he frame his ideas in ways that have tremendous impact, particularly given the time constraints of a typical speech?

This chapter delves into the techniques that Obama employs to convey vision in ways that are lucid, relevant, and compelling. We can learn lessons from the way Obama references history and frames ideas in familiar terms. We can glean best practices from the way he employs vivid language, relies on symbolic and dynamic imagery, and uses "backward loops." We can deepen our skills as we assess how he draws on the power of corollaries, personifies ideas, and provides "just enough" detail for significant impact. Together, these communication practices have enabled Barack Obama to communicate his vision with great effect.

⇥ REFERENCING HISTORY AND THE FAMILIAR ⇤

When Barack Obama articulates his vision to audiences, he employs many notable communication practices to present his ideas in ways that are clear, germane, and convincing. The way he references history serves as one of his techniques. Obama has demonstrated that when placing key ideas in a historical context, they can become more digestible because they are placed in a context that listeners understand. When Obama communicates his ideas as part of the cherished traditions with which audience members are familiar, the ideas can become perceived as a natural extension of or progression from those traditions. Consider this example, when Barack Obama articulates his vision of an America committed to addressing social issues, such as homelessness, violence, living wages, health care, and education. Obama skillfully places his ideas in an historical context, referencing the iconic American leader Robert Kennedy:

> I was only seven when Bobby Kennedy died. Many of the people in this room knew him as brother, as husband, as father, as friend. . . .
>
> [T]he idealism of Robert Kennedy—the unfinished legacy that calls us still—is a fundamental belief in the continued perfection of American ideals.
>
> It's a belief that says if this nation was truly founded on the principles of freedom and equality, it could not sit idly by while millions were shackled because of the color of their skin. That if we are to shine as a beacon of hope to the rest of the world, we must be respected not just for the might of our military, but for the reach of our ideals. That if this is a land where destiny is not determined by birth or circumstance, we have a duty to ensure that the child of a millionaire and the child of a welfare mom have the same

chance in life. That if out of many, we are truly one. Then we must not limit ourselves to the pursuit of selfish gain, but that which will help all Americans rise together. . . .

[O]ur greatness as a nation has depended on individual initiative, on a belief in the free market. But it has also depended on our sense of mutual regard for each other, the idea that everybody has a stake in the country, that we're all in it together and everybody's got a shot at opportunity.

Robert Kennedy reminded us of this. He reminds us still. He reminds us that we don't need to wait for a hurricane to know that third-world living conditions in the middle of an American city make us all poorer. We don't need to wait for the 3000th death of someone else's child in Iraq to make us realize that a war without an exit strategy puts all of our families in jeopardy. We don't have to accept the diminishment of the American Dream in this country now, or ever.

It's time for us to meet the whys of today with the why nots we often quote but rarely live—to answer "why hunger" and "why homeless," "why violence," and "why despair" with "why not good jobs and living wages," "why not better health care and world class schools," "why not a country where we make possible the potential that exists in every human being?"[2]

In linking his ideas not only to history, but also to an admirable historic American leader, Obama helps to substantiate his ideas as well as to make them more understandable and acceptable. He strengthens his ability to present a vision that will be embraced. Leaders seeking to convey vision effectively can learn from his successes. Are there ways in which you can reference history to make your ideas and your vision more understandable to listeners? Take time to consider how you might reference history and things that are familiar in ways that enhance your communication.

⇥ USING DESCRIPTIVE WORDS AS VISUAL AIDS ⇤

Another important practice that allows Barack Obama to convey his vision effectively is his excellent use of descriptive words. In many cases, speakers present their talks in settings in which they cannot, or should not, use visual aids, such as overhead slides or electronic presentations. For some speakers, the lack of visual aids might be a significant handicap. But outstanding orators master the art of using well-chosen descriptive words in lieu of visual aids. They paint pictures with vivid words, focusing at key points on words that call to mind rich images. If chosen carefully, rich language can affect a listener as significantly as any visual aid: a listener will visualize the ideas and themes and be more likely to remember them.

Several things make certain words rich in descriptive power—their precision or the specific image they call forth, for instance. Consider the difference in these two statements:

In this campaign, we won't employ harsh politicking.
vs.

What you won't hear from this campaign or this party is the kind of politics that uses religion as a wedge and patriotism as a bludgeon. (Obama, June 2008)[3]

In the latter statement, the use of the words *wedge* and *bludgeon* conjure up specific images that make a stronger impact. They are rich in descriptive power; they don't simply "tell," they "show." In creating imagery, the words help to convey vision.

Similarly, compare these remarks:

You came out to support us in large numbers.

vs.

They said this country was too divided; too disillusioned to ever come together around a common purpose.

But on this January night—at this defining moment in history—you have done what the cynics said we couldn't do. You have done what the state of New Hampshire can do in five days. You have done what America can do in this New Year, 2008. In lines that stretched around schools and churches; in small towns and big cities; you came together as Democrats, Republicans, and Independents to stand up and say that we are one nation; we are one people; and our time for change has come." (Obama, January 2008)[4]

Obama's reference above to "lines that stretched around schools and churches" brings forth images of people huddled for hours, perhaps cold and uncomfortable, yet willing to endure the long lines in order to have a chance to support him. This, in turn, implies that what Obama represents and his candidacy are very worthwhile. That is, the word choice that invokes "lines of people" implies many other things in addition to what is actually said, with all of the implied ideas contributing positively to

Obama's message. The language serves as an excellent example of well-chosen, richly descriptive words.

There are many examples of Obama's excellent use of vivid imagery and rich descriptive words. Consider his remarks during his 2009 inaugural address, when he stated:

> . . . let us mark this day with remembrance of who we are and how far we have traveled. In the year of America's birth, in the coldest of months, a small band of patriots huddled by dying campfires on the shores of an icy river. The capital was abandoned. The enemy was advancing. The snow was stained with blood. At the moment when the outcome of our revolution was most in doubt, the father of our nation ordered these words to be read to the people:
>
> "Let it be told to the future world . . . that in the depth of winter, when nothing but hope and virtue could survive . . . that the city and the country, alarmed at one common danger, came forth to meet [it]."
>
> America: In the face of our common dangers, in this winter of our hardship, let us remember these timeless words. With hope and virtue, let us brave once more the icy currents, and endure what storms may come. Let it be said by our children's children that when we were tested we refused to let this journey end, that we did not turn back nor did we falter; and with eyes fixed on the horizon and God's grace upon us, we carried forth that great gift of freedom and delivered it safely to future generations.

When issuing public remarks in 2011 following the military action that led to the death of Osama bin Laden, President Obama used very descriptive words to speak to Americans about the great tragedy of 9/11 and to place the pursuit and killing of Osama bin Laden in context, conveying a strong vision of his commitment to the fight against terrorism. He stated:

It was nearly 10 years ago that a bright September day was darkened by the worst attack on the American people in our history. The images of 9/11 are seared into our national memory—hijacked planes cutting through a cloudless September sky; the Twin Towers collapsing to the ground; black smoke billowing up from the Pentagon; the wreckage of Flight 93 in Shanksville, Pennsylvania, where the actions of heroic citizens saved even more heartbreak and destruction.

And yet we know that the worst images are those that were unseen to the world. The empty seat at the dinner table. Children who were forced to grow up without their mother or their father. Parents who would never know the feeling of their child's embrace. Nearly 3,000 citizens taken from us, leaving a gaping hole in our hearts.[5]

As President Obama spoke before government officials in India in 2010, he used vivid language—a reference to a tricolor flag—to evoke the memory of the important moment of India's political independence, in words that resonated with his Indian audience. He said:

An ancient civilization of science and innovation; a fundamental faith in human progress—this is the sturdy foundation upon which you have built ever since that stroke of midnight when the tricolor was raised over a free and independent India. [*Applause.*][6]

In 2012, when President Obama put forth a strong vision of his commitment to Israel, he employed a single descriptive word—fork—that helped emphasize his point. He remarked:

> . . . as you examine my commitment, you don't just have to count on my words. You can look at my deeds. Because over the last three years, as President of the United States, I have kept my commitments to the state of Israel. At every crucial juncture—at every fork in the road—we have been there for Israel. Every single time. [*Applause.*][7]

Likewise, President Obama used strong imagery to end his 2012 State of the Union address excellently when he remarked:

> Each time I look at that flag, I'm reminded that our destiny is stitched together like those 50 stars and those 13 stripes. No one built this country on their own. This nation is great because we built it together. This nation is great because we worked as a team. This nation is great because we get each other's backs. And if we hold fast to that truth, in this moment of trial, there is no challenge too great; no mission too hard. As long as we are joined in common purpose, as long as we maintain our common

resolve, our journey moves forward, and our future is hopeful, and the state of our Union will always be strong.

Obama illustrates that leaders who desire to use communication to convey vision in a compelling manner can benefit from using words that evoke rich imagery. Words filled with descriptive power can deepen the impact of speech. Employing richly descriptive words can create multilayered communication that enables speakers to articulate their vision with great efficacy.

DRAWING ON SYMBOLISM

Obama is also very good at conveying vision by using words rich with symbolism. Symbolic images often elicit emotional reactions. For example, referring to a national flag draped over a coffin evokes patriotism and notions of loyalty and sacrifice to a country. When Obama mentions that his grandfather was buried in a coffin draped with an American flag, therefore, he connects himself to all of those positive elements. The net effect: Those well-chosen words enhance Obama's standing. Drawing on symbolism when it will enhance your image can be considered a best practice.

LEVERAGING COROLLARIES

A practice closely related to the excellent use of symbolism is the practice of choosing words rich in corollary meaning. Obama does this with great skill. Unlike symbolic words, a word rich in corollary meaning is not necessarily laden with patriotic or emotional meanings. Nonetheless, such a word is multidimensional in the ideas and images it evokes. The effectiveness of Obama's communication demonstrates that, in choosing key words, selecting a word that "implies 20 others" can prove worthwhile. Think about this example:

> In the year I was born, President Kennedy let out word that the torch had been passed to a new generation of Americans. He was right. It had. It was passed to his youngest brother.
>
> From the battles of the 1960s to the battles of today, he has carried that torch, lighting the way for all who share his American ideals.
>
> It's a torch he's carried as a champion for working Americans, a fierce proponent of universal health care, and a tireless advocate for giving every child in this country a quality education.
>
> It's a torch he's carried as the lion of the senate, a man whose mastery of the issues and command of the levers of government—whose determined leadership and deft political skills—are matched only by his ability to tell a good story.[8]

Obama could have referred to some other light-bearing object, rather than a "torch," as being passed on. A torch, however, has positive corollary value. It elicits images of Olympic athletes and is associated with great achievement, great heroism, and the quest for excellence. The word choice sets powerful imagery dancing in the mind. Leaders seeking to convey vision excellently can leverage corollary meaning to achieve greater impact with their words.

PERSONIFYING IDEAS AND CONFERRING PHYSICALITY

Obama also employs the technique of personification very well. I use the term "personification" to refer to the act of giving inanimate objects or ideas human characteristics, such as emotions or actions. For example:

Every house on the street was sleeping.

The wind began to moan and the clouds wept down rain.[9]

More often than employing a personification technique, however, Obama gives ideas physicality, such as when he sees "hope" in the "light" of eyes. In doing so, Obama ties emotions or ideas to concrete images. Giving ideas physicality is a highly effective way to present ideas in ways a listener will remember. The embodiment of ideas gives the imagery power; the words resonate at a deeper level and listeners are more likely to remember how the imagery makes them feel. Consider this difference: suppose if Obama had simply stated, *"I know you all are hopeful; I can see this."* Contrast the impression of those words with the impact when Obama uses words that confer physicality, as he did after the Iowa primary on January 3, 2008:

But we always knew that hope is not blind optimism. It's not ignoring the enormity of the task ahead or the roadblocks that stand in our path. It's not sitting on the sidelines or shirking from a fight. Hope is that thing inside us that insists, despite all evidence to the contrary, that something better awaits us if we have the courage to reach for it and to work for it and to fight for it.

Hope is what I saw in the eyes of the young woman in Cedar Rapids who works the night shift after a full day of college and still can't afford health care for a sister who's ill; a young woman who still believes that this country will give her the chance to live out her dreams.

Hope is what I heard in the voice of the New Hampshire woman who told me that she hasn't been able to breathe since her nephew left for Iraq; who still goes to bed each night praying for his safe return.

Hope is what led a band of colonists to rise up against an empire; what led the greatest of generations to free a continent and heal a nation; what led young women and young men to sit at lunch counters and brave fire hoses and march through Selma and Montgomery for freedom's cause.

Hope. Hope is what led me here today—with a father from Kenya; a mother from Kansas; and a story that could only happen in the United States of America. Hope is the bedrock of this nation, the belief that our destiny will not be written for us, but by us, by all those men and women who are not content to settle for the world as it is—who have the courage to remake the world as it should be. [*Emphases added.*]

The first statement, "*I know you all are hopeful. I can see this,*" sounds flat and fails to stir a listener. In contrast, Obama's elaboration on "hope" above enables the listener to visualize the notion. The listener can see hopeful eyes. The image is vivid. Similarly, when Obama ties the notion of hope to honored history, he makes the notion more memorable and enables it to resonate at a deeper level. Obama's practice of conferring physicality to ideas often serves his purposes very well.

⇥ PROVIDING JUST ENOUGH DETAIL ⇤

Another very instructive practice Obama employs as he conveys vision involves his use of "just enough" detail. He has demonstrated on many occasions his ability to calibrate the amount of detail he provides in order to illustrate the depth of his knowledge about key issues. A master of using well-chosen detail, Obama also understands the value of vagueness. Consider the remarks below, through which Obama relates the Iraq War issue in terms of one specific soldier, Shamus:

> A while back, I met a young man named Shamus at the VFW Hall in East Moline, Illinois. He was a good-looking kid, six-two or six-three, clear-eyed, with an easy smile. He told me he'd joined the marines and was heading to Iraq the following week. As I listened to him explain why he'd enlisted, his absolute faith in our country and its leaders, his devotion to duty and service, I thought this young man was all any of us might hope for in a child. But then I asked myself: Are we serving Shamus as well as he was serving us? I thought of more than 900 service men and women, sons and daughters, husbands and

wives, friends and neighbors, who will not be returning to their hometowns. I thought of families I had met who were struggling to get by without a loved one's full income or whose loved ones had returned with a limb missing or with nerves shattered but who still lacked long-term health benefits because they were reservists. When we send our young men and women into harm's way, we have a solemn obligation not to fudge the numbers or shade the truth about why they're going, to care for their families while they're gone, to tend to the soldiers upon their return, and to never ever go to war without enough troops to win the war, secure the peace, and earn the respect of the world.[10]

With his choice of words, Obama paints a picture. He has met a soldier named Shamus, but he outlines only a broad image—the good looks, the clear eyes, the easy smile, his height. Nothing else. Given the lack of additional details, a fascinating thing can happen in the minds of many listeners. They fill in the gaps themselves. What ethnicity is Shamus? The only clue is his name—a name unfamiliar to many, thus many listeners will attribute no specific ethnicity at all, except for the one they see fit. With scant description, they are free to imagine Shamus as they please. In many cases, a listener will imagine Shamus to look a lot like themselves, their own ethnicity. If so, the character becomes in many ways more understandable to the listener, and the example can resonate closer to home. Free to imagine, the story can connect with a broad range of listeners, helping to create a powerful and lasting impact. This is also highly effective use of "just enough" detail.

⭑ CREATING DYNAMIC IMAGES ⭑

Dynamic images serve as another powerful tool for conveying vision effectively. By dynamic, I simply mean "not static." Consider this example:

> That is what we started here in Iowa, and that is the message we can now carry to New Hampshire and beyond: the same message we had when we were up and when we were down; the one that can change this country brick by brick, block by block, calloused hand by calloused hand—that together, ordinary people can do extraordinary things; because we are not a collection of red states and blue states, we are the United States of America; and at this moment, in this election, we are ready to believe again. Thank you, Iowa.[11]

The words "brick by brick, block by block, calloused hand by calloused hand" create moving images—dynamic rather than static. In the mind's eye, the image becomes an animated, living thing; it is in motion. This helps to create a sense of forward momentum.

Obama used similar words during his 2008 acceptance speech following his election as U.S. president, when he remarked:

> . . . above all, I will ask you to join in the work of remaking this nation the only way it's been done in America for two-hundred and twenty-one years—block by block, brick by brick, calloused hand by calloused hand.

At key times, leaders seeking to convey vision excellently can benefit from using words that create moving images. Dynamic words can be powerful. Imagery that becomes alive in the mind is likely to be remembered long after a speech is delivered.

⇥ LEVERAGING A BACKWARD LOOP ⇤

A much more rare technique that Obama has leveraged to great effect is what I call the "backward loop." Obama's knowledge and use of this unique technique helps demonstrate how he has mastered the art of highly effective communication. Many speakers, when seeking to create a dynamic image, put forth a picture of what they hope the future will bring. Obama, however, has also discerned the power of looping back in time. Examine this excerpt:

> The scripture tells us that when Joshua and the Israelites arrived at the gates of Jericho, they could not enter. The walls of the city were too steep for any one person to climb, too strong to be taken down with brute force. And so they sat for days, unable to pass on through.
>
> But God had a plan for his people. He told them to stand together and march together around the city, and on the seventh day he told them that when they heard the sound of the ram's horn, they should speak with one voice. And at the chosen hour, when the horn sounded and a chorus of voices cried out together, the mighty walls of Jericho came tumbling down.

There are many lessons to take from this passage, just as there are many lessons to take from this day, just as there are many memories that fill the space of this church. As I was thinking about which ones we need to remember at this hour, my mind went back to the very beginning of the modern civil rights era.

Because before Memphis and the mountaintop; before the bridge in Selma and the march on Washington; before Birmingham and the beatings; the fire hoses and the loss of those four little girls; before there was King the icon and his magnificent dream, there was King the young preacher and a people who found themselves suffering under the yoke of oppression.[12] [*Emphasis added.*]

This example demonstrates Obama's mastery of public speech. He skillfully uses imagery to illustrate a powerful point. Moving the motion backwards, Obama compares the launch of another significant American movement (the civil rights movement) to current-day efforts to bring positive social and political change. Obama begins with references to Memphis and Martin Luther King Jr.'s iconic "I Have a Dream" speech. The reference conjures up for many Americans images of hundreds of thousands of people marching on the Washington mall in a commendable effort to secure equality. Obama continues backward in time to Selma, and he refers to beatings and police use of water hoses against unarmed civil rights protestors. He finally rests on the image of Americans suffering amid discriminatory conditions at the very inception of the civil rights movement.

Consider how much more powerfully these remarks resonate than a more straightforward, succinct statement might have. Instead of stating, "supporters of the civil rights movement once stood like us, facing a big challenge," Obama takes listeners back in time, referencing the many accomplishments of civil rights supporters and illustrating that those protestors had once been just like his listeners, standing at the inception of a movement. Powerfully, the backward loop asks an implied question—if they did it, why can't we? The message transmitted becomes: *they did it, so can we!* Given the focus on a very laudable movement—the civil rights movement—a listener can be inspired, motivated, and stirred by the example. Obama makes his point powerfully.

⇥ ILLUSTRATING WITH ANECDOTES ⇤

Finally, Obama uses anecdotes as powerful tools for conveying vision. Anecdotes allow him to use brief narration to go into greater depth and illustrate points in memorable ways. When speaking about the United States and its future in 2008, for instance, Obama said:

> This union may never be perfect, but generation after generation has shown that it can always be perfected. And today, whenever I find myself feeling doubtful or cynical about this possibility, what gives me the most hope is the next generation—the young people whose attitudes and beliefs and openness to change have already made history in this election.

There is one story in particularly that I'd like to leave you with today—a story I told when I had the great honor of speaking on Dr. King's birthday at his home church, Ebenezer Baptist, in Atlanta.

There is a young, twenty-three-year-old white woman named Ashley Baia who organized for our campaign in Florence, South Carolina. She had been working to organize a mostly African American community since the beginning of this campaign, and one day she was at a roundtable discussion where everyone went around telling their story and why they were there.

And Ashley said that when she was nine years old, her mother got cancer. And because she had to miss days of work, she was let go and lost her health care. They had to file for bankruptcy, and that's when Ashley decided that she had to do something to help her mom.

She knew that food was one of their most expensive costs, and so Ashley convinced her mother that what she really liked and really wanted to eat more than anything else was mustard and relish sandwiches. Because that was the cheapest way to eat.

She did this for a year until her mom got better, and she told everyone at the roundtable that the reason she joined our campaign was so that she could help the millions of other children in the country who want and need to help their parents, too.

Now Ashley might have made a different choice. Perhaps somebody told her along the way that the source of her mother's problems were blacks who were on welfare and too lazy to work or Hispanics who were coming into the country illegally. But she didn't. She sought out allies in her fight against injustice.

Anyway, Ashley finishes her story and then goes around the room and asks everyone else why they're supporting the campaign. They all have different stories and reasons. Many bring up a specific issue. And finally they come to this elderly black man who's been sitting there quietly the entire time. And Ashley asks him why he's there. And he does not bring up a specific issue. He does not say health care or the economy. He does not say education or the war. He does not say that he was there because of Barack Obama. He simply says to everyone in the room, "I am here because of Ashley."

"I'm here because of Ashley." By itself, that single moment of recognition between that young white girl and that old black man is not enough. It is not enough to give health care to the sick or jobs to the jobless, or education to our children.

But it is where we start. It is where our union grows stronger. And as so many generations have come to realize over the course of the two-hundred and twenty-one years since a band of patriots signed that document in Philadelphia, that is where the perfection begins.[13]

The anecdote demonstrates in great detail the power of small changes in mind-set and the choice to unite across traditional societal divisions. It conveys these points excellently by focusing on one person listeners can relate to—Ashley. Focusing the discussion in this manner, Obama makes his points well and those points are more likely to linger with listeners.

President Obama also used an anecdote very powerfully during his 2008 acceptance speech, following his election as U.S. president. He spoke about a 106-year-old African American woman who had seen many changes in her lifetime. Earlier in her life, Obama elaborated, this woman could not vote in the United States both because of her race and because of her gender. But, in 2008 she was able to cast a vote for the first African American president. After speaking about this through his anecdote, Obama summarized the importance and tied it to his theme of change, saying:

[T]his year, in this election, she touched her finger to a screen, and cast her vote, because after 106 years in America, through the best of times and the darkest of hours, she knows how America can change. Yes we can.

While serving as U.S. president, Barack Obama has continued to use anecdotes as a means of connecting with his audiences, underscoring points and helping to convey his vision. During his comments before the National Governors Association Meeting in 2012 in Washington, DC, for example, Obama used an anecdote to relate more deeply with the audience while underscoring the importance of education as a means for spurring innovation. He said:

There was a kid—the kid who actually got the most attention was a young man named Joey Hudy of Arizona. That's because Joey let me fire off an extreme marshmallow cannon. We did it right here in this room. We shot it from here. We pumped it up—it almost hit that light. I thought it was a lot of fun. And while the cannon was impressive, Joey left a bigger impression because he had already printed out his own business cards—he was 14 years old. And he was handing them out to everybody, including me. He's on our short list for a Cabinet post.

Under his name on each card was a simple motto: "Don't be bored, do something." Don't be bored, do something. Don't be bored, make something.

All across this country there are kids like Joey who are dreaming big, and are doing things and making things. And we want them to reach those heights. They're willing to work hard. They are willing to dig deep to achieve. And we've got a responsibility to give them a fair shot. If we do, then I'm absolutely convinced that our future is going to be as bright as all of us want.[14]

In his 2011 State of the Union address, he used an anecdote equally well. When focusing on the need to meet the challenges of the globalizing world, Obama referred to the admirable efforts of a middle-aged mother. He stated:

One mother of two, a woman named Kathy Proctor, had worked in the furniture industry since she was 18 years old. And she told me she's earning her degree in biotechnology now, at 55 years old, not just because the furniture jobs are gone, but because she wants to inspire her children to pursue their dreams, too. As Kathy said, "I hope it tells them to never give up."

If we take these steps—if we raise expectations for every child, and give them the best possible chance at an education, from the day they are born until the last job they take—we will reach the goal that I set two years ago: By the end of the decade, America will once again have the highest proportion of college graduates in the world.[15]

Leaders seeking to use communication to convey vision excellently should consider whether an anecdote will allow them to crystallize a point or make a theme more memorable. Will listeners relate to the issues or key themes more readily? Carefully narrated anecdotes can enrich communication, enhancing a speaker's ability to convey their vision successfully.

⇥ WHAT WE'VE LEARNED—PRACTICES FOR ⇤ CONVEYING VISION

There is much to learn from the way Barack Obama conveys vision. Obama has shown a keen ability to convey vision in a compelling manner, which enables others to understand his vision and has inspired many people to ultimately embrace it.

Leaders can draw on the techniques that enable Obama to do this so well. When seeking to convey vision in a compelling manner, referencing history can make ideas more understandable and digestible. Listeners can relate to ideas more readily from a prism of shared history and cherished tradition, and may relate better with references to admired historical figures. Efforts to convey vision are more effective also when leaders "show, don't tell" at crucial times. That is, effective communicators will draw on vivid language at key times to paint pictures as effectively as they might with visual aids. They know to employ richly descriptive words—a torch instead of a light; a wedge; a bludgeon. They draw on symbolic language for emotional impact. They leverage the power of corollaries to bring about multilayered communication, saying 1 word while implying 20 others.

The practice of giving ideas physicality can also play a role in conveying vision effectively. "Embodiment" makes ideas more memorable, such as seeing "hope in the eyes." Highly skilled communicators also employ detail effectively, calibrating the ideal amount of detail they provide as they convey their vision. At times, ample detail establishes a depth of knowledge. But skillful speakers also recognize the value of vagueness, allowing listeners to imagine when appropriate with "just enough" detail.

Use of dynamic imagery represents another useful communication technique. Effective communicators find ways to make pictures move in the mind—"brick by brick, block by block, calloused hand by calloused hand." Similarly, backward loops can be powerful, as a speaker takes listeners back in time to imagine how it once was, comparing and contrasting the past with the present with great effect. Finally, effective communicators often employ anecdotes, which provide brief narration and short tales to breathe life into key themes. Together, these techniques enable leaders to use communication to convey their vision in highly compelling ways.

CHAPTER 6

DRIVING POINTS HOME

Highly effective leaders master the art of driving key messages home and achieving the designated goals of their speech—whether to inform, influence, persuade, motivate, or direct. Barack Obama has shown particular strength in his ability to share knowledge effectively, even amid the tight time constraints of a typical speech. In Chapter 5, we see how Obama employs communication practices that have enabled him to convey vision well; he knows how to articulate the "big picture." Obama is equally skilled in supporting the vision he puts forward with well-chosen details and themes that linger in the minds of listeners long after he has uttered a final word. Several additional practices have made Obama excellent at driving points home. Let's look at how he prioritizes his information, addresses rhetorical questions, employs effective repetition, leverages pace and tone, and communicates with slogans.

⇥ PRIORITIZING AND FOCUSING ON THEMES ⇤

Barack Obama demonstrates that when sharing knowledge, effective speakers understand and bear in mind the goal of their remarks—to influence, inform, motivate to action, or defuse controversy, for instance. Obama has developed the capacity to prioritize the points he will share. Based in part on his objectives, in the best of his speeches he sweeps aside low priority issues and promotes most assertively those ideas of greatest importance, shining a light on them. As he does this, Obama draws on an impressive array of rhetorical techniques to highlight his most important points and to present them memorably and with significant impact. Below, we examine many of these techniques.

⇥ USING RHETORICAL QUESTIONS ⇤

Often Obama raises rhetorical questions as a useful technique for focusing attention on key information. Rhetorical questions—questions whose answers are considered obvious and therefore are not answered by a speaker explicitly—help to emphasize points and crystallize attention around important issues. Obama has demonstrated how to employ rhetorical questions effectively to fix audience attention firmly on key issues or topics. He then proceeds to speak at greater length about his designated topics. Consider the example from Obama's 2004 keynote address:

In the end, that's what this election is about. *Do we participate in a politics of cynicism or do we participate in a politics of hope?* John Kerry calls on us to hope. John Edwards calls on us to hope. I'm not talking about blind optimism here—the almost willful ignorance that thinks unemployment will go away if we just don't think about it, or the health care crisis will solve itself if we just ignore it. That's not what I'm talking about. I'm talking about something more substantial. It's the hope of slaves sitting around a fire singing freedom songs; the hope of immigrants setting out for distant shores; the hope of a young naval lieutenant bravely patrolling the Mekong Delta; the hope of a millworker's son who dares to defy the odds; the hope of a skinny kid with a funny name who believes that America has a place for him, too. Hope in the face of difficulty. Hope in the face of uncertainty. The audacity of hope! [*Emphases added.*]

After drawing attention firmly to the notion of hope, Obama proceeds to elaborate on the notion. In another example, President Obama used rhetorical questions to drive home his points during his 2012 State of the Union address. He remarked:

Now, I recognize that people watching tonight have differing views about taxes and debt, energy and health care. But no matter what party they belong to, I bet most Americans are thinking the same thing right about now: Nothing will get done in Washington this year, or next year, or maybe even the year after that, because Washington is broken.

Can you blame them for feeling a little cynical?

The greatest blow to our confidence in our economy last year didn't come from events beyond our control. It came from a debate in Washington over whether the United States would pay its bills or not. Who benefited from that fiasco?

I've talked tonight about the deficit of trust between Main Street and Wall Street. But the divide between this city and the rest of the country is at least as bad—and it seems to get worse every year.

Rhetorical questions serve as valuable devices for focusing attention, laying the groundwork for delving into key themes.

⇥ EMPLOYING EFFECTIVE REPETITION ↤

A notable hallmark of Barack Obama's communication style is his use of unique variations of repetition. Obama draws on a wide variety of repetition techniques that give power to his oration—conduplicatio, anaphora, epistrophe, and mesodiplosis, among them. These rhetorical techniques help him to structure his key ideas and themes and drive key points home. Before delving into his remarks, however, let's take a look at definitions and examples.

Conduplicatio is the recurrence of a word or phrase found anywhere in one sentence or clause near the beginning of a successive clause or sentence. *Anaphora* is the recurrence of the same word, words, or phrases at the start of successive sentences, phrases, and clauses. Both are excellent tools for focusing attention on key words and ideas since those words or ideas are emphasized at the start of a successive sentence, phrase, or clause. Consider, for instance, these examples of anaphora:

> *To envision* the goal is good. *To envision* the execution is necessary. *To envision* the victory is crucial.

> *To give them* guidance is advisable. *To give them* motivation is required. *To give them* encouragement is imperative.

> *What does he* want? *What does he* hope for? *What does he* seek?

Repetition techniques such as anaphora have helped enhance the communicative power of many famous speeches. We find an excellent example in Dr. Martin Luther King Jr.'s famous "I Have a Dream" speech, delivered on August 28, 1963, at the Lincoln Memorial in Washington, DC:

> *I have a dream* that one day this nation will rise up and live out the true meaning of its creed: "We hold these truths to be self-evident: that all men are created equal."
>
> *I have a dream* that one day on the red hills of Georgia the sons of former slaves and the sons of former slave-owners will be able to sit down together at a table of brotherhood.
>
> *I have a dream* that one day even the state of Mississippi, a desert state, sweltering with the heat of injustice and oppression, will be transformed into an oasis of freedom and justice.

I have a dream that my four children will one day live in a nation where they will not be judged by the color of their skin but by the content of their character.

I have a dream today. [*Emphases provided.*]

A unique use of *anaphora* helped President Obama emphasize his desired points when speaking about American energy in 2012. He remarked:

Now, one of the reasons our oil—our dependence on foreign oil—is down is because of policies put in place by our administration, but also our predecessor's administration. And whoever succeeds me is going to have to keep it up. This is *not going to be* solved by one party; *it's not going to be* solved by one administration; *it's not going to be* solved by slogans; *it's not going to be* solved by phony rhetoric. It's going to be solved by a sustained, all-of-the-above energy strategy.[1] [*Emphases provided.*]

Epistrophe, the recurrence of the same word, words, or phrases at the end of successive sentences, phrases, or clauses, is also highly effective in focusing attention on key themes, adding emphasis. Think about this example:

The idea *was flawed*. The planning *was flawed*. The execution *was flawed*.

Epistrophe is effective in part because it fixes attention on the final word or words in a sentence, phrase, or paragraph. There are many famous examples. Consider this:

When I was a child, I spake *as a child*, I understood *as a child*, I thought *as a child*: but when I became a man, I put away childish things. (I Corinthians 13:11, King James Bible)

During his 2012 comments before AIPAC, President Obama used e*pistrophe* to underscore the significance of the U.S. relationship with Israel. He insisted:

If during this political season you hear some questions regarding my administration's support for Israel, remember that it's not backed up by the facts. And remember that the U.S.-Israel relationship is simply *too important* to be distorted by partisan politics. America's national security is *too important*. Israel's security is *too important*.[2] [*Emphases provided.*]

Mesodiplosis is the recurrence of a word or phrase near the midpoint of successive clauses or sentences. Here is an example:

We faced great obstacles, *yet we did not* give up; we felt great resistance, *yet we did not* give in; we grew weary from the long fight, *yet we did not* lie down.

Obama is famous for using variations of repetition to yield powerful oration. He draws on a full range of techniques and often extends his use of repetition across multiple paragraphs. This gives the paragraphs parallel structure—helping him to communicate his messages with greater efficacy. We look at several excellent examples below. We begin with Obama's remarks about John McCain, delivered on the final Democratic primary night in St. Paul, Minnesota, on June 3, 2008:

> John McCain has spent a lot of time talking about trips to Iraq in the last few weeks, but *maybe if he* spent some time taking trips to the cities and towns that have been hardest hit by this economy—cities in Michigan, and Ohio, and right here in Minnesota—he'd understand the kind of change that people are looking for.
>
> *Maybe if he* went to Iowa and met the student who works the night shift after a full day of class and still can't pay the medical bills for a sister who's ill, he'd understand that she can't afford four more years of a health-care plan that only takes care of the healthy and wealthy. She needs us to pass a health-care plan that guarantees insurance to every American who wants it and brings down premiums for every family who needs it. That's the change we need.
>
> *Maybe if he* went to Pennsylvania and met the man who lost his job but can't even afford the gas to drive around and look for a new one, he'd understand that we can't afford four more years of our addiction to oil from dictators. That man needs us to pass an energy policy that works with automakers to raise fuel standards and makes corporations pay for their pollution and oil companies invest their record profits in a clean energy future—an energy policy that will create millions of new jobs that pay well and can't be outsourced. That's the change we need.
>
> And *maybe if he* spent some time in the schools of South Carolina or St. Paul or where he spoke tonight in New

Orleans, he'd understand that we can't afford to leave the money behind for No Child Left Behind; that we owe it to our children to invest in early childhood education, to recruit an army of new teachers and give them better pay and more support, to finally decide that in this global economy the chance to get a college education should not be a privilege for the wealthy few, but the birthright of every American. That's the change we need in America. That's why I'm running for president.[3] [*Emphases added.*]

The repetition of the words "maybe if" help to provide a high level of structure to Obama's remarks and ideas. The dismissive words also focus attention on the main themes, which aim to cast doubt in the minds of listeners about McCain's credibility and the degree to which McCain is in touch with the plight of everyday Americans. Obama uses this repetition, therefore, in a way that enhances the impression he seeks to convey.

Similarly, in the remarks below, Obama skillfully uses repetition to create a sense of common identity among the diverse members of the audience, underscoring the principles they share and adding to a sense of unity:

This is our moment. This is our time for change. Our party—the Democratic party—has always been at its best when we've led not by polls, but by principle; not by calculation, but by conviction; when we've called all Americans to a common purpose—a higher purpose.

We are the party of Jefferson, who wrote the words that we are still trying to heed—that all of us are created equal, that all of us deserve the chance to pursue our happiness.

We're the party of Jackson, who took back the White House for the people of this country.

We're the party of a man who overcame his own disability to tell us that the only thing we had to fear was fear itself; who faced down fascism and liberated a continent from tyranny.

And we're the party of a young president who asked what we could do for our country and then challenged us to do it.

That is who we are. That is the party that we need to be, and can be, if we cast off our doubts and leave behind our fears and choose the America that we know is possible. Because there is a moment in the life of every generation, if it is to make its mark on history, when its spirit has to come through, when it must choose the future over the past, when it must make its own change from the bottom up.

This is our moment. This is our message—the same message we had when we were up, and when we were down. The same message that we will carry all the way to the convention. And in seven months' time we can realize this promise; we can claim this legacy; we can choose new leadership for America. Because there is nothing we cannot do if the American people decide it is time.[4] [*Emphases added.*]

Below, Obama uses repetition to stress unity, a strong image of forward action, a sense of urgency, and the importance of action on the part of the listener:

Let us begin this hard work together. *Let us* transform this nation.

Let us be the generation that reshapes our economy to compete in the digital age. *Let's* set high standards for our schools and give them the resources they need to succeed. *Let's* recruit a new army of teachers and give them better pay and more support in exchange for more accountability. *Let's* make college more affordable, and *let's* invest in scientific research, and *let's* lay down broadband lines through the heart of inner cities and rural towns all across America.

And as our economy changes, *let's be* the generation that ensures our nation's workers are sharing in our prosperity. *Let's* protect the hard-earned benefits their companies have promised. *Let's* make it possible for hard-working Americans to save for retirement. And *let's* allow our unions and their organizers to lift up this country's middle class again.

Let's be the generation that ends poverty in America. Every single person willing to work should be able to get job training that leads to a job and earn a living wage that can pay the bills and afford child care so their kids have a safe place to go when they work. *Let's* do this.

Let's be the generation that finally tackles our healthcare crisis. We can control costs by focusing on prevention, by providing better treatment to the chronically ill, and using technology to cut the bureaucracy. *Let's be* the generation that says right here, right now, that we will have universal health care in America by the end of the next president's first term.

Let's be the generation that finally frees America from the tyranny of oil. We can harness homegrown, alternative fuels like ethanol and spur the production of more fuel-efficient cars. We can set up a system for capping greenhouse gases. We can turn this crisis of global warming into a moment of opportunity for innovation and job creation and an incentive for businesses that will serve as a model for the world. *Let's be* the generation that makes future generations proud of what we did here.

Most of all, let's be the generation that never forgets what happened on that September day and confront the terrorists with everything we've got. Politics doesn't have to divide us on this anymore—we can work together to keep our country safe. I've worked with Republican Senator Dick Lugar to pass a law that will secure and destroy some of the world's deadliest, unguarded weapons. We can work together to track terrorists down with a stronger military, we can tighten the net around their finances, and we can improve our intelligence capabilities. But let us also understand that ultimate victory against our enemies will come only by rebuilding our alliances and exporting those ideals that bring hope and opportunity to millions around the globe.[5] [*Emphases added.*]

Repetition was the rhetorical tool of choice when Barack Obama underscored powerfully the consistent and deep commitment of the USA to Israel during his remarks before AIPAC in 2012. He stated:

Now our assistance is expanding Israel's defensive capabilities, so that more Israelis can live free from the fear of rockets and ballistic missiles. Because no family, no citizen, should live in fear.

And just as we've been there with our security assistance, we've been there through our diplomacy. *When* the Goldstone report unfairly singled out Israel for criticism, *we* challenged it. *When* Israel was isolated in the aftermath of the flotilla incident, *we* supported them. *When* the Durban conference was commemorated, *we* boycotted it, and we will always reject the notion that Zionism is racism.

When one-sided resolutions are brought up at the Human Rights Council, *we* oppose them. *When* Israeli diplomats feared for their lives in Cairo, *we* intervened to save them. *When* there are efforts to boycott or divest from Israel, *we* will stand against them. And whenever an effort is made to de-legitimize the state of Israel, my administration has opposed them. So there should not be a shred of doubt by now—when the chips are down, I have Israel's back.[6] [*Emphases added.*]

Repetition helped President Obama persuade the American people that all would be well following the forced resignation of General Stanley McChrystal amid a scandal in 2010. Obama used repetition to underscore that General Petraeus could fill the void effectively and seamlessly. He remarked:

Let me say to the American people, this is a change in personnel but it is not a change in policy. General Petraeus fully participated in our review last fall, and he both supported and helped design the strategy that we have in place. In his current post at Central Command, *he has worked closely* with our forces in Afghanistan. *He has worked closely* with Congress. *He has worked closely* with the Afghan and Pakistan governments and with all our partners in the region. He has my full confidence, and I am urging the Senate to confirm him for this new assignment as swiftly as possible.[7] [*Emphases provided.*]

President Obama's skillful use of repetition also allowed him to paint a vivid portrait of India's achievements and current successes, as he spoke before a Joint Session of the Indian Parliament in 2010. He stated:

And despite the skeptics who said this country was simply *too poor*, or *too vast*, or *too diverse* to succeed, you surmounted overwhelming odds and became a model to the world.

Instead of slipping into starvation, you launched a Green Revolution that fed millions. Instead of becoming dependent on commodities and exports, *you* invested in science and technology and in your greatest resource—the Indian people. And the world sees the results, from the supercomputers you build to the Indian flag that you put on the moon.

Instead of resisting the global economy, *you* became one of its engines—reforming the licensing raj and unleashing an economic marvel that has lifted tens of millions of people from poverty and created one of the world's largest middle classes.

Instead of succumbing to division, *you* have shown that the strength of India—the very idea of India—is its embrace of all colors, all castes, all creeds. It's the diversity represented in this chamber today. It's the richness of faiths celebrated by a visitor to my hometown of Chicago more than a century ago—the renowned Swami Vivekananda. He said that, "holiness, purity and charity are not the exclusive possessions of any church in the world, and that every system has produced men and women of the most exalted character."

And instead of being lured by the false notion that progress must come at the expense of freedom, *you* built the institutions upon which true democracy depends.[8]

⇥ LEVERAGING PACE AND TONE ⇤

In driving points home with skill, Barack Obama also employs variations of pace and tone excellently. He draws on a full range of effective rhetorical techniques that focus the listener on his key points. Here are of some of his more prominent techniques.

Adding Emphasis and Eloquence—Alliteration

At times, Obama uses *alliteration,* the repetition of the sounds of the initial consonants of words, to help drive key points home. In general, with alliteration the recurrence of initial consonant sounds may be sprinkled throughout a sentence. For example:

In *long lines* that *led* to the ballot boxes, you *demonstrated* the *depth* of your *determination.*

His *policy position pleased* many.

The repetition of the starting consonant sound draws attention to those particular words and serves as a valuable technique for underscoring key words and ideas. Obama draws on alliteration as needed to emphasize words and concepts, and often to add eloquence to the beginning of his speeches. Alliteration can provide a musical beginning, which is pleasant to the ears. Consider how Obama began his 2004 Democratic National Convention keynote address:

> On behalf of the great state of Illinois, crossroads of a nation, *land* of *Lincoln, let* me express my deep gratitude for the privilege of addressing this convention. [*Emphases added.*]

Many of Obama's most powerful speeches are sprinkled with alliteration, adding to the sense that he is an eloquent speaker. Consider his words as he announced his candidacy for the U.S. presidency in Springfield, Illinois, on February 10, 2007:

> But through his *will* and his *words*, he moved a nation and helped free a people. [*Emphases added.*]

Similarly, Obama employed alliteration multiple times in his speech following his loss of the Pennsylvania primary in 2008. For example, he stated:

> It was a creed written into the founding *documents* that *declared* the *destiny* of a nation. [*Emphases added.*]

During his remarks about the resignation of General Stanley McChrystal in 2010, alliteration helped President Obama underscore his mission to keep America safe from terrorism and terrorists' efforts. He stated:

> . . . I have a responsibility to do what is—whatever is necessary to succeed in Afghanistan, and in our broader effort to *disrupt, dismantle*, and *defeat* al Qaeda. I believe that this mission demands unity of effort across our alliance and across my national security team.[9] [*Emphases provided.*]

When informing the American public about the military success in killing Osama bin Laden in 2011, alliteration also helped Obama emphasize the importance of the work in the fight against terrorism. He remarked:

> After nearly 10 years of *service, struggle*, and *sacrifice*, we know well the costs of war. These efforts weigh on me every time I, as Commander-in-Chief, have to sign a *letter* to a family that has *lost* a *loved* one, or *look* into the eyes of a service member who's been gravely wounded.[10] [*Emphases added.*]

President Obama also used alliteration to close his August 2011 comments about the S&P downgrade of the U.S. credit rating, when he stated:

> But no matter what differences they might have as individuals, they serve this nation as a team. They meet their responsibilities together. And some of them—like the 30 Americans who were lost this weekend—give their lives for their country. Our responsibility is to ensure that their legacy is an America that reflects their *courage*,

their *commitment,* and their sense of *common* purpose.[11] [*Emphases provided.*]

Alliteration, used even subtly, can draw attention to words and enhance the eloquence of speech.

Picking Up Speed—Asyndeton

Asyndeton occurs when a speaker deliberately omits conjunctions (such as "and," "but," "or," "nor," and "for") between successive words, phrases, or clauses. The omission quickens the pace of spoken words. It also gives a sense that a list of words is only partial or is more far-reaching than the words appearing in the list. Specifically, the omission of the word "and" can imply that the given list is only partially representative, and in fact, goes on. Here is an example:

To win, we demonstrated *vision, hard work, dedication, perseverance.*

Asyndeton can also serve to emphasize or amplify a point, when successive words seem to represent or echo the word immediately prior in an amplified form. For example:

We learned to *rise, stand, brace, fight.*

There are many famous examples of asyndeton, such as in Abraham Lincoln's Gettysburg Address:

But in a larger sense, we *cannot dedicate, we cannot consecrate, we cannot hallow* this ground.[12] [*Emphases added.*]

Like many great orators before him, Obama also uses asyndeton to enhance the power of his comments. In the speech in which he announced his presidential candidacy on February 10, 2007, for instance, Obama used this technique to make his words sound more emphatic:

> . . . you believe we can be one people, reaching for what's possible, building that more perfect union.

When emphasizing America's need to strengthen itself tocompete in the changing world during his 2011 State of the Union address, President Obama used asyndeton as he remarked:

> Our infrastructure used to be the best, but our lead has slipped. South Korean homes now have greater Internet access than we do. Countries in Europe and Russia invest more in their roads and railways than we do. China is building faster trains and newer airports. Meanwhile, when our own engineers graded our nation's infrastructure, they gave us a "D."
>
> We have to do better. *America is the nation that built the transcontinental railroad, brought electricity to rural communities, constructed the Interstate Highway System.* The jobs created by these projects didn't just come from laying down track or pavement. They came from businesses that opened near a town's new train station or the new off-ramp.[13] [*Emphases provided.*]

President Obama used asyndeton to emphasis his belief in America's greatness, as he remarked in his August 2011 remarks on the S&P downgrade of the U.S. credit rating:

For all of the challenges we face, we continue to have the best universities, some of the most productive workers, the most innovative companies, the most adventurous entrepreneurs on Earth.[14]

Similarly, asyndeton added to the richness of President Obama's 2012 State of the Union address. He said:

One of my proudest possessions is the flag that the SEAL Team took with them on the mission to get bin Laden. On it are each of their names. Some may be Democrats. Some may be Republicans. But that doesn't matter. Just like it didn't matter that day in the Situation Room, when I sat next to Bob Gates—a man who was George Bush's defense secretary—and Hillary Clinton—a woman who ran against me for president.

All that mattered that day was the mission. No one thought about politics. No one thought about themselves. One of the young men involved in the raid later told me that he didn't deserve credit for the mission. It only succeeded, he said, because every single member of that unit did their job—*the pilot who landed the helicopter that spun out of control; the translator who kept others from entering the compound; the troops who separated the women and children from the fight; the SEALs who charged up the stairs.* More than that, the mission only succeeded because every member of that unit trusted each other—because you can't charge up those stairs, into darkness and danger, unless you know that there's somebody behind you, watching your back. [*Emphases provided.*]

During his remarks in 2012 about the U.S. relationship with Israel, President Obama also used asyndeton effectively. He commented:

> We may not agree on every single issue—no two nations do, and our democracies contain a vibrant diversity of views. But we agree on the big things—the things that matter. And together, we are working to build a better world—one where our people can live free from fear; one where peace is founded upon justice; one where our children can know a future that is more hopeful than the present.[15]

Amplifying Ideas—Polysyndeton

Polysyndeton occurs when a conjunction, such as *and*, is used between every word, clause, or phrase, or between a series of more than two successive clauses or phrases. It serves as a valuable technique for building up or amplifying a point, in part because the repetition of conjunctions stands out and hence the list of words seems to go on at greater length than normal. In the example below, for instance, the use of polysyndeton gives the impression of an arduous and extensive breadth of activity:

> We brainstormed *and* planned *and* executed *and* achieved our goal.
>
> We studied *and* shared *and* learned *and* succeeded.

This technique can be powerful when used for negations ("nor") or extended comparison ("as"):

As with the rebels, *as* with the freedom riders, *as* with occupy movement supporters, we . . .

Obama uses polysyndeton with great effect. Consider these instances. On January 3, 2008, during his remarks on Iowa caucus night in Des Moines, Iowa, he said:

I know this—I know this because while I may be standing here tonight, I'll never forget that my journey began on the streets of Chicago doing what so many of you have done for this campaign and all the campaigns here in Iowa—*organizing and working and fighting to* make people's lives just a little bit better.[16] [*Emphases added.*]

In the same speech, he asserted:

This was the moment when we finally beat back the politics of *fear and doubt and cynicism* . . . [*Emphases added.*]

President Obama employed this rhetorical technique in his 2009 inaugural address, when he said:

To those leaders around the globe who seek to sow conflict, or blame their society's ills on the West, know that your people will judge you on what you can build, not what you destroy.

To those who cling to power through corruption and deceit and the silencing of dissent, know that you are on the wrong side of history, but that we will extend a hand if you are willing to unclench your fist.

He used polysyndeton in 2011 to emphasize America's ability to innovate and transform American energy sources, products, and practices. In his remarks on American energy, he said:

> We may not have a silver bullet to bring down gas prices tomorrow, or reduce our dependence on foreign oil overnight. But what we do have in this country are limitless sources of energy, and a boundless supply of ingenuity *and* imagination *and* talent that we can put to work to develop the energy of the future. We've got you. We've got you.[17] [*Emphases provided.*]

During his 2011 State of the Union address, this same technique allowed President Obama to stress his belief that in spite of issues that divide Americans, we can unite for a greater purpose. He said:

> But there's a reason the tragedy in Tucson gave us pause. Amid all the noise *and* passion *and* rancor of our public debate, Tucson reminded us that no matter who we are or where we come from, each of us is a part of something greater—something more consequential than party or political preference.[18] [*Emphases provided.*]

Driving Points Home with the Power of Three

When seeking to drive points home and paint clear pictures, Obama sometimes uses three words, three phrases, or even three parallel paragraphs, to underscore his points. These practices are variations of "tricolon." I will refer to them here as "triadic extension." For example, on the night of his 2008 Iowa caucus win, Obama stated:

> I know how hard it is. It comes with *little sleep*, *little pay*, and *a lot of sacrifice*. [*Emphases added.*]

In an example from Obama's announcement for president, in Springfield, Illinois, on February 10, 2007, he stated:

> It will take *your time*, *your energy*, and *your advice* to push us forward when we're doing right, and to let us know when we're not. This campaign has to be about *reclaiming* the meaning of citizenship, *restoring* our sense of common purpose, and *realizing* that few obstacles can withstand the power of millions of voices calling for change. [*Emphases added.*]

In the preceding example, triadic phrases help to provide structure to thoughts. They also help to underscore the breadth of what must be achieved: *reclaiming, restoring, realizing*.

Triadic extensions can also be used to paint a picture more fully and to add eloquence to delivery. Speaking of President Abraham Lincoln during his announcement for president in February 2007, Obama used a loose variation of triadic extension:

> *He tells us that* there is power in words.
> *He tells us that* there is power in conviction.

That beneath all the differences of race and region, faith and station, we are one people.

He tells us that there is power in hope.[19] [*Emphases added.*]

Using Triadic Extensions for Forward Momentum

There are other, more specific uses of triadic phrases. Obama sometimes uses triadic extension to establish a sense of a continuum or a movement forward. This helps amplify his points. For example, in his announcement for president on February 10, 2007, he said:

> *In the face of tyranny*, a band of patriots brought an empire to its knees. *In the face of secession*, we unified a nation and set the captives free. *In the face of Depression*, we put people back to work and lifted millions out of poverty. [*Emphases added.*]

Using Triadic Extensions to Reiterate Key Aspects

Triadic extensions are also useful for emphasizing important aspects or traits about the subject under discussion. To do this, the three words of the triadic extension should represent a succession of synonymous words that underscore similar ideas. Referred to generally as *scesis onomaton*, when used in a triadic extension it helps drive points home. For example:

> She displayed *enthusiasm*, demonstrated *fervor*, exuded *passion*.

In his remarks in Des Moines, Iowa, on December 27, 2007, Obama stated:

> In the end, the argument we are having between the candidates in the last seven days is not just about the meaning of change. It's about the meaning of hope. Some of my opponents appear scornful of the word; they think it speaks of *naïveté, passivity, and wishful thinking.*[20] [*Emphases added.*]

During his remarks following his win in the Iowa caucus on January 3, 2008, Obama said:

> You said the time has come to move beyond *the bitterness and pettiness and anger* that's consumed Washington; to end the political strategy that's been all about division and instead make it about addition; to build a coalition for change that stretches through red states and blue states. [*Emphases added.*]

In this example from his announcement for president on February 10, 2007, Obama combines triadic extensions with *scesis onomaton* to elaborate on one idea, reiterated in three slightly varying ways. This amplifies the point he is making, causing it to stand out:

> That's what Abraham Lincoln understood. *He had his doubts. He had his defeats. He had his setbacks.* But through his will and his words, he moved a nation and helped free a people. [*Emphases added.*]

President Obama used triadic extension to underscore his message during his February 2009 remarks at the Lincoln bicentennial celebration, when he stated:

. . . as we meet here today, in a moment when we are far less divided than in Lincoln's day, but when we are once again debating the critical issues of our time—and debating them sometimes fiercely—let us remember that we are doing so as *servants of the same flag*, as *representatives of the same people*, and as *stakeholders in a common future*. That is the most fitting tribute we can pay—the most lasting monument we can build—to that most remarkable of men, Abraham Lincoln. [*Emphases added.*]

Indeed, a key technique found in President Obama's 2012 State of the Union address was triadic extension. He remarked:

The Taliban's momentum has been broken, and some troops in Afghanistan have begun to come home. These achievements are a testament to the *courage, selflessness, and teamwork* of America's Armed Forces. [*Emphases added.*]

When speaking about the economic hardships of the American people in this same speech, he stated:

Folks at the top saw their incomes rise like never before, but most hardworking Americans struggled with *costs that were growing, paychecks that weren't, and personal debt that kept piling up*. [*Emphases added.*]

Using Triadic Extensions for a Multiplier Effect

To add a multiplier effect, Obama sometimes also employs extra conjunctions such as "and" along with triadic extension. In his announcement for president on February 10, 2007, he stated:

> [A]s people have looked away in disillusionment and frustration, we know what's filled the void. *The cynics,* and *the lobbyists,* and the *special interests* who've turned our government into a game only they can afford to play. [*Emphases added.*]

We see this same technique reflected in his 2012 State of the Union address when President Obama remarked:

> We're also making it easier for American businesses to sell products all over the world. Two years ago, I set a goal of doubling U.S. exports over five years. With the bipartisan trade agreements we signed into law, we're on track to meet that goal ahead of schedule. And soon, there will be millions of new customers for American goods in *Panama, Colombia, and South Korea.* Soon, there will be new cars on the streets of Seoul imported from *Detroit, and Toledo, and Chicago.* [*Emphases added.*]

Using Triadic Extensions to Enhance the Sense of Logic

To give power to his points, Obama sometimes uses triadic words or phrases with a sequenced order. This establishes both a strong sense of logic and an amplification, underscoring a particular point of view. During his 2004 Democratic National Convention keynote address, for example, he said:

> When we send our young men and women into harm's way, we have a solemn obligation not to fudge the numbers or shade the truth about why they're going, to care for their families while they're gone, to tend to the soldiers upon their return, and to never ever go to war without enough troops to *win the war, secure the peace,* and *earn the respect* of the world. [*Emphases added.*]

Similarly, in the same speech, he stressed:

> We have real enemies in the world. These enemies must be *found,* they must be *pursued,* and they must be *defeated.* [*Emphases added.*]

Here is an example where Obama structures paragraphs using the broad concept of triadic extension, presenting his thoughts in three sets that reinforce a theme. When conveying how intimately he understands the plight of the average American, Obama mentioned:

> *I've heard from seniors* who were betrayed by CEOs who dumped their pensions while pocketing bonuses, and from those who still can't afford their prescriptions because Congress refused to negotiate with the drug companies for the cheapest available price.

I've met Maytag workers who labored all their lives only to see their jobs shipped overseas; who now compete with their teenagers for $7-an-hour jobs at Wal-Mart.

I've spoken with teachers who are working at doughnut shops after school just to make ends meet; who are still digging into their own pockets to pay for school supplies.[21] [*Emphases added.*]

⇝ COMMUNICATING WITH SLOGANS AND REFRAINS ⇜

Obama also employs slogans and refrains to emphasize his key themes and takeaways. This helps focus audience attention. A *slogan* is a catchphrase or short sentence that reflects the themes a speaker wants people to remember. A *refrain*—originally a musical term, but increasingly used in the media to describe elements of public speech—can be thought of as a concise chant phrase that underscores a main idea, like a chorus emphasizes a song's theme. Obama often uses repetition as he seeks to fix the slogans or refrains in the minds of listeners. He has been so highly effective in conveying his slogans and refrains that many Americans can recite with ease at least one from his 2008 presidential campaign, such as *"Yes we can." "Change we can believe in." "There is something happening." "Our moment is now."*

We see a powerful example of the use of slogans when examining Obama's remarks following his primary loss in Pennsylvania. It was an important loss, because pundits questioned whether the loss signaled that Obama would fail to gain sufficient support among working-class Americans. To quell any sense that he was losing momentum, Obama came out strong, conveying a slogan that enabled listeners to fix their sights on future possibilities and remain motivated. He also used alliteration to add power to his words, making them sound more eloquent and hopeful, and encouraging supporters to remain inspired:

[I]n the unlikely story that is America, there has never been anything false about hope. For when we have faced down impossible odds; when we've been told that we're not ready or that we shouldn't try or that we can't, generations of Americans have responded with a simple creed that sums up the spirit of a people.

Yes we can.

It was a creed written into the founding *documents* that *declared* the *destiny* of a nation. [*Alliteration.*]

Yes we can.

It was whispered by slaves and abolitionists as they blazed a *trail toward* freedom through the darkest of nights. [*Alliteration.*]

Yes we can.

It was *sung* by immigrants as they *struck* out from distant *shores* and *pioneers* who *pushed* westward against an unforgiving wilderness. [*Alliteration.*]

Yes we can.

It was the call of *workers who* organized; *women who* reached for the ballot; a president who chose the moon as our new frontier; and a King who took us to the mountaintop and pointed the way to the promised land. [*Alliteration.*]

Yes we can to justice and equality. *Yes we can* to opportunity and prosperity. *Yes we can* heal this nation. *Yes we can* repair this world. *Yes we can.*[22] [*Emphases added.*]

Consider another example:

The choice in this election is not between regions or religions or genders. It's not about rich versus poor; young versus old; and it is not about black versus white.

It's about the past versus the future.

It's about whether we settle for the same divisions and distractions and drama that passes for politics today, or whether we reach for a politics of common sense, and innovation—a shared sacrifice and shared prosperity.

There are those who will continue to tell us we cannot do this. That we cannot have what we long for. That we are peddling false hopes.

But here's what I know. I know that when people say we can't overcome all the big money and influence in Washington, I think of the elderly woman who sent me a contribution the other day—an envelope that had a money order for $3.01 along with a verse of scripture tucked inside. So don't tell us change isn't possible.

When I hear the cynical talk that blacks and whites and Latinos can't join together and work together, I'm reminded of the Latino brothers and sisters I organized with and stood with and fought with side by side for jobs and justice on the streets of Chicago. So don't tell us change can't happen.

When I hear that we'll never overcome the racial divide in our politics, I think about that Republican woman who used to work for Strom Thurmond, who's now devoted to educating inner-city children and who went out onto the streets of South Carolina and knocked on doors for this campaign. Don't tell me we can't change.

Yes we can change.

Yes we can heal this nation.

Yes we can seize our future.

And as we leave this state with a new wind at our backs and take this journey across the country we love with the message we've carried from the plains of Iowa to the hills of New Hampshire; from the Nevada desert to the South Carolina coast; the same message we had when we were up and when we were down—that out of many, we are one; that while we breathe, we hope; and where we are met with cynicism and doubt and those who tell us that we can't, we will respond with that timeless creed that sums up the spirit of a people in three simple words:

Yes. We. Can.[23] [*Emphases added.*]

The repetition drives "yes we can" home as a key theme and slogan.

⇥ WHAT WE'VE LEARNED—PRACTICES ⇤ FOR DRIVING POINTS HOME

In this chapter, we have taken a look at key communication techniques that allow Barack Obama to drive home points effectively. We can learn much from these techniques. When constructing remarks, for example, highly effective communicators prioritize and focus well, casting aside lower priority issues and shining a light on ideas of greatest importance. They draw on a wide range of valuable rhetorical devices to promote assertively the most significant ideas and themes. Rhetorical questions help crystallize attention on key ideas. Repetition and parallel paragraph structures emphasize key points and help build to a climax. Alliteration draws attention to key words and adds a musical eloquence to speech. A choice to omit conjunctions enables skilled speakers to pick up speed, presenting emphatic words. Adding extra conjunctions amplifies points and creates a multiplier effect. When leveraging the "power of three," skilled communicators underscore key points, building momentum or enhancing a sense of logic. Communicating with slogans and refrains can help leaders emphasize themes to be remembered.

CHAPTER 7

PERSUADING

Throughout his political career, Barack Obama has delivered a striking number of momentum-building speeches that demonstrate his ability to use communication as a means to persuade others.

Persuasion is central to effective leadership. It is the act—or, as some would say, the "art"—of influencing someone to do something by advising, encouraging, or convincing them. Beyond informing, persuasion involves ways of conveying information that convince listeners to agree with a particular perspective. The goal is to get to "yes," a nod, or that glimmer in the eye of a listener that indicates you've achieved agreement—you've gotten through and the listener is embracing your ideas.

Persuasion plays a central role in enabling leaders to motivate and guide others to achieve designated goals. It is considered so central to effective leadership that scores of books have been written on variations of the topic—*the power of persuasion, the importance of persuasion, the craft of persuasion.*

Barack Obama's speeches have often served as core tools that have enabled his success. His persuasive power was evident through the 2 million individual donors he motivated to contribute to his 2008 presidential campaign. Obama's notable ability to persuade was also evident through the tremendous momentum he experienced during his 2008 primary campaign, his ability to fill a stadium with as many as 75,000 eager listeners, his success in drawing a German audience of 200,000 for a single speech, and his success in inspiring millions to help support his 2012 reelection bid. What is Barack Obama doing that people find so compelling? How has his effective communication style persuaded so many people to consider his views? How does he inspire people to embrace and ultimately support his perspectives and vision? We have much to learn from his practices—how he sequences ideas, answers nonrhetorical questions, addresses objections, uses antithesis, and crystallizes his points through juxtaposition, comparisons, and contrasts.

⫷ ELICITING A NOD ⫸

There are many dimensions to persuasion, and many types of tools can facilitate effective persuasion. Body language plays a role. Oratory delivery techniques make an impact. Voice and intonation can sway listeners, as can techniques such as employing dramatic pauses, using emphatic words, and employing effective gestures. Descriptive language paints lucid pictures and also serves the cause. Barack Obama demonstrates that other key practices also aid the quest to persuade. As a master of the craft, several of Obama's additional practices are worth exploring.

⇥ SEQUENCING IDEAS ⇤

Barack Obama illustrates that orators skilled in the art of persuasion know how to create a strong sense of logic to their ideas and remarks. The clarity of their reasoning is apparent and they demonstrate the merit of their ideas with sharp arguments.

One key to creating a strong sense of logic involves sequencing ideas. There is no "right" order, as such—only an *effective* order. The listener must be able to understand the flow of thoughts and find that this flow makes logical, compelling sense. This lays the foundation for agreement. Sequencing information should help achieve the goal of conveying ideas effectively and, if possible, help elicit a yes or a nod.

In his public remarks, Obama sequences his ideas and themes well. It is possible to observe this sequencing within a concise series of sentences. For example, during his 2004 keynote address, Obama sequenced his ideas in a way that conveyed logic and strong determination:

We have real enemies in the world. These enemies must be found. They must be pursued, and they must be defeated.

When issuing a public statement about the resignation of General Stanley McChrystal in 2010, President Obama also employed a concise series of logically flowing sequenced ideas to convey the U.S. military approach. He stated:

> So make no mistake: We have a clear goal. We are going to break the Taliban's momentum. We are going to build Afghan capacity. We are going to relentlessly apply pressure on al Qaeda and its leadership, strengthening the ability of both Afghanistan and Pakistan to do the same.[1]

In his remarks before AIPAC in 2012, President Obama employed a similar style. He commented:

> I have said that when it comes to preventing Iran from obtaining a nuclear weapon, I will take no options off the table, and I mean what I say. That includes all elements of American power: A political effort aimed at isolating Iran; a diplomatic effort to sustain our coalition and ensure that the Iranian program is monitored; an economic effort that imposes crippling sanctions; and, yes, a military effort to be prepared for any contingency.[2]

Obama also sequences ideas and themes in parallel order, paragraph by paragraph, which lends his remarks a strong sense of order and helps persuade the listener. In the following example, Obama structured his points with themes that— sequenced effectively one after the other, by paragraph— successfully reinforced his commitment to the community and ultimately helped persuade many listeners of his sincere dedication to their interests:

I walked away from a job on Wall Street to bring job training to the jobless and after school programs to kids on the streets of Chicago.

I turned down the big-money law firms to win justice for the powerless as a civil rights lawyer.

I took on the lobbyists in Illinois and brought Democrats and Republicans together to expand health care to 150,000 people and pass the first major campaign finance reform in twenty-five years; and I did the same thing in Washington when we passed the toughest lobbying reform since Watergate. I'm the only candidate in this race who hasn't just talked about taking power away from lobbyists; I've actually done it.[3] [*Emphasis added.*]

Here's another example. When speaking about American energy in 2012 in New Hampshire, President Obama asked a question as a means of underscoring his points:

In five years, the number of cars on the road in China more than tripled. Over the last five years, the number of cars tripled. Nearly 10 million cars were added in China alone in 2010—10 million cars just in one country in one year. So that's using up a lot of oil. And those numbers are only going to get bigger over time. As places like China and India get wealthier, they're going to want to buy cars like we do, and they're going to want to fill them up like we do, and that's going to drive up demand.

So what does this mean for us? What does this mean for America? It means that anybody who tells you that we can just drill our way out of this problem does not know what they're talking about or they're not telling you the truth. [*Applause.*][4]

Similarly, when speaking to the Joint Session of the Indian Parliament in New Delhi in 2010, President Obama used a nonrhetorical question to lead into a deeper discussion. He remarked:

So since that time, people in both our countries have asked: What's next? How can we build on this progress and realize the full potential of our partnership? That's what I want to address today—the future that the United States seeks in an interconnected world, and why I believe that India is indispensable to this vision; how we can forge a truly global partnership—not just in one or two areas, but across many; not just for our mutual benefit, but for the benefit of the world.[5]

For leaders seeking to develop outstanding communication skills, a best practice is to sequence your ideas in a highly effective manner. Make sure to communicate your points so that you make *compelling sense*.

⇥ ADDRESSING NONRHETORICAL QUESTIONS ⇤

Another way to enhance persuasion is by addressing non-rhetorical questions. Asking a nonrhetorical question—one you intend to answer—is a valuable way to replicate a sense of two-way conversation. The use of nonrhetorical questions, addressed at appropriate length, makes the listener feel as if the speaker is raising and addressing commonly held concerns. Referred to as *hypophora*, the practice enables speakers to act as if they are vetting key questions from the audience. A well-developed answer demonstrates depth of knowledge and aids effective knowledge sharing. Nonrhetorical questions also focus attention on key concerns and make remarks more engaging.

Barack Obama has shown great skill in employing nonrhetorical questions. Before he delivers his remarks, Obama seems to often consider: *What does the audience most want to know and learn? What will it most doubt or question?* The next task: ask and answer. Obama has demonstrated the power of asking nonrhetorical questions and providing the answers, replicating effective dialogue. Consider this example, as Obama spoke of Robert Kennedy at the Robert F. Kennedy Human Rights Award Ceremony on November 16, 2005. Obama asked:

> Why is it that this man who was never president, who was our attorney general for only three years, who was New York's junior senator for just three and a half, still calls to us today? Still inspires our debate with his words, animates our politics with his ideas, and calls us to make gentle the life of a world that's too often coarse and unforgiving?
>
> Obviously, much has to do with charisma and eloquence—that unique ability, rare for most but common among Kennedys, to sum up the hopes and dreams of the most diverse nation on Earth with a simple phrase or sentence; to inspire even the most apathetic observers of American life.

Part of it is his youth—both the time of life and the state of mind that dared us to hope that even after John was killed; even after we lost King; there would come a younger, energetic Kennedy who could make us believe again.

But beyond these qualities, there's something more.

Obama proceeded to elaborate about the relevant attributes of Kennedy. As he often does when using this technique, Obama answers the question at length to underscore his points. In asking a germane question and then answering it, Obama succeeded in creating the feel of an engaging, two-way dialogue and in advancing his key points. This technique can be applied with great success. Leaders aspiring to use their words to persuade others should seek to identify a question or two that listeners would most like to understand. Consider asking and answering a question or two as you deliver your remarks.

⊰ ADDRESSING OBJECTIONS ⊱

Obama also understands the value of addressing objections. This technique, known as *procatalepsis*, is a useful rhetorical device and an excellent persuasion tool. By airing a potential objection and responding to it, speakers can persuade listeners by providing logical reasons why key counterarguments should be dismissed. Addressing objections demonstrates awareness of key counterarguments and provides the speaker with opportunities to illustrate why their chosen positions are more sensible. In addressing key counterarguments, a speaker can skillfully undercut those arguments, strengthening their own positions.

Consider this example from December 27, 2007, when Obama addressed concerns that his emphasis on hope was naïve:

> In the end, the argument we are having between the candidates in the last seven days is not just about the meaning of change. It's about the meaning of hope. *Some of my opponents appear scornful of the word; they think it speaks of naïveté, passivity, and wishful thinking.*
>
> *But that's not what hope is.* Hope is not blind optimism. It's not ignoring the enormity of the task before us or the roadblocks that stand in our path. Yes, the lobbyists will fight us. Yes, the Republican attack dogs will go after us in the general election. Yes, the problems of poverty and climate change and failing schools will resist easy repair. I know. I've been on the streets, I've been in the courts. I've watched legislation die because the powerful held sway, and good intentions weren't fortified by political will. And I've watched a nation get mislead into war because no one had the judgment or the courage to ask the hard questions before we sent our troops to fight.
>
> But I also know this: I know that hope has been the guiding force behind the most improbable changes this country has ever made. In the face of tyranny, it's what led a band of colonists to rise up against an empire. In the face of slavery, it's what fueled the resistance of the slave and the abolitionist, and what allowed a president to chart a treacherous course to ensure that the nation would not continue half slave and half free. In the face of war and Depression, it's what led the greatest of generations to free a continent and heal a nation. In the face of oppression, it's what led young men and women to sit at

lunch counters and brave fire hoses and march through the streets of Selma and Montgomery for freedom's cause. That's the power of hope—to imagine, and then work for, what had seemed impossible before. [*Emphasis added.*]

President Obama also used this technique of addressing objections when he stated during his 2009 inaugural address:

Now, there are some who question the scale of our ambitions, who suggest that our system cannot tolerate too many big plans. Their memories are short, for they have forgotten what this country has already done, what free men and women can achieve when imagination is joined to common purpose, and necessity to courage. What the cynics fail to understand is that the ground has shifted beneath them, that the stale political arguments that have consumed us for so long no longer apply.

We see above that when preparing remarks with the aim of persuading, addressing objections can prove a useful exercise. For a speaker seeking to persuade, identify key counterarguments and consider whether your remarks can be enhanced by drawing attention to those counterarguments and explaining why your ideas are best.

⇥ USING JUXTAPOSITION AND ANTITHESIS— ⇤ COMPARING AND CONTRASTING

One of the hallmarks of Barack Obama's powerful oration is his outstanding use of juxtaposition. Through juxtaposition,

Obama places opposing ideas side by side, allowing him to crystallize key points about the ideas or concepts by comparing or contrasting them.

When contrasting the ideas, Obama frequently uses antithesis, a technique that places two ideas side by side in a sentence or paragraph, often using balancing or parallel structures. Antithesis enables a speaker to present "counter propositions," clarifying differences in ideas and contrasting opposite ideas or beliefs.

There are many examples of antithesis in famous American speeches:

> [We] observe today not a victory of party, but a celebration of freedom—symbolizing an end as well as a beginning— signifying renewal as well as change. (John F. Kennedy's inaugural address, January 20, 1961)

Obama uses antithesis to great effect in his public remarks. In some instances, the comparisons are succinct—simple statements that make profound points. For example, Obama commented after the final primary night in St. Paul, Minnesota, on June 3, 2008:

> We must be as careful getting out of Iraq as we were careless getting in . . .

During his remarks on the final primary night in Minnesota, he also stated:

> [T]he chance to get a college education should not be a privilege for the wealthy few, but the birthright of every

American. That's the change we need in America. That's why I'm running for president.

During his comments in his speech "Our Kids, Our Future," in November 2007, Obama noted:

And so while I know hopelessness, I also know hope.

These are examples of succinct uses of antithesis that bring clarity to thought and aid persuasion. Obama is also highly skilled in using a longer antithesis/contrast structure to extend his clarification of ideas. In his remarks following his historic win of the Iowa caucus in January 2008, Obama said:

But we always knew that hope is not blind optimism. It's not ignoring the enormity of the task ahead or the road-blocks that stand in our path. It's not sitting on the sidelines or shirking from a fight. Hope is that thing inside us that insists, despite all evidence to the contrary, that something better awaits us if we have the courage to reach for it, and to work for it, and to fight for it.

Below, Obama juxtaposes ideas in succession in order to clarify the character of the Democratic party:

Our party—the Democratic party—has always been at its best when we've led not by polls, but by principle; not by calculation, but by conviction; when we've called all Americans to a common purpose—a higher purpose.[6]

President Obama used antithesis with great effect when he took command of the crisis at hand, asking for the resignation of General Stanley McChrystal in 2010. When issuing public remarks about the matter, antithesis helped him project his resoluteness and insistence on unity. He said:

I've just told my national security team that now is the time for all of us to come together. Doing so is not an option, but an obligation.[7]

Following the death of Osama bin Laden in 2011, President Obama used antithesis to underscore that in pursuing and killing Osama bin Laden, America was not at war with Islam. He stated:

I've made clear, just as President Bush did shortly after 9/11, that our war is not against Islam. Bin Laden was not a Muslim leader; he was a mass murderer of Muslims.[8]

During his 2011 State of the Union address, Obama sought to encourage cooperation across party lines with his use of antithesis. He commented:

Now, by itself, this simple recognition won't usher in a new era of cooperation. What comes of this moment is up to us. What comes of this moment will be determined not by whether we can sit together tonight, but whether we can work together tomorrow.[9]

Obama draws on many additional variations of juxtaposition/ antithesis. Their net effect is to sharpen the persuasive power of his remarks. Let's delve into some of his key practices.

Juxtaposition and Tricolon

At times Obama combines juxtaposition with other rhetorical techniques such as triadic extension to bring precision to his contrast of ideas. During his announcement for president in Springfield, Illinois, on February 10, 2007, for example, he blended juxtaposition with triadic extension to compare what Americans face and what they desire:

> It's humbling, but in my heart I know you didn't come here just for me. You came here because you believe in what this country can be. In the face of war, you believe there can be peace. In the face of despair, you believe there can be hope. In the face of a politics that's shut you out, that's told you to settle, that's divided us for too long, you believe we can be one people, reaching for what's possible, building that more perfect union.

Extended Juxtaposition

One of the hallmarks of Barack Obama's effective communication is his use of creative variations of juxtaposition. At times, Obama structures whole paragraphs around opposing ideas. In this example, he presents extended juxtaposition through a series of contrasts and comparisons in back-and-forth succession:

We have a choice in this election.

We can be a party that says there's no problem with taking money from Washington lobbyists—from oil lobbyists and drug lobbyists and insurance lobbyists. *We can* pretend that they represent real Americans and look the other way when they use their money and influence to stop us from reforming health care or investing in renewable energy for yet another four years.

Or this time, we can recognize that you can't be the champion of working Americans if you're funded by the lobbyists who drown out their voices. *We can do* what we've done in this campaign and say that we won't take a dime of their money. We can do what I did in Illinois, and in Washington, and bring both parties together to rein in their power so we can take our government back. *It's our choice.*

We can be a party that thinks the only way to look tough on national security is to talk, and act, and vote like George Bush and John McCain. We can use fear as a tactic, and the threat of terrorism to scare up votes.

Or we can decide that real strength is asking the tough questions before we send our troops to fight. We can see the threats we face for what they are—a call to rally all Americans and all the world against the common challenges of the twenty-first century—terrorism and nuclear weapons; climate change and poverty; genocide and disease. That's what it takes to keep us safe in the world. That's the real legacy of Roosevelt and Kennedy and Truman.

We can be a party that says and does whatever it takes to win the next election. We can calculate and poll-test our positions and tell everyone exactly what they want to hear.

Or we can be the party that doesn't just focus on how to win but why we should. We can tell everyone what they need to hear about the challenges we face. We can seek to regain not just an office, but the trust of the American people that their leaders in Washington will tell them the truth. That's the choice in this election.

We can be a party of those who only think like we do and only agree with all our positions. We can continue to slice and dice this country into red states and blue states. We can exploit the divisions that exist in our country for pure political gain.

Or this time, we can build on the movement we've started in this campaign—a movement that's united Democrats, Independents, and Republicans; a movement of young and old, rich and poor; white, black, Hispanic, Asian, and Native American. Because one thing I know from traveling to forty-six states this campaign season is that we're not as divided as our politics suggests. We may have different stories and different backgrounds, but we hold common hopes for the future of this country.

In the end, this election is still our best chance to solve the problems we've been talking about for decades—as one nation; as one people. Fourteen months later, that is still what this election is about.

Millions of Americans who believe we can do better—that we must do better—have put us in a position to bring about real change. Now it's up to you, Indiana. You can decide whether we're going to travel the same worn path, or whether we chart a new course that offers real hope for the future.[10] [*Emphasis added.*]

This back-and-forth comparison, aided by the parallel structures of paragraphs, can bring great clarity to the comparison and contrast of ideas.

Broad-Stroked Juxtaposition

Another key technique Obama employs to sharpen the persuasive power of his communication is an "idea-pivot-contrasting idea" structure for presenting contrary ideas. In this broad-stroked style of juxtaposition, Obama devotes ample space for the discussion of an initial view, usually the view with which he disagrees. Next, he provides a powerful transition sentence, indicating that a contrasting idea or view will follow. Then Obama expounds upon a contrasting position, usually the one he supports. This structure enables Obama to elaborate at length about why he believes his position is superior to the contrary one. Consider this example:

It's not change when John McCain decided to stand with George Bush ninety-five percent of the time, as he did in the senate last year.

It's not change when he offers four more years of Bush economic policies that have failed to create well-paying jobs, or insure our workers, or help Americans afford the skyrocketing cost of college—policies that have lowered the real incomes of the average American family, widened the gap between Wall Street and Main Street, and left our children with a mountain of debt.

And it's not change when he promises to continue a policy in Iraq that asks everything of our brave men and women in uniform and nothing of Iraqi politicians—a policy where all we look for are reasons to stay in Iraq, while we spend billions of dollars a month on a war that isn't making the American people any safer.

So I'll say this—*there are many words to describe* John McCain's attempt to pass off his embrace of George Bush's policies as bipartisan and new. *But change is not one of them.*

Change is a foreign policy that doesn't begin and end with a war that should've never been authorized and never been waged. I won't stand here and pretend that there are many good options left in Iraq, but what's not an option is leaving our troops in that country for the next hundred years—especially at a time when our military is over-stretched, our nation is isolated, and nearly every other threat to America is being ignored.

We must be as careful getting out of Iraq as we were careless getting in—but start leaving we must. It's time for Iraqis to take responsibility for their future. It's time to rebuild our military and give our veterans the care they need and the benefits they deserve when they come home. It's time to refocus our efforts on al Qaeda's leadership and Afghanistan, and rally the world against the common threats of the twenty-first century—terrorism and nuclear weapons; climate change and poverty; genocide and disease. That's what change is.

Change is realizing that meeting today's threats requires not just our firepower, but the power of our diplomacy—tough, direct diplomacy where the president of the United States isn't afraid to let any petty dictator know where America stands and what we stand for. We must once again have the courage and conviction to lead the free world. That is the legacy of Roosevelt and Truman and Kennedy. That's what the American people want. That's what change is.

Change is building an economy that rewards not just wealth, but the work and workers who created it. It's understanding that the struggles facing working families can't be solved by spending billions of dollars on more tax breaks for big corporations and wealthy CEOs, but by giving the middle-class a tax break, and investing in our crumbling infrastructure, and transforming how we use energy, and improving our schools, and renewing our commitment to science and innovation. It's understanding that fiscal responsibility and shared prosperity can go hand in hand, as they did when Bill Clinton was president.[11] [*Emphasis added.*]

The use of broad-stroked juxtaposition and parallel structures makes Obama's remarks excellent in their capacity to contrast positions and strengthens their persuasive power. Consider another example from Obama's remarks titled "A More Perfect Union," delivered in Philadelphia in March 2008:

For we have a choice in this country. *We can* accept a politics that breeds division and conflict and cynicism. *We can* tackle race only as spectacle—as we did in the OJ trial—or in the wake of tragedy, as we did in the aftermath of Katrina—or as fodder for the nightly news. *We can* play Reverend Wright's sermons on every channel, every day, and talk about them from now until the election, and make the only question in this campaign whether or not the American people think that I somehow believe or sympathize with his most offensive words. We can pounce on some gaffe by a Hillary supporter as evidence that she's playing the race card, or we can speculate on whether white men will all flock to John McCain in the general election regardless of his policies.

We can do that.

But if we do, I can tell you that in the next election, we'll be talking about some other distraction. And then another one. And then another one. And nothing will change.

That is one option. Or, at this moment, in this election, we can come together and say, "Not this time." *This time* we want to talk about the crumbling schools that are stealing the future of black children and white children and Asian children and Hispanic children and Native American children. *This time* we want to reject the cynicism that tells us that these kids can't learn; that those kids who don't look like us are somebody else's problem. The children of America are not those kids, they are our kids, and we will not let them fall behind in a twenty-first century economy. Not this time.

This time we want to talk about how the lines in the emergency room are filled with whites and blacks and Hispanics

who do not have health care; who don't have the power on
their own to overcome the special interests in Washington,
but who can take them on if we do it together.

This time we want to talk about the shuttered mills
that once provided a decent life for men and women of
every race, and the homes for sale that once belonged to
Americans from every religion, every region, every walk of
life. This time we want to talk about the fact that the real
problem is not that someone who doesn't look like you
might take your job; it's that the corporation you work for
will ship it overseas for nothing more than a profit.

This time we want to talk about the men and women
of every color and creed who serve together, and fight
together, and bleed together under the same proud flag.
We want to talk about how to bring them home from
a war that never should've been authorized and never
should've been waged, and we want to talk about how
we'll show our patriotism by caring for them and their
families and giving them the benefits they have earned.

I would not be running for president if I didn't believe
with all my heart that this is what the vast majority of
Americans want for this country. [*Emphases added.*]

In the example that follows, Obama's outstanding use of
parallel structure reinforces his use of juxtaposition and paints
a clear contrast between his assertions of what John McCain
believes and what he believes:

John McCain is an American hero and a worthy opponent,
but he's proven time and time again that he just doesn't

understand this. It took him three tries in seven days just to figure out that the home foreclosure crisis was an actual problem. He's had a front-row seat to the last eight years of disastrous policies that have widened the income gap and saddled our children with debt, and now *he's promising* four more years of the very same thing.

He's promising to make permanent the Bush tax breaks for the wealthiest few who didn't need them and didn't ask for them—tax breaks that are so irresponsible that John McCain himself once said they offended his conscience.

He's promising four more years of trade deals that don't have a single safeguard for American workers—that don't help American workers compete and win in a global economy.

He's promising four more years of an administration that will push for the privatization of Social Security—a plan that would gamble away people's retirement on the stock market; a plan that was already rejected by Democrats and Republicans under George Bush.

He's promising four more years of policies that won't guarantee health insurance for working Americans, that won't bring down the rising cost of college tuition, that won't do a thing for the Americans who are living in those communities where the jobs have left and the factories have shut their doors.

And yet, despite all this, the other side is still betting that the American people won't notice that John McCain is running for George Bush's third term. They think that they'll forget about all that's happened in the last eight years, that they'll be tricked into believing that it's either me or our party is the one that's out of touch with what's going on in their lives.

Well I'm making a different bet. I'm betting on the American people.

The men and women I've met in small towns and big cities across this country see this election as a defining moment in our history. They understand what's at stake here because they're living it every day. And they are tired of being distracted by fake controversies. They are fed up with politicians trying to divide us for their own political gain. And I believe they'll see through the tactics that are used every year, in every election, to appeal to our fears, or our biases, or our differences—because they've never wanted or needed change as badly as they do now.

The people I've met during this campaign know that government cannot solve all of our problems, and they don't expect it to. They don't want our tax dollars wasted on programs that don't work or perks for special interests who don't work for us. They understand that we cannot stop every job from going overseas or build a wall around our economy, and they know that we shouldn't.

But *they believe* it's finally time that we make health care affordable and available for every single American; that we bring down costs for workers and for businesses; that we cut premiums and stop insurance companies from denying people care or coverage who need it most.

They believe it's time we provided real relief to the victims of this housing crisis; that we help families refinance their mortgage so they can stay in their homes; that we start giving tax relief to the people who actually need it—middle-class families, and seniors, and struggling homeowners.

They believe that we can and should make the global economy work for working Americans; that we might not be able to stop every job from going overseas, but we certainly can stop giving tax breaks to companies who send them there and start giving tax breaks to companies who create good jobs right here in America. We can invest in the types of renewable energy that won't just reduce our dependence on oil and save our planet, but create up to five million new jobs that can't be outsourced.

They believe we can train our workers for those new jobs and keep the most productive workforce the most competitive workforce in the world if we fix our public education system by investing in what works and finding out what doesn't; if we invest in early childhood education and finally make college affordable for everyone who wants to go; if we stop talking about how great our teachers are and start rewarding them for their greatness.

They believe that if you work your entire life, you deserve to retire with dignity and respect, which means a pension you can count on, and Social Security that's always there.

This is what the people I've met believe about the country they love. It doesn't matter if they're Democrats or Republicans; whether they're from the smallest towns or the biggest cities; whether they hunt or they don't; whether they go to church, or temple, or mosque, or not. We may come from different places and have different stories, but we share common hopes and one very American dream.

That is the dream I am running to help restore in this election. If I get the chance, that is what I'll be talking about from now until November. That is the choice that I'll offer the American people—four more years of what we had for the last eight or fundamental change in Washington. [*Emphases added.*]

Finally, in this additional example, Obama draws on the experience of Martin Luther King Jr. He uses juxtaposition to present his ideas in ways that might provide them greater influence:

[I]f Dr. King could love his jailor; if he could call on the faithful who once sat where you do to forgive those who set dogs and fire hoses upon them, then surely we can look past what divides us in our time, and bind up our wounds, and erase the empathy deficit that exists in our hearts.

But if changing our hearts and minds is the first critical step, we cannot stop there. *It is not enough* to bemoan the plight of poor children in this country and remain unwilling to push our elected officials to provide the resources to fix our schools. *It is not enough* to decry the disparities of health care and yet allow the insurance companies and the drug companies to block much needed reforms. *It is not enough* for us to abhor the costs of a misguided war, and yet allow ourselves to be driven by a politics of fear that sees the threat of attack as way to scare up votes instead of a call to come together around a common effort.

The scripture tells us that we are judged not just by word, but by deed. And if we are to truly bring about the unity that is so crucial in this time, *we must* find it within ourselves to act on what we know; to understand that living up to this country's ideals and its possibilities will require great effort and resources; sacrifice and stamina.

And that is what is at stake in the great political debate we are having today. The changes that are needed are not just a matter of tinkering at the edges, and they will not come if politicians simply tell us what we want to hear. All of us will be called upon to make some sacrifice. None of us will be exempt from responsibility. *We will have* to fight to fix our schools, but *we will also* have to challenge ourselves to be better parents. We will have to confront the biases in our criminal justice system, but *we will also have* to acknowledge the deep-seated violence that still resides in our own communities and marshal the will to break its grip.

That is how we will bring about the change we seek. *That is how* Dr. King led this country through the wilderness. He did it with words—words that he spoke not just to the children of slaves, but the children of slave owners. Words that inspired not just black but also white; not just the Christian but the Jew; not just the Southerner but also the Northerner.

He led with words, but he also led with deeds. He also led by example. *He led by* marching and going to jail and suffering threats and being away from his family. *He led by* taking a stand against a war, knowing full well that it would diminish his popularity. *He led by* challenging our economic structures, understanding that it would cause discomfort. Dr. King understood that unity cannot be won on the cheap; that we would have to earn it through great effort and determination.[12] [*Emphases provided.*]

Obama's varied uses of juxtaposition and comparison/contrast offer many best practices. For leaders seeking to use communication to persuade others, consider the many variations of juxtaposition, comparing, and contrasting. Draw on these useful techniques when they will help you crystallize your arguments, clarify your points, or draw attention to why your positions or ideas are worth adopting.

⇥ WHAT WE'VE LEARNED— ⇤ PRACTICES FOR PERSUADING

Obama has mastered an ability to persuade others, eliciting a nod, a glimmer in the eye, the "yes." In this chapter, we have examined some of the valuable communication techniques that allow Barack Obama to persuade others effectively. Leaders can glean many lessons from his successful techniques. When constructing remarks, for example, sequencing ideas can be useful—within a single sentence, among multiple sentences, even among paragraphs. Sequencing helps provide a strong sense of logic to remarks, crystallizing the clarity of reasoning so that speakers seem to make *compelling sense*.

Addressing nonrhetorical questions is also a useful practice. This helps communicators replicate two-way conversation, as if they are vetting questions. Excellent communicators will often identify questions the audience would most like to probe. Then, they ask and answer. Well-developed answers impress listeners and enhance effective knowledge sharing.

Addressing key objections is a valuable persuasion technique. In addressing objections, the skilled communicator demonstrates awareness of key counterarguments and undercuts those counterarguments, showing why their own position is superior. In the quest to persuade, comparison and contrast can also play a role. Leaders can clarify key points by placing ideas side by side for comparison and contrast within a single sentence, among multiple sentences or among paragraphs. A skilled communicator will draw as needed on a wide variety of techniques—whether presenting comparison with a back-and-forth succession or with an "idea-pivot-contrasting idea" construction. In their many variations, comparison and contrast, juxtaposition and antithesis give remarks greater potency as excellent communicators sharpen the differences between their ideas and opposing views in order to persuade listeners that their ideas are best.

CHAPTER 8

FACING AND OVERCOMING CONTROVERSY

Most leaders face controversy at some point in their careers. A slip of the tongue. An unintended slight. A miscommunication. A surrogate misspeaking. These and other circumstances can all give rise to difficult situations. Barack Obama has demonstrated a notable ability to survive controversy and thrive in the aftermath. He illustrates that, oftentimes, how you respond to controversy is more important than the controversy itself. Various controversies have derailed other shining political careers—Gary Hart's affair, Gerald Ford's pardon of Richard Nixon, public doubts arising after "swiftboat" attacks on John Kerry. Barack Obama has faced his share as well— his association with Reverend Jeremiah Wright, who uttered incendiary comments that undercut Obama's messages of unity;

the unsolicited endorsement of Minister Louis Farrakhan; and Obama's own poorly worded remarks about middle Americans clinging to guns and religion. How has Barack Obama successfully used strong communication skills to weather these storms and thrive in their wake, with his reputation largely in tact and his brand scarcely tarnished?

There are valuable lessons to be learned from how Obama addresses and overcomes controversy. He skillfully resets the tone of the conversation as he employs gracious beginnings, focuses on his goals, exudes humility, and leverages props. His ability to address controversy head-on, accepting responsibility when appropriate, has helped bring relatively quick resolutions. His skill in standing strong in his beliefs and continuing to deliver tough messages, even in the wake of controversy, has also enabled him to thrive. Let's delve into these communication practices that have aided Obama's ability to face and overcome controversy.

⇥ KNOWING YOUR GOALS: REJECTING ⇤ *AND* DENOUNCING

When addressing controversy, it helps to clearly identify your goals. This can guide subsequent choices—how humbly you should act, your ideal body language, the props you might gather around you, or the venue where you might offer your apology. When considered with care, these factors can work together to help yield good resolutions. Barack Obama has shown considerable skill in identifying his goals before he addresses controversy in public settings. A good example occurred when he addressed, during a presidential debate with Senator Hillary

Clinton, an issue regarding Nation of Islam leader Louis Farrakhan. Days before the debate, Farrakhan backed Obama's candidacy at a national convention. During the February 26, 2008 presidential debate, moderator Tim Russert asked Obama, "Do you accept the support of Louis Farrakhan?"

Aware of the endorsement, Obama tried to defuse any controversy arising from the unsolicited support. He replied:

I have been very clear in my denunciation of Minister Farrakhan's anti-Semitic comments. I think they are unacceptable and reprehensible. I did not solicit this support. He expressed pride in an African American who seems to be bringing the country together. I obviously can't censor him. But it is not support that I sought, and we're not doing anything, I assure you, formally or informally with Mr. Farrakhan. . . .

Tim, I have some of the strongest support from the Jewish community in my hometown of Chicago and in this presidential campaign. And the reason is because I have been a stalwart friend of Israel's. I think they are one of our most important allies in the region, and I think that their security is sacrosanct and that the United States is in a special relationship with them, as is true with my relationship with the Jewish community.

And the reason that I have such strong support is because they know that not only would I not tolerate anti-Semitism in any form, but also because of the fact that what I want to do is rebuild what I consider to be a historic relationship between the African American community and the Jewish community.

You know, I would not be sitting here were it not for a whole host of Jewish Americans who supported the civil rights movement and helped to ensure that justice was served in the South. And that coalition has frayed over time around a whole host of issues, and part of my task in this process is making sure that those lines of communication and understanding are reopened.

However, seizing on the fact that Obama did not use the term *reject* in his repudiation of Farrakhan, Senator Hillary Clinton said:

I just want to add something here, because I faced a similar situation when I ran for the Senate in 2000 in New York. . . . The Independence Party was under the control of people who were anti-Semitic, anti-Israel. And I made it very clear that I did not want their support. I rejected it. . . . I was willing to take that stand. . . .

When Russert asked Clinton, "Are you suggesting Senator Obama is not standing on principle?" she replied, "No. I'm just saying that you asked specifically if he would reject it. And there's a difference between denouncing and rejecting."

Obama understood that Clinton's comments had put him in a bad spot and that he could potentially emerge from the debate more deeply enveloped in controversy. Obama kept his eyes on his goals of distancing himself from Farrakhan and articulating unwavering support for Israel. He reacted quickly, without further prompting from Russert, saying:

I have to say I don't see a difference between denouncing and rejecting. There's no formal offer of help from Minister Farrakhan that would involve me rejecting it. But if the word "reject" Senator Clinton feels is stronger than the word "denounce," then I'm happy to concede the point, and I would reject and denounce.

The audience burst into applause. They recognized that Obama had just doused a potential firestorm. Keeping his eyes on his goals, Obama had spoken the right words in a firm manner and quelled a controversy that could have lingered for weeks and done considerable damage to his campaign. An important lesson: before facing controversy, be clear about your goals; while addressing the difficult situation, align your actions, words, and behavior in ways that are consistent with your goals.

⊰ RECASTING THE TONE: HUMILITY ⊱ AND GRACIOUS BEGINNINGS

Humility and graciousness have also played a role in Obama's success in weathering controversies. His success teaches many lessons. For example, from his behavior we can see that the way you initially present yourself to people as you face controversy is very important. In some ways, it is like making a first impression all over again. In light of a prevailing controversy, your character or judgment may have been placed in doubt. You need to impress people all over again. First and foremost, don't appear defiant. Additionally, bear in mind that defensiveness normally undercuts your purpose. If possible, appear humble and gracious as you begin to address a difficult situation. "To err is to be human"—this is well accepted and people are often willing to forgive, but they are more *likely* to forgive when you convey a sense of humility or remorse.

To this end, when addressing controversy, body language plays a large role in your success. Just as with first impressions, body language communicates important messages about whether you are sorry, empathetic, defensive, or defiant. Obama has shown the importance of remorsefulness and strength. The ideal body language often involves a fine line between looking too weak with contriteness and looking unapologetic with strength. It would be counterproductive to come into a room with slouched shoulders and your head bowed—that conveys weakness. A strong back—chin up—"look them in the eye" approach is better; that conveys strength. But while appearing strong, other nonverbal language must communicate humility or remorse—the look in your eyes and your tone, for instance. Allow body language and nonverbal communication to set the tone together, taking as much care with these elements as you do when making a "first impression."

RESETTING YOUR IMAGE: LEVERAGING PROPS

Obama has also demonstrated that when addressing controversy, gathering the right props around you can help send a message that echoes your sentiments as effectively as your body language and vocal tone. Obama illustrated this very well when he delivered remarks in response to the Reverend Jeremiah

Wright controversy. Large segments of the American public wished to know why Obama had associated himself with such a fiery preacher. Obama delivered his explanation from a lectern flanked on each side by large American flags. The image conveyed patriotism and a deep respect for America. This served as a frame in which Obama offered apologetic statements and affirmed his commitment to uniting people of disparate backgrounds in an effort to attain cherished American goals. The backdrop for his comments sent submessages highly consistent with his words and helped to underscore them. When facing controversy, this should be considered a "best practice": the backdrop and props around you should reinforce your intent and words.

⊰ RECASTING THE DIALOGUE: ⊱
LANGUAGE CHOICE

Taking strides to quickly recast the prevailing dialogue is also a best practice when facing difficult situations. Your aim should be to nip controversy in the bud as much as possible. If the controversy has already grown relatively large, then you should seek to take the bull by its horns.

A good example of when Obama recast the dialogue quickly occurred when he addressed the controversy surrounding his relationship with Jeremiah Wright. Given the divisive comments Wright had uttered over the prior weeks, Obama needed to address accusations that he must secretly support Wright's view since Obama had attended Wright's church for years. Obama came out strong, drawing on patriotic sentiments as he led into his so-called race speech. He began by quoting the Declaration of Independence: "We the people, in order to form a more perfect union."

Before uttering another word, Obama's choice of this initial quotation rooted his response firmly within American tradition and underscored his commitment to core American values. The words helped to place Obama on moral high ground and changed the tone of the conversation. Obama was able to speak from that moral high ground, rather than from a strictly defensive position about his relationship with Reverend Wright. He continued on, speaking about the intricacies of American race relations and the challenges to equality, and he clarified how deeply he disapproved of Wright's fiery comments.

⇥ ADDRESSING ERROR HEAD-ON: ⇤
ACCEPTING RESPONSIBILITY

Another lesson we can glean from Obama's communication practices is that, when addressing controversy, he usually offers an apology early on in his remarks. His apologies are usually very clear and forthright. He admits he's wrong when it's appropriate, and he takes responsibility when it's appropriate. For example, in April 2008 Obama used a poor choice of words as he referred to working-class voters in old and economically ailing Midwest industrial towns. He said that those Americans "get bitter, they cling to guns or religion or antipathy to people who aren't like them or anti-immigrant sentiment or antitrade sentiment as a way to explain their frustrations." The comments caused an uproar.

When referring to his inappropriate remarks before an AP luncheon in Washington, DC, on April 14, 2008, Obama began with a direct acknowledgment of his error:

> Good afternoon. I know I kept a lot of you guys busy this weekend with the comments I made last week. Some of you might even be a little bitter about that.
>
> As I said yesterday, I regret some of the words I chose, partly because the way that these remarks have been interpreted have offended some people and partly because they have served as one more distraction from the critical debate that we must have in this election season.

The forthright acknowledgment was well received. Reporters and the public appeared to concur with the motto, "If you make a mistake, say so."

RESTATING ETHICS AND DELIVERING TOUGH MESSAGES

Finally, Obama often adheres to a practice of restating his beliefs when he addresses controversies or offers an apology. He does not shy away from, but rather stands strong in his beliefs, and he has proceeded to deliver tough messages even after tenderly addressing his own errors. For example, after addressing the ill-chosen words he had used when speaking about Midwest rural voters, Obama took the opportunity to outline his true beliefs:

> I'm a person of deep faith, and my religion has sustained me through a lot in my life. I even gave a speech on faith

before I ever started running for president where I said that Democrats "make a mistake when we fail to acknowledge the power of faith in people's lives." I also represent a state with a large number of hunters and sportsmen, and I understand how important these traditions are to families in Illinois and all across America. And, contrary to what my poor word choices may have implied or my opponents have suggested, I've never believed that these traditions or people's faith has anything to do with how much money they have.

But I will never walk away from the larger point that I was trying to make. For the last several decades, people in small towns and cities and rural areas all across this country have seen globalization change the rules of the game on them. When I began my career as an organizer on the South Side of Chicago, I saw what happens when the local steel mill shuts its doors and moves overseas. You don't just lose the jobs in the mill. You start losing jobs and businesses throughout the community. The streets are emptier. The schools suffer.

I saw it during my campaign for the Senate in Illinois when I'd talk to union guys who had worked at the local Maytag plant for twenty, thirty years before being laid off at fifty-five years old when it picked up and moved to Mexico; and they had no idea what they're going to do without the paycheck or the pension that they counted on. One man didn't even know if he'd be able to afford the liver transplant his son needed now that his health care was gone.

I've heard these stories almost every day during this campaign, whether it was in Iowa or Ohio or Pennsylvania. And the people I've met have also told me that every year, in every election, politicians come to their towns, and they tell them what they want to hear, and they make big promises, and then they go back to Washington when the campaign's over, and nothing changes. There's no plan to address the downside of globalization. We don't do anything about the skyrocketing cost of health care or college or those disappearing pensions. Instead of fighting to replace jobs that aren't coming back, Washington ends up fighting over the latest distraction of the week.

And after years and years and years of this, a lot of people in this country have become cynical about what government can do to improve their lives. They are angry and frustrated with their leaders for not listening to them, for not fighting for them, for not always telling them the truth. And yes, they are bitter about that. . . .

I may have made a mistake last week in the words that I chose, but the other party has made a much more damaging mistake in the failed policies they've chosen and the bankrupt philosophy they've embraced for the last three decades.

It's a philosophy that says there's no role for government in making the global economy work for working Americans, that we have to just sit back [and] watch those factories close and those jobs disappear, that there's nothing we can do or should do about workers without health care or children in crumbling schools or families who are losing their homes, and so we should just hand out a few tax breaks and wish everyone the best of luck.[1] [*Emphases added.*]

Similarly, in March 2008, after repudiating Reverend Wright's divisive comments and clarifying that he affirmed principles of unity, not division, Obama proceeded to stand strong in his conviction that, at that time, he could not fully disown Reverend Wright. He explained at length, in what has since been called a "seminal" speech on race relations in America:

Throughout the first year of this campaign, against all predictions to the contrary, we saw how hungry the American people were for this message of unity. Despite the temptation to view my candidacy through a purely racial lens, we won commanding victories in states with some of the whitest populations in the country. In South Carolina, where the Confederate flag still flies, we built a powerful coalition of African Americans and white Americans.

This is not to say that race has not been an issue in the campaign. At various stages in the campaign, some commentators have deemed me either "too black" or "not black enough." We saw racial tensions bubble to the surface during the week before the South Carolina primary. The press has scoured every exit poll for the latest evidence of racial polarization, not just in terms of white and black, but black and brown as well.

And yet, it has only been in the last couple of weeks that the discussion of race in this campaign has taken a particularly divisive turn. . . .

I have already condemned, in unequivocal terms, the statements of Reverend Wright that have caused such controversy. For some, nagging questions remain. Did I know him to be an occasionally fierce critic of American domestic and foreign policy? Of course. Did I ever hear him make remarks that could be considered controversial while I sat in church? Yes. Did I strongly disagree with many of his political views? Absolutely—just as I'm sure many of you have heard remarks from your pastors, priests, or rabbis with which you strongly disagreed.

But the remarks that have caused this recent firestorm weren't simply controversial. They weren't simply a religious leader's effort to speak out against perceived injustice. Instead, they expressed a profoundly distorted view of this country—a view that sees white racism as endemic and that elevates what is wrong with America above all that we know is right with America; a view that sees the conflicts in the Middle East as rooted primarily in the actions of stalwart allies like Israel instead of emanating from the perverse and hateful ideologies of radical Islam.

As such, Reverend Wright's comments were not only wrong but divisive, divisive at a time when we need unity; racially charged at a time when we need to come together to solve a set of monumental problems—two wars, a terrorist threat, a falling economy, a chronic health-care crisis, and potentially devastating climate change; problems that are neither black or white or Latino or Asian, but rather problems that confront us all.

Given my background, my politics, and my professed values and ideals, there will no doubt be those for whom my statements of condemnation are not enough. Why associate myself with Reverend Wright in the first place, they may ask? Why not join another church? And I confess that if all that I knew of Reverend Wright were the snippets of those sermons that have run in an endless loop on the television and YouTube, or if Trinity United Church of Christ conformed to the caricatures being peddled by some commentators, there is no doubt that I would react in much the same way.

But the truth is, that isn't all that I know of the man. The man I met more than twenty years ago is a man who helped introduce me to my Christian faith, a man who spoke to me about our obligations to love one another; to care for the sick and lift up the poor. He is a man who served his country as a U.S. marine; who has studied and lectured at some of the finest universities and seminaries in the country, and who for over thirty years led a church that serves the community by doing God's work here on Earth—by housing the homeless, ministering to the needy, providing day care services and scholarships and prison ministries, and reaching out to those suffering from HIV/AIDS. . . .

As imperfect as [Reverend Wright] may be, he has been like family to me. He strengthened my faith, officiated my wedding, and baptized my children. Not once in my conversations with him have I heard him talk about any ethnic group in derogatory terms, or treat whites with whom he interacted with anything but courtesy and respect. He contains within him the contradictions—the good and the bad—of the community that he has served diligently for so many years.

I can no more disown him than I can disown the black community. I can no more disown him than I can my white grandmother—a woman who helped raise me, a woman who sacrificed again and again for me, a woman who loves me as much as she loves anything in this world, but a woman who once confessed her fear of black men who passed by her on the street and who on more than one occasion has uttered racial or ethnic stereotypes that made me cringe.

These people are a part of me. And they are a part of America, this country that I love. . . .

For the men and women of Reverend Wright's generation, the memories of humiliation and doubt and fear have not gone away; nor has the anger and the bitterness of those years. That anger may not get expressed in public, in front of white coworkers or white friends. But it does find voice in the barbershop or around the kitchen table. At times, that anger is exploited by politicians, to gin up votes along racial lines, or to make up for a politician's own failings.

And occasionally it finds voice in the church on Sunday morning, in the pulpit and in the pews. . . .

This is where we are right now. It's a racial stalemate we've been stuck in for years. Contrary to the claims of some of my critics, black and white, I have never been so naive as to believe that we can get beyond our racial divisions in a single election cycle, or with a single candidacy—particularly a candidacy as imperfect as my own.

But I have asserted a firm conviction—a conviction rooted in my faith in God and my faith in the American people—that working together we can move beyond some of our old racial wounds and that in fact we have no choice if we are to continue on the path of a more perfect union. [*Emphases added.*]

Obama's clarification above was quite bold. Not all listeners were pleased. On the whole, however, the public and press seemed satisfied to hear a clear denunciation of Wright's remarks and a clarification of how Obama viewed those remarks. Given Obama's forthrightness and the sincerity with which he spoke of wanting to unite Americans, the public and the press seemed largely accepting of Obama's choice to also assert that at the time he could not "disown" Wright any more than he could his own grandmother but that he hoped to help move America beyond its "old racial wounds." Obama's choice to stand strong in his convictions won the respect of many listeners.

⇥ WHAT WE'VE LEARNED—PRACTICES FOR ⇤ FACING AND OVERCOMING OBSTACLES

Obama has demonstrated tremendous skill in facing and overcoming controversy. We have learned many lessons from the communication practices that have enabled him to weather storms and thrive in their aftermath. Notably, leaders should always remember that how they respond to controversy is as or more important than the controversy itself. They should address controversy head-on and accept responsibility when appropriate. When offering apologies, skilled communicators seek to appear remorseful but strong. Because their character and judgment may have been placed in doubt, skilled communicators realize they must make strong impressions all over again. They avoid the appearance of defiance and defensiveness; humility and graciousness characterize their words. As with first impressions, body language, image, and voice have considerable impact on the impressions made. Effective communicators identify their goals before they offer apologies or remarks, and they stay focused, making sure to articulate the words necessary to achieve their goals. Skilled communicators remember to use props and physical location to reset their image amid controversy, as well as to reinforce their key messages. They offer their apologies early on in their remarks, in a forthright manner. They also avoid appearing as if they are wavering in their commitment to admirable ethics. Instead, when offering their remarks, they communicate their strong ethics again, standing strong in their beliefs.

CHAPTER 9

MOTIVATING OTHERS TO ACTION AND LEAVING STRONG LAST IMPRESSIONS

Strong finishes are indispensable for communicating messages that impact listeners and endure in their minds. Ideally, during their remarks, leaders will convey their visions and points effectively enough to successfully achieve the goal of their talk. Ideally also, when delivering closing remarks, leaders will succeed in motivating their listeners, wielding a strong impact and leaving a strong last impression. Barack Obama has shown considerable skill in ending his speeches and public remarks with great power and efficacy. Just as a strong start helps to capture attention and engage and direct a listener, an excellent end to a set of remarks leaves listeners with a positive impression that can influence their subsequent opinions, choices, and actions. With his strong concluding comments, Obama inspires listeners, helps build momentum, creates a sense of importance and urgency to future actions, and at times directs listeners toward "low-hanging fruit"—the small actions they can take immediately to help a cause. By the time Obama finishes speaking, he has built to a crescendo, and he leaves on that high. Below, we glean some lessons from the practices that have enabled Obama to end "strong" and that helped inspire not just a campaign, but a "movement."

⇥ INSPIRING OTHERS TO ↤ GREAT ACHIEVEMENTS

As Obama ends his talks strong, he often employs words that set forth great aspirations, inspiring and motivating his listeners. Several types of language fulfill this task. Sometimes the words are simply eloquent. Other times the language incorporates patriotic words, cherished principles, or biblical truths. Most of the time, the words evoke an emotional reaction. Consider this example.

It is the light of opportunity that led my father across an ocean.

It is the founding ideals that the flag draped over my grandfather's coffin stands for—it is life, and liberty, and the pursuit of happiness.

It's the simple truth I learned all those years ago when I worked in the shadows of a shuttered steel mill on the South Side of Chicago—that in this country, justice can be won against the greatest of odds; hope can find its way back to the darkest of corners; and when we are told that we cannot bring about the change that we seek, we answer with one voice—yes we can.

So don't ever forget that this election is not about me, or any candidate. Don't ever forget that this campaign is about you—*about your hopes, about your dreams, about your struggles, about securing your portion of the American Dream.*

Don't ever forget that we have a choice in this country—that we can choose not to be divided; that we can choose not to be afraid; that we can still choose this moment to finally come together and solve the problems we've talked about all those other years in all those other elections.

This time can be different than all the rest. This time we can face down those who say our road is too long; that our climb is too steep; that we can no longer achieve the change that we seek. This is our time to answer the call that so many generations of Americans have answered before—by insisting that by hard work, and by sacrifice, the American Dream will endure. Thank you, and may God bless the United States of America.[1] [*Emphases added.*]

In another example, Obama uses language to encourage audience members to respond to a call to service, to think of things bigger than themselves, and to realize this represents a legacy from America's great past. His emphasis helps lend an "aspire to great things" feel to the ending of this speech. It helps to inspire listeners:

Through service, I found a community that embraced me, a church to belong to, citizenship that was meaningful, the direction I'd been seeking. Through service, I found that my own improbable story fit into a larger American story.

In America, each of us seeks our own dreams, but the sum of those dreams must be greater than ourselves. Because the America we inherited is the legacy of those who struggled and those who served in so many ways before us.

It's the legacy of a band of unlikely patriots who overthrew the tyranny of a king.

It's the legacy of abolitionists who stood up, and soldiers who fought for a more perfect union.

It's the legacy of those who started to teach in our schools and tend to the sick in our cities; who laid the rails and volunteered to uphold the law as America moved west.

It's the legacy of men who faced the Depression by putting on the uniform of the Civilian Conservation Corps; of women who worked on that Arsenal of Democracy and built the tanks and ships and bomber aircraft to fight fascism.

It's the legacy of those women's suffragists and freedom riders who stood up for justice; and young people who answered President Kennedy's call to go forth in a Peace Corps.

The sacrifices made by previous generations have never been easy. But America is a great nation precisely because Americans have been willing to stand up when it was hard, to serve on stages both great and small, to rise above moments of great challenge and terrible trial.[2]

↠ CREATING A SENSE OF MOMENTUM ↞
AND URGENCY

Another practice Obama draws on as he ends his talks strong is the practice of drawing attention to successes and establishing a sense of momentum, in addition to creating a sense of importance and urgency to future actions. He employs language that adds to the sense that the stakes are high and that what each individual listener does can matter. Consider this excerpt, where his language establishes a sense of urgency:

I did not run for the presidency to fulfill some long-held ambition or because I believed it was somehow owed to me. I chose to run in this election—at this moment—because of what Dr. King called "the fierce urgency of now." Because we are at a defining moment in our history. Our nation is at war. Our planet is in peril. Our health-care system is broken, our economy is out of balance, our education system fails too many of our children, and our retirement system is in tatters.

At this defining moment, we cannot wait any longer for universal health care. We cannot wait to fix our schools. We cannot wait for good jobs, and living wages, and pensions we can count on. We cannot wait to halt global warming, and we cannot wait to end this war in Iraq.[3]

Consider this additional example, in which Obama draws attention to facts that demonstrate momentum:

We can change the electoral math that's been all about division and make it about addition—about building a coalition for change and progress that stretches through blue states and red states. That's how I won some of the reddest, most Republican counties in Illinois. That's why the polls show that I do best against the Republicans running for president—because we're attracting more support from Independents and Republicans than any other candidate. That's how we'll win in November, and that's how we'll change this country over the next four years.[4]

The example below is even more explicit in pointing to specific achievements that illustrate increasing momentum. Pointing to these specifics has the effect of persuading listeners that they can help continue the momentum and that their efforts will matter:

It has now been one year since we began this campaign for the presidency on the steps of the Old State Capitol in Springfield, Illinois—just me and 15,000 of my closest friends.

At the time, there weren't too many who imagined we'd be standing where we are today. I knew I wouldn't be Washington's favorite candidate. I knew we wouldn't get all the big donors or endorsements right off the bat. I knew I'd be the underdog in every contest from January to June. I knew it wouldn't be easy.

But then something started happening. As we met people in their living rooms and on their farms; in churches and town hall meetings, they all started telling a similar story about the state of our politics today. Whether they're young or old; black or white; Latino or Asian; Democrat, Independent, or even Republican, the message is the same:

We are tired of being disappointed by our politics. We are tired of being let down. We're tired of hearing promises made and ten-point plans proposed in the heat of a campaign only to have nothing change when everyone goes back to Washington. Because the lobbyists just write another check. Or because politicians start worrying about how they'll win the next election instead of why they should. Or because they focus on who's up and who's down instead of who matters.

And while Washington is consumed with the same drama and division and distraction, another family puts up a "for sale" sign in the front yard. Another factory shuts its doors forever. Another mother declares bankruptcy because she cannot pay her child's medical bills.

And another soldier waves goodbye as he leaves on another tour of duty in a war that should've never been authorized and never been waged. It goes on and on and on, year after year after year.

But in this election—at this moment—Americans are standing up all across the country to say, not this time.

Not this year. The stakes are too high and the challenges too great to play the same Washington game with the same Washington players and expect a different result. And today, voters from the West Coast to the Gulf Coast to the heart of America stood up to say that it is time to turn the page. We won Louisiana, and Nebraska, and the state of Washington, and I believe that we can win in Virginia on Tuesday if you're ready to stand for change.[5]

When examining the preceding excerpt, particular wording helps to make the language especially effective. When Obama says, "Then something started happening," he draws attention to change and momentum. When he refers to "living rooms," "churches," and "town hall meetings," he illustrates the breadth of the increasing support. Similarly, when he talks about support coming from young, old, black, white, Latino, Asian, Democrat, Independent, and Republican, he reinforces the notion that the support levels are broad and increasing. Pointing to his primary wins in Louisiana, Nebraska, and Washington helps to show that "things are rolling." Emphasizing the mood—"not this time"— and indicating that "the stakes are too high" helps underscore the urgency and importance of events and potential actions.

Below, we can see another valuable example where Obama builds a sense of momentum and urgency. In this example, he uses repetition skillfully to help create this sense:

A few weeks ago, no one imagined that we'd have accomplished what we did here tonight. For most of this campaign, we were far behind, and we always knew our climb would be steep.

But in record numbers, you came out and spoke up for change. And with your voices and your votes, you made it clear that at this moment—in this election—*there is something happening in America.*

There is something happening when men and women in Des Moines and Davenport; in Lebanon and Concord come out in the snows of January to wait in lines that stretch block after block because they believe in what this country can be.

There is something happening when Americans who are young in age and in spirit—who have never before participated in politics—turn out in numbers we've never seen because they know in their hearts that this time must be different.

There is something happening when people vote not just for the party they belong to but the hopes they hold in common—that whether we are rich or poor; black or white; Latino or Asian; whether we hail from Iowa or New Hampshire, Nevada or South Carolina, we are ready to take this country in a fundamentally new direction. *That is what's happening* in America right now. *Change is what's happening in America.*

You can be the new majority who can lead this nation out of a long political darkness—Democrats, Independents, and Republicans who are tired of the division and distraction that has clouded Washington; who know that we can disagree without being disagreeable; who understand that if we mobilize our voices to challenge the money and influence that's stood in our way and challenge ourselves to reach for something better, there's no problem we can't solve—no destiny we cannot fulfill.[6] [*Emphases added.*]

⇥ Building to a Crescendo ⇤

In other arenas, such as in fiction writing, a good practice might be to build up to a climax and then wind down. Not so in highly effective speeches and public remarks. To end strong means to end on a high. Outstanding orators move to the peak of their comments and end there, leaving the audiences inspired, moved, motivated, and focused on a memorable thought or call to action. Obama understands the importance of building to a crescendo (the climactic point) and ending a speech on a high. Consider this example from his remarks following his loss in the 2008 Pennsylvania primary. Here, Obama ends his remarks with an anecdote describing a meeting during which an old black man indicated he was choosing to support Obama because he had been inspired by the example of a young white woman, Ashley, who was already an Obama supporter. Obama uses the anecdote to underscore the possibility of transcending traditional lines of division and uniting for change. Through this narration, as Obama ends his speech, he builds to a high point:

> By itself, that single moment of recognition between that young white girl and that old black man is not enough. It is not enough to give health care to the sick, or jobs to the jobless, or education to our children.
>
> But it is where we begin. It is why the walls in that room began to crack and shake.
>
> And if they can shake in that room, they can shake in Atlanta.
>
> And if they can shake in Atlanta, they can shake in Georgia.

And if they can shake in Georgia, they can shake all across America. And if enough of our voices join together, we can bring those walls tumbling down. The walls of Jericho can finally come tumbling down. That is our hope—but only if we pray together, and work together, and march together.

Brothers and sisters, we cannot walk alone.

In the struggle for peace and justice, we cannot walk alone.

In the struggle for opportunity and equality, we cannot walk alone.

In the struggle to heal this nation and repair this world, we cannot walk alone.

So I ask you to walk with me, and march with me, and join your voice with mine, and together we will sing the song that tears down the walls that divide us and lift up an America that is truly indivisible, with liberty and justice, for all. May God bless the memory of the great pastor of this church, and may God bless the United States of America.[7]

In the language above, we see how Obama moves to a climax through the cadence of the sentences and use of repetition techniques. In places, too, words or phrases are arranged in succession, with the words of greater impact following those of lesser impact: this is also building to a crescendo. In the example above, we see how Obama ends with a call to action. Consider this additional example:

In our country, I have found that this cooperation happens not because we agree on everything, but because behind all the labels and false divisions and categories that define us; beyond all the petty bickering and point-scoring in Washington, Americans are a decent, generous, compassionate people, united by common challenges and common hopes. And every so often, there are moments which call on that fundamental goodness to make this country great again.

So it was for that band of patriots who declared in a Philadelphia hall the formation of a more perfect union; and for all those who gave on the fields of Gettysburg and Antietam their last full measure of devotion to save that same union.

So it was for the Greatest Generation that conquered fear itself, and liberated a continent from tyranny, and made this country home to untold opportunity and prosperity.

So it was for the workers who stood out on the picket lines; the women who shattered glass ceilings; the children who braved a Selma bridge for freedom's cause.

So it has been for every generation that faced down the greatest challenges and the most improbable odds to leave their children a world that's better, and kinder, and more just.

And so it must be for us.

America, this is our moment. This is our time. Our time to turn the page on the policies of the past. Our time to bring new energy and new ideas to the challenges we face. Our time to offer a new direction for the country we love.

The journey will be difficult. The road will be long. I face this challenge with profound humility and knowledge of my own limitations. But I also face it with limitless faith in the capacity of the American people. Because if we are willing to work for it, and fight for it, and believe in it, then I am absolutely certain that generations from now, we will be able to look back and tell our children that this was the moment when we began to provide care for the sick and good jobs to the jobless; this was the moment when the rise of the oceans began to slow and our planet began to heal; this was the moment when we ended a war and secured our nation and restored our image as the last, best hope on Earth. This was the moment—this was the time—when we came together to remake this great nation so that it may always reflect our very best selves and our highest ideals. Thank you, God bless you, and may God bless the United States of America.[8]

⇥ REPEATING TAKEAWAYS AND SLOGANS ⇤

When ending strong, Obama takes steps to restate key themes and slogans. His efficacy in doing this is evident by how widely known some of those slogans became: *Yes we can, Change that works for you, The past versus the future, Reclaim the American Dream, Our moment is now, Change we can believe in.*

As we saw in an early chapter, introducing refrains and slogans is a valuable way to drive points home. Reiterating refrains and slogans in the closing words of a speech serves as a means of keeping themes dominant in a listener's mind long after the speech concludes. Consider the earlier example, in which Obama restates the refrain "yes we can" in order to move to a climax and end the speech on an upbeat. Obama also uses alliteration in many spots, which adds to the eloquence of his final words:

We have been told we cannot do this by a chorus of cynics who will only grow louder and more dissonant in the weeks to come. We've been asked to pause for a reality check. We've been warned against offering the people of this nation false hope.

But in the unlikely story that is America, there has never been anything false about hope. For when we have faced down impossible odds; when we've been told that we're not ready, or that we shouldn't try, or that we can't, generations of Americans have responded with a simple creed that sums up the spirit of a people.

Yes we can.

It was a creed written into the founding documents that declared the destiny of a nation.

Yes we can.

It was whispered by slaves and abolitionists as they blazed a trail toward freedom through the darkest of nights.

Yes we can.

It was sung by immigrants as they struck out from distant shores and pioneers who pushed westward against an unforgiving wilderness.

Yes we can.

It was the call of workers who organized; women who reached for the ballot; a president who chose the moon as our new frontier; and a King who took us to the mountaintop and pointed the way to the Promised Land.

Yes we can to justice and equality. *Yes we can* to opportunity and prosperity. *Yes we can* heal this nation. *Yes we can* repair this world. *Yes we can.*

And so tomorrow, as we take this campaign south and west; as we learn that the struggles of the textile worker in Spartanburg are not so different than the plight of the dishwasher in Las Vegas; that the hopes of the little girl who goes to a crumbling school in Dillon are the same as the dreams of the boy who learns on the streets of LA; we will remember that there is something happening in America; that we are not as divided as our politics suggests; that we are one people; we are one nation; and together, we will begin the next great chapter in America's story with three words that will ring from coast to coast; from sea to shining sea—*Yes. We. Can.*[9] [*Emphases added.*]

⇥ DIRECTING TO LOW-HANGING FRUIT ⇤

Another important practice that Obama sometimes uses as he ends strong is a call to action, directing audience members to "low-hanging fruit"—the small actions they can take immediately to help a cause. Sometimes the call to action is very specific; other times, it is a general call to participate. In the speech that follows, Obama builds to a crescendo, underscores key points, and then ends with inspiring words and a call to action:

That is why this campaign can't only be about me. It must be about us. It must be about what we can do together. This campaign must be the occasion, the vehicle, of your hopes, and your dreams. It will take your time, your energy, and your advice to push us forward when we're doing right and to let us know when we're not. This campaign has to be about reclaiming the meaning of citizenship, restoring our sense of common purpose, and realizing that few obstacles can withstand the power of millions of voices calling for change.

By ourselves, this change will not happen. Divided, we are bound to fail.

But the life of a tall, gangly, self-made Springfield lawyer tells us that a different future is possible.

He tells us that there is power in words.

He tells us that there is power in conviction, that beneath all the differences of race and region, faith and station, we are one people.

He tells us that there is power in hope.

As Lincoln organized the forces arrayed against slavery, he was heard to say: "Of strange, discordant, and even hostile elements, we gathered from the four winds, and formed and fought to battle through."

That is our purpose here today.

That's why I'm in this race.

Not just to hold an office, but to gather with you to transform a nation.

I want to win that next battle—for justice and opportunity.

I want to win that next battle—for better schools, and better jobs, and health care for all.

I want us to take up the unfinished business of perfecting our union and building a better America.

And if you will join me in this improbable quest, if you feel destiny calling, and *see as I see*, a future of endless possibility stretching before us; *if you sense, as I sense*, that the time is now to shake off our slumber, and slough off our fear, and make good on the debt we owe past and future generations, *then I'm ready to take up the cause, and march with you, and work with you. Together, starting today, let us finish the work* that needs to be done, and usher in a new birth of freedom on this Earth.[10] [*Emphases added.*]

In issuing those closing remarks, Obama issued a challenge to generate support for future participation. This communication style has proven highly effective for Obama, as manifested by the momentum he built during the 2008 presidential campaign and the unprecedented levels of participation he secured.

⇥ PUTTING IT ALL TOGETHER ⇤ TO END STRONG

Finally, we take a look at an excerpt from Obama's December 2007 speech titled "Our Moment Is Now." It demonstrates how to blend some excellent communication techniques in order to end strong. Here, Obama uses vivid language—"slash and burn politics." He creates a sense of unity through the repetition of

"If you believe." He builds a sense of forward movement through the use of dynamic language that helps create a moving picture in the mind: "the task before us of remaking this country block by block, precinct by precinct, county by county, state by state." Obama rallies the audience with patriotic words that resonate: "keep the American dream alive"; "change the course of history." He also uses words that evoke biblical references: "hunger for," "thirst for." Obama makes certain to point out the challenges that have been faced and the achievements and momentum that have resulted: "They said we wouldn't have a chance"; "we resisted"; "I know that this time can be different." He stresses the mind shift that must take place in order to achieve success, driving this home through use of triadic phrases: "to shed our fears and our doubts and our cynicism." He offers words of affirmation while also building a sense of urgency: "Because I know that when the American people believe in something, it happens. . . . And now, in seven days, you have a chance once again to prove the cynics wrong." Obama reiterates the takeaway slogans just before he closes: "This is the moment. This is our time." He ends with a call to action, pointing to some low-hanging fruit: "stand with me in seven days." Let's see how he brings this all together masterfully:

> They said we wouldn't have a chance in this campaign unless we resorted to the same old negative attacks. But we resisted, even when we were written off, and ran a positive campaign that pointed out real differences and rejected the politics of slash and burn.
>
> And now, in seven days, you have a chance once again to prove the cynics wrong. In seven days, what was

improbable has the chance to beat what Washington said was inevitable. And that's why in these last weeks, Washington is fighting back with everything it has—with attack ads and insults; with distractions and dishonesty; with millions of dollars from outside groups and undisclosed donors to try and block our path.

We've seen this script many times before. But I know that this time can be different.

Because I know that when the American people believe in something, it happens.

If you believe, then we can tell the lobbyists that their days of setting the agenda in Washington are over.

If you believe, then we can stop making promises to America's workers and start delivering—jobs that pay, health care that's affordable, pensions you can count on, and a tax cut for working Americans instead of the companies who send their jobs overseas.

If you believe, we can offer a world-class education to every child, and pay our teachers more, and make college dreams a reality for every American.

If you believe, we can save this planet and end our dependence on foreign oil.

If you believe, we can end this war, close Guantanamo, restore our standing, renew our diplomacy, and once again respect the Constitution of the United States of America.

That's the future within our reach. That's what hope is—that thing inside us that insists, despite all evidence to the contrary, that something better is waiting for us around the corner. But only if we're willing to work for it and fight for it. To shed our fears and our doubts and our cynicism. To glory in the task before us of remaking this country block by block, precinct by precinct, county by county, state by state.

There is a moment in the life of every generation when, if we are to make our mark on history, this spirit must break through.

This is the moment.

This is our time.

And if you will stand with me in seven days, if you will stand for change so that our children have the same chance that somebody gave us; if you'll stand to keep the American dream alive for those who still hunger for opportunity and thirst for justice; if you're ready to stop settling for what the cynics tell you you must accept, and finally reach for what you know is possible, then we will win this caucus, we will win this election, we will change the course of history, and the real journey—to heal a nation and repair the world—will have truly begun.

Thank you.[11]

⇥ WHAT WE'VE LEARNED—PRACTICES FOR ⇤ MOTIVATING OTHERS TO ACTION AND LEAVING STRONG LAST IMPRESSIONS

When seeking to use communication to deliver messages that will influence listeners and endure, several techniques prove useful. A speaker can inspire others to great achievements by employing words that resonate, including words that evoke shared values, patriotic values, cherished principles, or biblical truths. Speaking in ways that create a sense of momentum and urgency to future actions can also be important. Obama has done this repeatedly with great effect as he has pointed to successes that continued to build his momentum, noted the increasing levels of support for his ideas, and demonstrated through the details he offered that "things are rolling."

Another best practice for leaving a strong last impression is to "finish strong." Outstanding orators will build to a high point and end on that high, leaving listeners stirred, inspired, motivated, and focused on key themes. Speakers can also consider repeating takeaways or slogans in the closing minutes of their talks. This helps to keep those themes and ideas dominant in the minds of audience members. Issuing a call to action or directing listeners to low-hanging fruit—the small actions they can take to aid a cause—can also help increase the motivating impact of communication.

CHAPTER 10

SPEECHES THAT MADE HISTORY

This chapter contains speeches that Barack Obama gave both shortly before and after he assumed the office of the U.S. presidency. These are speeches that have made history and include Barack Obama's nomination acceptance speech, delivered at the Democratic National Convention on August 28, 2008; his 2008 election night victory speech; his 2009 presidential inaugural address; his 2009 Middle East speech "On a New Beginning"; his 2009 remarks about financial reform; his 2009 speech before the United Nations; his 2011 announcement of the death of Osama bin Laden; and his 2012 State of the Union address.

⇥ **2008 NOMINATION ACCEPTANCE SPEECH** ⇤

Barack Obama moves on stage with a confident gait and bright smile, stretching his arm and waving to the live Denver audience of approximately 80,000 and to millions of TV viewers. He walks with a "presidential" air, exuding authority. He claps his hands along with his audience at times, an early sign of his connection with the audience and his comfort. He moves to the lectern and stands with a commanding posture, feet planted firmly, and shoulders squared. Dressed in a formal dark suit, his tie blends the colors of blue and red stripes, sending a subtle yet significant message of unity that is underscored by an American flag pin adorning his lapel.

The physical background reinforces his image and body language, which are intended to project him as a leader. Numerous large American flags flank the podium behind him. The staging itself—adorned with large columns—evokes memories of Washington's Lincoln Memorial, the site of Martin Luther King Jr.'s 1963 "I Have a Dream" speech. Obama stands before the formal wooden lectern as applause rings on for some time, his lips pressed together in a close-mouthed smile. His expression is humble, not gratifying—a look of appreciation and seriousness of purpose. After a long while, the applause begins to subside. Obama takes a deep breath and the timbre of his voice resonates as he begins his historic 2008 Democratic presidential nomination acceptance address:

> Thank you! [*The applause continues on.*]
>> Thank you, everybody. [*More applause.*]
>> To Chairman Dean and my great friend Dick Durbin, and to all my fellow citizens of this great nation, with *profound*

gratitude [*emphasis*] and *great humility* [*emphasis*], I accept your nomination for presidency of the United States. [*He amplifies his volume. The words electrify the listeners. The audience applauds and claps and waves American flags.*]

Let me express my thanks to the historic slate of candidates who accompanied me on this journey [*his tone is filled with gratitude*], and especially the one who traveled the farthest, a *champion* [*emphasis*] for working Americans and an *inspiration* [*emphasis*] to my daughters and yours, Hillary Rodham Clinton. [*He pinches his fingers to underscore Clinton's importance. The audience rings with applause.*]

To President Clinton, to President Bill Clinton, who made last night the case for change as only *he* can make it. [*He motions his hands widely, indicating the words are heartfelt. Applause.*] To Ted Kennedy, who embodies the spirit of service. [*Applause.*] And to the next vice president of the United States [*slight pause*], Joe Biden, I thank you. [*Enthusiastic applause.*]

I am *grateful* [*emphasis*] to finish this journey with one of the finest statesmen of our time, a man at ease with everyone [*he motions his hands wide*] from world leaders to the conductors on the Amtrak train he still takes home every night.

To the love of my life [*his eyes twinkle with emotion*], our next first lady, Michelle Obama [*pause for applause; Obama flashes a bright smile*]. And to Malia and Sasha, I love you *so much* [*emphasis*], and I am *so proud* [*emphasis*] of you. [*His tone is filled with adoration. Applause.*]

Four years ago [*he draws out the words*], I stood before you and told you my story, of the brief union between a young man from Kenya and a young woman from Kansas who weren't well off or well known, but shared a belief that in America their son could *achieve* whatever he put his mind to. [*He pinches his fingers; his tone is wistful.*]

It is that *promise* [*he holds the "s," drawing a little more attention to the word "promise"*] that's always set this country apart [*he motions his hands widely, underscoring the greatness of the country*], that through hard work and sacrifice *each of us* [*he enunciates each word with extra care*] can pursue our individual dreams, but still come together [*he motions his hands together*] as one American family, to *ensure* [*emphasis; he points an index finger*] that the next generation can pursue their dreams, as well. That's why I stand here tonight. Because for 232 years [*he motions his hand widely, conveying the magnitude of time and he stresses each word: two-hundred-thirty-two*], at each moment when that promise was in jeopardy, *ordinary* [*he points his finger in the air, underscoring the word*] men and women—students and soldiers, farmers and teachers, nurses and janitors [*his voice rises and falls, conveying the breadth of people involved*]—found the courage to keep it alive.

We meet at one of those *defining moments* [*he pinches his fingers and stresses the words, sounding wistful*], a moment when our nation is at war, our economy is in turmoil, and the American promise has been threatened once more.

Tonight [*he dips his voice, adding emphasis*], more Americans are out of work and more are working harder for less. More of you have lost your homes and even more are watching your home values plummet. More of you have cars you can't afford to drive, credit cards, bills you can't afford to pay, and tuition that's beyond your reach. [*He motions his hands widely.*]

These challenges are not all of government's making. But the failure to respond [*he moves his index finger in a chastising manner*] is a direct result of a broken politics in Washington and the failed policies of George W. Bush. [*He points his finger in the air again; he amplifies his volume. Applause.*]

America! [*A challenge rings beneath his tone as he nearly sings out the name, America!*] We are better than these last eight years. We are *a better country* than this. [*A challenge rings in his tone. Applause.*]

This country is more *decent* [*emphasis*] than one where a woman in Ohio, on the brink of retirement, finds herself one illness away [*he points his index finger*] from disaster after a lifetime of hard work. We're a better country [*he motions his hands widely*] than one where a man in Indiana has to pack up the equipment that he's worked on for twenty years and watch as it's shipped off to China [*he brushes a hand dismissively to the side*], and then chokes up as he explains how he felt like a failure when he went home to tell his family the news. [*He dips his pitch low, conveying disapproval.*]

We are more *compassionate* than a government that lets veterans sleep on our streets and families *slide* into poverty . . . [*Applause.*] . . . that sits on its hands while a major American city drowns before our eyes. [*The audience applauds his disapproving reference to the crisis suffered in New Orleans.*]

Tonight [*emphasis*], I say to the people of America—to Democrats *and* Republicans *and* Independents [*his tone crests and dips to emphasize the diverse political backgrounds*] across this great land: *Enough!* [*He puts tremendous volume behind the word. Dramatic pause.*] This moment [*emphasis; applause*]—this moment [*slight pause; applause*], this election [*emphasis*] is *our chance* [*emphasis*] to keep, in the twenty-first century [*he points an index finger in the air*], the American promise alive. [*He pinches his fingers to underscore the importance.*]

Because next week, in Minnesota, the same party that brought you two terms of George Bush and Dick Cheney will ask this country for a third. [*The audience boos.*]

And we are here [*he motions both hands toward himself*]— we are here because we love this country *too much* [*emphasis*] to let the next four years look just like the last eight. [*He glides his voice subtly up and down to underscore the words, eliciting a strong audience response of support. Applause.*]

On November 4th, we must stand up and say: *Eight is enough!* [*Applause. He flashes a bright, confident smile and utters a slight chuckle. The cheers go on.*]

Now, now, let there be no doubt. The Republican nominee, John McCain, has worn the uniform of our country with bravery and distinction [*his tone is respectful and full of gratitude*], and for that we owe him our gratitude and our respect. [*He nods to affirm his point further. Applause.*]

And next week [*he points an index finger*], we'll also hear about those occasions when he's broken with his party as evidence that he can deliver the change that we need. But the record's clear: John McCain has voted with George Bush

90 percent [*he pinches his fingers*] of the time. Senator McCain likes to talk about judgment, but, really [*his pitch rises; he wags an index finger in the air, expressing disapproval*], what does it say about your judgment when you think George Bush has been right more than 90 percent of the time? [*His tone is mocking. Applause.*] I don't know about you, but I am not ready to take a *10 percent* chance on change. [*He pinches his fingers. Applause.*]

The truth is [*he waves an index finger in the air*], on issue after issue that would make a difference in your lives—on health care, and education, and the economy [*he motions his hands wide, indicating the breadth and importance of the issues*]— Senator McCain has been anything *but* [*emphasis*] independent.

He said that our economy has made great progress under this president. He *said* [*he draws out the word, adding emphasis*] that the fundamentals of the economy are strong. And when one of his chief advisers, the man who wrote his economic plan, was talking about the anxieties that Americans are feeling, he said that we were just suffering from a *mental recession* [*he enunciates each word, his tone conveying disapproval*] and that we've become—and I quote [*he raises an index finger*]—"a nation of whiners." [*The audience boos.*]

A nation of whiners? Tell that to the proud autoworkers at a Michigan plant who, after they found out it was closing, kept showing up every day and working as hard as ever, because they knew [*he points his index finger*] there were people who counted on the brakes that they made. [*His tone is indignant.*] Tell that to the military families who shoulder their burdens silently [*his voice dips*] as they watch their loved ones leave for their third, or fourth, or fifth tour of duty. *These are not whiners.* [*Emphasis.*] They work *hard, and* [*emphasis*] they give back, *and* [*emphasis*] they keep going without complaint. *These* [*emphasis*] are the Americans I know. [*Applause.*]

Now, I don't believe that Senator McCain doesn't care what's going on in the lives of Americans; I just think he doesn't know. [*He quickens his cadence, as if delivering a humorous punch line. The audience rings with laughter.*]

Why else would he define middle class as someone making under $5 million a year? [*He waves an index finger in the air.*] How else could he propose hundreds of billions [*slight mocking chuckle*] in tax breaks for big corporations and oil companies, but *not one penny* [*he stresses each word*] of tax relief to more than *100 million* Americans? [*He jabs an index finger, accusingly; emphasis.*] How else could he offer a health care plan that would actually *tax* [*he pinches his fingers*] people's benefits, or an education plan that would do *nothing* [*he motions his hands wide, highlighting "nothing"*] to help families pay for college, or a plan [*he increases his cadence, giving the sense that the list could go on and on*] that would privatize Social Security and gamble your retirement? [*The audience boos.*]

It's not because John McCain doesn't care [*his pitch dips*]; it's because John McCain doesn't get it. [*Applause.*]

For over two decades, he's subscribed to that old, discredited Republican philosophy: Give more and more to those with the most [*his pitch rises, emphasizing the point*] and hope that prosperity trickles down to everyone else. [*He dips his pitch disapprovingly.*]

In Washington, they call this the "Ownership Society" [*he pinches his fingers*], but what it really means is that you're on your own. [*He jabs his index finger in the air, as if issuing a warning. The audience laughs.*] Out of work? *Tough luck* [*he punches the words and waves a dismissive hand that mocks the words*], you're on your own. [*His tone is mocking.*] No health care? The market will fix it. [*He waves a hand dismissively.*] You're on your own. Born into poverty? Pull yourself up by your *own* bootstraps, even if you don't have boots. You are *on your own*. [*He enunciates each word with care: on-your-own. He draws a strong audience reaction of disapproval to the idea.*]

Well [*he draws the word out*], it's time for them to *own* their failure. [*His voice is stern and chastising; he points a finger in the air.*] *It's time for us* to *change* America. [*He points a finger in the air determinedly.*] And that's why I'm running for president of the United States. [*His tone is resolute. Enthusiastic applause.*]

You see [*he draws the words out*], we Democrats have a very different measure of what constitutes *progress* [*he pinches his fingers*] in this country. We measure progress by how many people can find a job that pays the mortgage [*his tone rings with rightness*], whether you can put a little extra money away [*he pinches his fingers to underscore the point*] at the end of each month so you can someday watch your child receive her college diploma. We measure progress in the 23 million new jobs that were created when *Bill Clinton* [*he speaks a tad bit more closely into the microphone, pointing an index finger to emphasize the point*] was president [*applause*] . . . when the average American family saw its income go up $7,500 [*he motions his hand upwards*] instead of go down $2,000 [*he motions his other hand downward*], like it has under George Bush. [*Applause.*]

We measure the strength of our economy not by the number of billionaires we have or the profits of the Fortune 500, but by whether someone with a good idea can take a risk and start a new business, or whether the waitress who lives on tips [*he points an index finger*] can take a day off and look after a sick kid without losing her job—an economy that honors the dignity of work.

The fundamentals [*his hand gestures convey that "the fundamentals" are precious*] we use to measure economic strength are whether we are living up to that fundamental promise that has made this country great—a promise that is the only reason I am standing here tonight. [*He motions a hand gently toward his chest.*]

Because, in the faces of those young veterans who come back from Iraq and Afghanistan, I see my grandfather, who signed up after Pearl Harbor, marched in Patton's army, and was rewarded by a grateful nation with the chance to go to college on the GI Bill.

In the face of that young student, who sleeps just three hours before working the night shift, I think about my mom, who raised my sister and me on her own while she worked and earned her degree; who once turned to food stamps, but was still able to send us to the *best schools* in the country with the help of student loans and scholarships. [*Applause.*]

When I listen to another worker tell me that his factory has shut down, I remember all those men and women on the South Side of Chicago who I *stood by* [*emphasis*] and *fought for* [*emphasis*] two decades ago after the local steel plant closed.

And when I hear a woman talk about the difficulties of starting her own business or making her way in the world, I think about my grandmother, who worked her way up from the secretarial pool to middle management, despite years of being passed over for promotions because she was a woman.

She's the one who taught me about *hard work.* [*He pinches his fingers, underscoring the point.*] She's the one who put off buying a new car or a new dress for herself so that I could have a better life. [*He touches both hands to his chest, underscoring the precious nature of his grandmother's sacrifice.*] She poured everything she had into me. And although she can no longer travel, I know that she's watching tonight and that tonight is *her night* as well. [*Emphasis; enthusiastic applause.*]

Now [*he draws the word out*], I don't know what kind of lives John McCain thinks that celebrities lead [*his tone is mocking as he makes an allusion to McCain's assertions that he is a celebrity*], but this has been mine. [*Applause.*]

These [*emphasis*] are my heroes; *theirs* [*emphasis*] are the stories that shaped my life. And it is on behalf of them that I intend to win this election and keep our promise alive as president of the United States. [*He amplifies his words; his tone is determined. Applause.*]

What is that American promise? [*Pause for impact.*] It's a promise that says each of us has the freedom to make of our own lives what we will, but that we also have obligations to treat each other with *dignity* [*slight pause*] and *respect.*

It's a promise that says the market should reward *drive and innovation and generate growth* [*his cadence quickens, underscoring the importance*], but that businesses should live up to their responsibilities to create American jobs, to look out for American workers, and play by the rules of the road. [*He motions his hands to underscore the points.*]

Ours [*he draws out the word, adding emphasis*] is a promise that says government cannot solve all our problems [*his pitch dips*], but what it *should do* [*emphasis*] is that which we cannot do for ourselves [*he motions both hands toward himself*]: protect us from harm [*he holds a vertical palm in a stop sign*] and provide every child a decent education [*he motions his hands widely, signifying the importance*]; keep our water clean and our toys safe; invest in new schools, *and* new roads, *and* science, *and* technology.

Our government should work *for us* [*he stresses the words*], not against us. [*His pitch rises and falls, adding emphasis.*] It should *help us* [*he stresses the words*], not hurt us. [*His pitch rises and falls.*] It should ensure opportunity not just for those with the most money and influence, but for every American who's willing to work. [*He increases his cadence, underscoring the point.*]

That's the promise of America, the idea that we are responsible for ourselves, but that we also rise or fall as one nation, the fundamental belief that I am my brother's keeper, I am my sister's keeper. [*He slices his hand through the air, signifying the rightness of the principles.*]

That's the promise we need to keep. [*He point an index finger.*] That's the change we need right now. [*He points the index finger of his other hand. Applause.*]

So let me spell out *exactly* what that change would mean [*he pinches his fingers, as if addressing a criticism*] if I am president. [*Applause.*]

Change means a tax code that doesn't reward the lobbyists who wrote it, but the American workers and small businesses who deserve it. [*He moves a hand toward the audience. Applause.*] You know, unlike John McCain, I will *stop* [*emphasis*] giving tax breaks to companies that ship jobs overseas, and I will start giving them to companies that create good jobs right here in America. [*He points his index finger in the air. Applause.*] I'll eliminate capital gains taxes for the small businesses and start-ups that will create the *high-wage, high-tech jobs* of tomorrow. [*He cups his hand in a "C," as if placing the words in the air. Applause.*] I will—listen now [*he points his finger in the air*]—I will cut taxes [*pause*]—cut taxes [*emphasis*]—for 95 percent [*he jabs an index finger*] of *all* [*emphasis*] working families, because, in an economy like this [*he leans into the microphone, accentuating the point*], the last thing we should do is raise taxes on the middle class. [*He amplifies his volume. Applause.*] And for the sake of our economy, our security, and the future of our planet, I will set a clear goal [*he cuts a hand through the air*] as president: In 10 years [*he points an index finger*], we will finally [*he points the index finger of his other hand*] end our dependence on oil from the Middle East. [*Enthusiastic applause.*]

We will do this. Washington—Washington has been talking about our oil addiction for the last thirty years. And, by the way, John McCain has been there for twenty-six of them. [*His tone is mocking. Laughter rings from the audience.*] And in that time, he has said *no* [*emphasis; slight pause*] to higher fuel-efficiency standards for cars, *no* [*emphasis*] to investments in renewable energy, *no* to renewable fuels. And today, we import *triple* the amount of oil than we had on the day that Senator McCain took office.

Now [*he draws out the word*] is the time to *end* [*emphasis*] this addiction and to understand that drilling is a stop-gap measure, not a long-term solution, not even close. [*He slices a horizontal hand, palm down, through the air. Applause.*] As president [*he moves a hand toward the audience, exuding sincerity*], as president, I will tap our natural gas reserves [*he motions his hands wide, conveying the importance*], invest in clean coal technology, and find ways to safely harness nuclear power. I'll help our auto companies re-tool, so that the fuel-efficient cars of the future are built right here [*he taps an index finger as if pointing to the very ground on which he stands*] in America. [*Applause.*]

I'll make it easier for the American people to afford these new cars. [*He points an index finger in the air.*] And I'll invest *$150 billion* over the next decade in affordable, renewable sources of energy—wind power, *and* solar power, *and* the next generation of biofuels—an investment that will lead to new industries and *5 million* [*emphasis*] new jobs that pay well and can't be outsourced. [*He varies his pitch. Dramatic pause. Applause.*]

America [*he draws out the word*], *now* is not the time for small plans. *Now* [*emphasis*] is the time [*he points an index finger in the air*] to *finally* meet our *moral obligation* [*he enunciates the words with care*] to provide every child a world-class education [*he motions his hands widely*], because it will take nothing less to compete in the global economy. [*He points an index finger.*] You know, Michelle and I are only here tonight because we were given a chance at an education. And I will not settle for an America where some kids don't have that chance. [*His tone is stern. Applause.*]

I'll invest in early childhood education [*he motions his hands widely*]. I'll recruit an army of new teachers [*he stretches his arm to the side, as if reaching to pull something from far away*], *and pay* [*emphasis*] them higher salaries, *and give* [*emphasis*] them more support. [*He motions his hand widely, signifying the importance.*] And in exchange, I'll ask for higher standards and more accountability. And we will keep our promise to every young American: If you commit to serving your community or our country, we will make sure you can afford a college education. [*He varies his volume and pitch to accentuate key words. Applause.*]

Now [*slight pause*]—now is the time to finally keep the promise of affordable, accessible health care for *every single* [*emphasis*] American. [*Applause.*]

If you have health care, my plan will lower your premiums. If you *don't* [*emphasis*], you'll be able to get the same kind of coverage that members of Congress give themselves. [*Applause.*]

And [*he draws the word out*]—and as someone who watched my mother argue with insurance companies while she lay in bed [*slight pause*] dying of cancer, I will make certain those companies stop discriminating against those who are sick and need care the most. [*He amplifies his volume. His tone is indignant. Applause.*]

Now [*he draws the word out*] is the time to help families with paid sick days and better family leave, because nobody in America [*he slices his hand through the air*] should have to choose between keeping their job and caring for a sick child or an ailing parent.

Now [*emphasis*] is the time to change our bankruptcy laws, so that your pensions are protected ahead of CEO bonuses, and the time to protect Social Security for future generations.

And now [*emphasis*] is the time to keep the promise of *equal pay* [*he amplifies his voice*] for an *equal day's work* [*he jabs an index finger in the air; emphasis*], because I want my daughters to have the exact same opportunities as your sons. [*He jabs his index finger again and generates enthusiastic applause.*]

Now, many of these plans will cost money, which is why I've laid out how I'll pay for every dime: by closing corporate loopholes and tax havens that don't help America grow. But I will also go through the federal budget *line by line* [*he punches the words*], eliminating programs that no longer work and making the ones we do need *work better* [*emphasis*] and cost *less* [*emphasis*], because we cannot meet *twenty-first-century* challenges with a *twentieth-century* bureaucracy. [*Applause.*]

And, Democrats—Democrats—we must also admit that fulfilling America's promise will require more than just money. It will require a renewed sense of responsibility [*he softens his tone, speaking the words solemnly and touching his fingertips together*] from each of us to recover what John F. Kennedy called our intellectual and moral strength.

Yes, government must lead on energy independence, but *each of us* [*he stresses each word*] must do our part to make our homes and businesses more efficient. [*Applause.*]

Yes [*emphasis*], we must provide more ladders [*he motions his hands widely*] to success for young men who fall into lives of crime and despair. But we must also admit that programs alone can't replace parents [*his tone is emphatic*], that government can't turn off the television and make a child do her homework [*he motions a hand downward*], that *fathers* must take more responsibility [*he stretches a hand toward the audience, to emphasize the importance*] to provide love and guidance to their children. [*He amplifies his voice and lets the words linger.*]

Individual responsibility [*he pinches the fingers of one hand*] and mutual responsibility [*he pinches the fingers of his other hand, underscoring the significance of the twin responsibilities*], that's the *essence* [*emphasis*] of America's promise. And just as we keep our promise to the next generation here at home, so must we keep America's promise abroad. [*He points an index finger in the air.*]

If John McCain wants to have a debate about who has the *temperament and judgment* [*emphasis*] to serve as the next commander-in-chief, that's a debate I'm ready to have. [*A strong, direct challenge lies beneath his words; his tone is unwavering and he elicits enthusiastic applause.*]

[*He stretches his hand in a stop sign, emphasizing the gravity of the words to follow.*] For while Senator McCain was turning his sights to Iraq [*he stretches his arm and motions his hand, indicating "far away"*] just days after 9/11, I stood up and opposed this war, knowing that it would distract us from the real threats that we face. [*He points his finger in a chastising manner.*]

When John McCain said we could just muddle through [*he motions his hands, accentuating the words*] in Afghanistan, I argued for more resources and more troops to finish the fight against the terrorists who actually attacked us on 9/11, and made clear that we must *take out* [*he points a finger toward the audience, determinedly*] Osama bin Laden and his lieutenants if we have them in our sights. You know, John McCain likes to say that he'll follow bin Laden to the gates of Hell, but he *won't even follow him to the cave where he lives.* [*He colors his tone with disappointment. Applause.*]

And today, today, as my call for a timeframe to remove our troops from Iraq has been echoed by the Iraqi government and *even* [*emphasis*] the Bush administration, even after we learned that Iraq has $79 *billion* [*emphasis*] in surplus while we are *wallowing* in deficit, John McCain stands alone in his *stubborn* [*emphasis*] refusal to end a misguided war.

That's not the judgment we need [*his tone is indignant*]; that won't keep America safe. We need a president who can face the threats of the future [*his pitch rises*], not keep *grasping* [emphasis] at the ideas of the past. [*He lowers his pitch and stretches an arm, palm downward, conveying disapproval. Applause.*]

You don't defeat a terrorist network that operates in eighty countries by occupying Iraq. [*The audience laughs.*] You don't protect Israel and deter Iran just by talking tough in Washington. [*The audience cheers.*] You can't truly stand up for Georgia when you've strained our oldest alliances.

If John McCain wants to follow George Bush with more tough talk and bad strategy, that is his choice [*he motions both hands to the left—as if indicating their choice is far from him*], but that is not the change that America needs. [*He pinches his fingers. Applause.*]

We are the party of Roosevelt. [*He moves both hands toward his chest and amplifies his voice.*] We are the party of Kennedy. So don't tell me [*he amplifies his voice more, conveying indignation*] that Democrats won't defend this country. *Don't tell me* [*amplified voice*] that Democrats won't keep us safe. [*His tone mocks the notion that Democrats are weak.*]

The Bush-McCain foreign policy has *squandered* [*emphasis*] the legacy that generations of Americans, Democrats *and* [*emphasis*] Republicans, have built, and we are here to restore that legacy. [*He cuts a hand through the air with resoluteness. Applause.*]

As commander-in-chief [*his face is stern*], I will never hesitate to defend this nation, but I will only send our troops into harm's way with a clear mission and a sacred commitment to give them the equipment they need in battle and the care and benefits they deserve when they come home. [*His tone is resolute. Applause.*]

I will end this war in Iraq responsibly and finish the fight against Al Qaida and the Taliban in Afghanistan. I will rebuild [*he points the index finger of one hand toward the audience*] our military to meet future conflicts, but I will also renew the tough, direct diplomacy [*he points the index finger of his other hand toward the audience*] that can prevent Iran from obtaining nuclear weapons and curb Russian aggression.

I will build new partnerships [*he motions his hands widely, signifying the importance*] to defeat the threats of the twenty-first century: terrorism and nuclear proliferation, poverty and genocide, climate change and disease.

And I will *restore* [*emphasis*] our moral standing so that America [*he slices his hand through the air*] is once again that *last, best hope* [*emphasis*] for *all* [*he stretches his arm, palm down, emphasizing the word*] who are called to the cause of freedom, who *long* [*emphasis*] for lives of peace, and who *yearn* [*emphasis*] for a better future. [*He progressively amplifies his voice for great effect and he generates tremendous applause. The audience begins chanting "USA! USA!"*]

These [*emphasis*] are the policies I will pursue. And in the weeks ahead, I look forward to debating them with John McCain. [*His tone is determined.*]

But [*pause*] what I will *not* do is suggest that the senator takes his positions for political purposes [*his tone rings with moral rightness*], because one of the things that we have to change in our politics is the idea that people cannot disagree without challenging each other's character and each other's patriotism. [*Applause.*]

The times are too serious [*pause*], the stakes are too high for this same partisan playbook. So let us agree that patriotism has no party. I love this country [*he places a hand to his chest*], and so do you [*he points his finger toward the audience*], and so does John McCain. [*He point his finger again, indicating McCain.*]

The men and women who serve in our battlefields may be Democrats *and* Republicans *and* Independents, but they have fought together, *and bled* together, *and* some *died* together under the same *proud* flag. They have not served a *red* [*emphasis*] America or a *blue* [*emphasis*] America; they have served the *United States of America* [*he thumps a finger against the lectern emphatically and enunciates each word: U-ni-ted-States-of-A-mer-i-ca. The audience erupts in thunderous applause and chants "USA! USA!" Listeners wave flags throughout the stadium.*]

[*He motions a vertical palm in a stop sign.*] So I've got news for you, John McCain [*his face is stern; he amplifies his voice, making his challenge is clear*]: We *all* [*emphasis*] put our country first. [*He cuts a hand through the air. Dramatic pause. Applause.*]

America, our work will not be easy. The challenges we face require tough choices. And Democrats, as well as Republicans, will need to cast off the worn-out ideas [*he motions a hand as if pushing away the antiquated ideas*] and politics of the past, for part of what has been lost these past eight years can't just be measured by lost wages or bigger trade deficits. What has also been lost is our sense of common purpose [*he softens his voice, giving the words gravity*], and *that's* [*emphasis*] what we have to restore.

We may not agree on abortion, but surely we can agree on reducing the number of unwanted pregnancies in this country. [*He quickens his cadence to underscore the point. Applause.*]

The reality of gun ownership may be different for hunters in rural Ohio than they are for those plagued by gang violence in Cleveland, *but* [*emphasis*] don't tell me we can't uphold the Second Amendment while keeping AK-47s out of the hands of criminals. [*His tone ridicules any notion this cannot be done and generates applause.*]

I know there are differences on same-sex marriage, but *surely* [*emphasis*] we can agree that our gay and lesbian brothers and sisters deserve to visit the person they love in a hospital and to live lives free of discrimination. [*Applause.*]

You know, passions may fly on immigration, but I don't know anyone who benefits when a mother is separated from her infant child [*he motions his hands apart*] or an employer undercuts American wages by hiring illegal workers.

But this, too, is part of America's promise [*he touches his hands together gently, underscoring the preciousness of the promise*], the promise of a democracy where we can find the strength [*slight pause*] and grace [*his voice lingers on the "c," highlighting the word "grace"*] to bridge divides and unite in common effort.

I know there are those who dismiss such beliefs as happy talk. They claim that our insistence on something *larger* [*slight pause*], something *firmer*, and more *honest* in our public life is just a Trojan horse for higher taxes and the abandonment of traditional values. And that's to be expected, because if you don't have any fresh ideas, then you use stale tactics to scare voters. [*He points a finger accusingly. Applause.*]

If you don't have a record to run on [*he wags an index finger back and forth*], then you paint your opponent as someone people should run *from* [*emphasis*]. You make a big election [*he moves both hands apart, indicating something large*] about small things [*he brings his hands together, motioning to indicate smallness*]. And you know what? It's worked before, because it *feeds* into the cynicism we all have about government. When Washington doesn't work, all its promises seem empty [*he motions a hand away, as if pushing a false promise far away*]. If your hopes have been dashed again and again, then it's best to stop hoping and settle for what you already know. [*His pitch dips slightly, conveying disapproval.*]

I get it. I realize that I am not the likeliest candidate for this office [*he moves both hands toward his chest*]. I don't fit the typical pedigree, and I haven't spent my career in the halls of Washington. But I stand before you tonight because all across America something is stirring [*he motions his hands widely*]. What the naysayers don't understand is that this election has never been about me [*his pitch dips and he pauses*]; it's about you. [*His pitch rises; he points a finger toward the audience. Enthusiastic applause.*]

It's about you. [*More applause.*]

For eighteen long months, you have stood up, *one by one*, and said, "*Enough,*" [*emphasis*] to the politics of the past. *You* [*he draws out the word and points a finger at the audience*] understand that, in this election, the greatest risk we can take is to try the *same, old politics* with the *same, old players* [*emphasis*] and expect a different result.

You have shown what history teaches us—that at defining moments like this one, the change we need doesn't come *from* [*emphasis*] Washington. Change comes *to* [*emphasis*] Washington. [*He motions his hands widely. Applause.*]

Change [*he nearly sings the word and cuts a hand through the air, adding emphasis*] happens—change happens because the American people *demand* it, because they *rise up* [*he motions his hands emphatically*] and insist on *new* ideas [*slight pause*] and *new* leadership [*slight pause*], a *new* politics [*he slices a hand through the air*] for a *new* time. [*He pinches his fingers.*]

America, this is one of those moments.

I believe [*he nearly sings the words, letting them linger*] that, as hard as it will be [*slight pause*], the change we need is coming [*he dips his pitch*], because I've *seen* it [*he motions his hands to his chest; slight pause for impact*], because I've *lived* it. [*Slight pause.*]

Because I've seen it in Illinois, when we provided health care to more children [*he motions his hands widely*] and moved more families from welfare to work. I've seen it in Washington, where we worked across party lines to open up government and hold lobbyists more accountable, to give better care for our veterans, and keep nuclear weapons out of the hands of terrorists. [*He glides his voice up and down to emphasize the breadth of change.*] And I've *seen* it in this campaign [*his tone is filled with admiration*], in the young people who voted for the *first time* [*pride sounds in his voice*] and the young at heart, those who got involved again after a *very long* time; in the Republicans who never thought [*slight chuckle, slight smile*] they'd pick up a Democratic ballot [*he gives a dramatic pause to underscore the importance*], but did. [*He smiles. Applause.*]

I've seen it—I've seen it in the workers who would rather cut their hours back a day [*he pinches his fingers*], even though they can't afford it, than see their friends lose their jobs; in the soldiers who reenlist after losing a limb; in the good neighbors who take a stranger in when a hurricane strikes and the floodwaters rise.

You know, this country of ours has more wealth than any nation, but that's not what makes us rich. We have the most powerful military on Earth, but that's not what makes us strong [*his pitch rises and falls, underscoring his point*]. Our universities and our culture are the envy of the world [*his pitch crests; he motions his hands wide, signifying the grandness of the USA*], but that's not what keeps the world coming to our shores [*his pitch dips*].

Instead [*he dips his voice again*], it is that American spirit [*pause*], that American promise, that pushes us forward even when the path is uncertain; that binds us together in spite of our differences; that makes us fix our eye not on what is seen, but what is *unseen* [*emphasis*], that better place around the bend. [*His tone is wistful and filled with hope.*]

That promise [*his voice lingers on the "s," emphasizing "promise"*] is our greatest inheritance. It's a promise I make to my daughters when I tuck them in at night and a promise [*his voice stresses the "s," highlighting the word "promise"*] that you make to yours, a promise that has led immigrants to *cross oceans* [*he amplifies his voice, highlighting the greatness of this*] and pioneers to travel west, a promise that led workers to picket lines and women to reach for the ballot. [*He quickens his cadence; his pitch rises and falls. Applause.*]

And [*slight pause*] it is that promise that, forty-five years ago today [*pause*], brought Americans from every corner of this land to *stand together* on a Mall in Washington, before Lincoln's Memorial, and hear a young preacher from Georgia speak of his dream [*he progressively amplifies his voice, giving great effect to his words and rousing listeners with his reference to Martin Luther King Jr. He lets the words linger. The audience rings with enthusiastic applause.*]

The men and women who gathered there could've heard many things. They could've heard words of anger and discord. They could've been told to succumb to the *fear and frustrations* of so many dreams deferred.

But what the people heard instead—people of every *creed and color*, from every walk of life—is that, *in America* [*emphasis*], our destiny is inextricably linked, *that together* [*emphasis*] our dreams can be one. [*He pinches his fingers, accentuating the points.*]

"*We cannot walk alone,*" [*he slices his hand emphatically through the air*] the preacher cried. "And as we walk, we must make the pledge that we shall always march ahead. [*He cuts his hand through the air again.*] We cannot turn back." [*He stresses each word.*]

America, we cannot turn back . . . [*His tone remains determined; he wags his index finger high in the air. Applause.*] . . . *Not* [*emphasis*] with so much work to be done [*he amplifies his volume and keeps it raised and he points repeatedly to the audience, challenging listeners*]; not [*emphasis*] with so many children to educate, and so many veterans to care for; not [*emphasis*] with an economy to fix, *and* cities to rebuild, *and* farms to save; not [*emphasis*] with so many families to protect and so many lives to mend.

America! We cannot turn back. [*His tone issues a challenge. Pause.*] We cannot walk alone. [*His tone is unwavering and resolute as he builds to a crescendo.*]

At this moment, in this election [*his tone underscores a sense of urgency as he reaches his crescendo*], we must pledge once more to march into the future. Let us *keep* [*emphasis*] that promise [*his tone issues a challenge*], that *American promise* [*his tone is wistful*], and in the words of Scripture hold firmly [*he speaks the word "Scripture" with reverence*], without *wavering*, to the hope that we confess.

Thank you! [*Slight pause.*] God bless you! [*Slight pause.*] And *God bless* [*emphasis*] the United States of America! [*Emphases added.*]

[*The audience rises in an ovation. Obama stretches his arm wide, waving to the audience. He claps his hands briefly with the audience, underscoring their unity. The audience continues on in applause.*]

The media, many listeners, and political pundits immediately praised Barack Obama's 2008 presidential nomination acceptance speech as "magnificent," "extraordinary," "electrifying," "rousing," "unifying," and "the best since President Kennedy." The masterful and powerful delivery solidified Obama's place as one of the most effective and outstanding orators of recent times.

Here are some additional history-making speeches. As valuable pieces of both American and, in many cases, international history, these speeches are printed in their entirety. Are you able to identify his rhetorical techniques?

⇥ ELECTION NIGHT VICTORY SPEECH, ⇤ GRANT PARK, CHICAGO, NOVEMBER 4, 2008

If there is anyone out there who still doubts that America is a place where all things are possible; who still wonders if the dream of our founders is alive in our time; who still questions the power of our democracy, tonight is your answer.

It's the answer told by lines that stretched around schools and churches in numbers this nation has never seen; by people who waited three hours and four hours, many for the very first time in their lives, because they believed that this time must be different; that their voice could be that difference.

It's the answer spoken by young and old, rich and poor, Democrat and Republican, black, white, Latino, Asian, Native American, gay, straight, disabled and not disabled—Americans who sent a message to the world that we have never been a collection of Red States and Blue States: we are, and always will be, the United States of America.

It's the answer that led those who have been told for so long by so many to be cynical, and fearful, and doubtful of what we can achieve to put their hands on the arc of history and bend it once more toward the hope of a better day.

It's been a long time coming, but tonight, because of what we did on this day, in this election, at this defining moment, change has come to America.

I just received a very gracious call from Senator McCain. He fought long and hard in this campaign, and he's fought even longer and harder for the country he loves. He has endured sacrifices for America that most of us cannot begin to imagine, and we are better off for the service rendered by this brave and selfless leader. I congratulate him and Governor Palin for all they have achieved, and I look forward to working with them to renew this nation's promise in the months ahead.

I want to thank my partner in this journey, a man who campaigned from his heart and spoke for the men and women he grew up with on the streets of Scranton and rode with on that train home to Delaware, the Vice President-elect of the United States, Joe Biden.

I would not be standing here tonight without the unyielding support of my best friend for the last sixteen years, the rock of our family and the love of my life, our nation's next First Lady, Michelle Obama. Sasha and Malia, I love you both so much, and you have earned the new puppy that's coming with us to the White House. And while she's no longer with us, I know my grandmother is watching, along with the family that made me who I am. I miss them tonight, and know that my debt to them is beyond measure.

To my campaign manager David Plouffe, my chief strategist David Axelrod, and the best campaign team ever assembled in the history of politics—you made this happen, and I am forever grateful for what you've sacrificed to get it done.

But above all, I will never forget who this victory truly belongs to—it belongs to you.

I was never the likeliest candidate for this office. We didn't start with much money or many endorsements. Our campaign was not hatched in the halls of Washington—it began in the backyards of Des Moines and the living rooms of Concord and the front porches of Charleston.

It was built by working men and women who dug into what little savings they had to give five dollars and ten dollars and twenty dollars to this cause. It grew strength from the young people who rejected the myth of their generation's apathy; who left their homes and their families for jobs that offered little pay and less sleep; from the not-so-young people who braved the bitter cold and scorching heat to knock on the doors of perfect strangers; from the millions of Americans who volunteered, and organized, and proved that more than two centuries later, a government of the people, by the people, and for the people has not perished from this Earth. This is your victory. I know you didn't do this just to win an election and I know you didn't do it for me. You did it because you understand the enormity of the task that lies ahead. For even as we celebrate tonight, we know the challenges that tomorrow will bring are the greatest of our lifetime—two wars, a planet in peril, the worst financial crisis in a century. Even as we stand here tonight, we know there are brave Americans waking up in the deserts of Iraq and the mountains of Afghanistan to risk their lives for us. There are mothers and fathers who will lie awake after their children fall asleep and wonder how they'll make the mortgage, or pay their doctor's bills, or save enough for college. There is new energy to harness and new jobs to be created; new schools to build and threats to meet and alliances to repair.

The road ahead will be long. Our climb will be steep. We may not get there in one year or even one term, but America— I have never been more hopeful than I am tonight that we will get there. I promise you—we as a people will get there.

There will be setbacks and false starts. There are many who won't agree with every decision or policy I make as President, and we know that government can't solve every problem. But I will always be honest with you about the challenges we face. I will listen to you, especially when we disagree. And above all, I will ask you to join in the work of remaking this nation the only way it's been done in America for two-hundred and twenty-one years—block by block, brick by brick, calloused hand by calloused hand.

What began twenty-one months ago in the depths of winter must not end on this autumn night. This victory alone is not the change we seek—it is only the chance for us to make that change. And that cannot happen if we go back to the way things were. It cannot happen without you.

So let us summon a new spirit of patriotism; of service and responsibility where each of us resolves to pitch in and work harder and look after not only ourselves, but each other. Let us remember that if this financial crisis taught us anything, it's that we cannot have a thriving Wall Street while Main Street suffers—in this country, we rise or fall as one nation; as one people.

Let us resist the temptation to fall back on the same partisanship and pettiness and immaturity that has poisoned our politics for so long. Let us remember that it was a man from this state who first carried the banner of the Republican Party to the White House—a party founded on the values of self-reliance, individual liberty, and national unity. Those are values we all share, and while the Democratic Party has won a great victory tonight, we do so with a measure of humility and determination to heal the divides that have held back our progress.

As Lincoln said to a nation far more divided than ours, "We are not enemies, but friends . . . though passion may have strained it must not break our bonds of affection." And to those Americans whose support I have yet to earn—I may not have won your vote, but I hear your voices, I need your help, and I will be your President too.

And to all those watching tonight from beyond our shores, from parliaments and palaces to those who are huddled around radios in the forgotten corners of our world—our stories are singular, but our destiny is shared, and a new dawn of American leadership is at hand. To those who would tear this world down—we will defeat you. To those who seek peace and security—we support you. And to all those who have wondered if America's beacon still burns as bright—tonight we proved once more that the true strength of our nation comes not from the might of our arms or the scale of our wealth, but from the enduring power of our ideals: democracy, liberty, opportunity, and unyielding hope.

For that is the true genius of America—that America can change. Our union can be perfected. And what we have already achieved gives us hope for what we can and must achieve tomorrow.

This election had many firsts and many stories that will be told for generations. But one that's on my mind tonight is about a woman who cast her ballot in Atlanta. She's a lot like the millions of others who stood in line to make their voice heard in this election except for one thing—Ann Nixon Cooper is 106 years old.

She was born just a generation past slavery; a time when there were no cars on the road or planes in the sky; when someone like her couldn't vote for two reasons—because she was a woman and because of the color of her skin.

And tonight, I think about all that she's seen throughout her century in America—the heartache and the hope; the struggle and the progress; the times we were told that we can't, and the people who pressed on with that American creed: Yes we can.

At a time when women's voices were silenced and their hopes dismissed, she lived to see them stand up and speak out and reach for the ballot. Yes we can.

When there was despair in the dust bowl and depression across the land, she saw a nation conquer fear itself with a New Deal, new jobs, and a new sense of common purpose. Yes we can.

When the bombs fell on our harbor and tyranny threatened the world, she was there to witness a generation rise to greatness and a democracy was saved. Yes we can.

She was there for the buses in Montgomery, the hoses in Birmingham, a bridge in Selma, and a preacher from Atlanta who told a people that "We Shall Overcome." Yes we can.

A man touched down on the moon, a wall came down in Berlin, a world was connected by our own science and imagination. And this year, in this election, she touched her finger to a screen, and cast her vote, because after 106 years in America, through the best of times and the darkest of hours, she knows how America can change. Yes we can.

America, we have come so far. We have seen so much. But there is so much more to do. So tonight, let us ask ourselves—if our children should live to see the next century; if my daughters should be so lucky to live as long as Ann Nixon Cooper, what change will they see? What progress will we have made?

This is our chance to answer that call. This is our moment. This is our time—to put our people back to work and open doors of opportunity for our kids; to restore prosperity and promote the cause of peace; to reclaim the American Dream and reaffirm that fundamental truth—that out of many, we are one; that while we breathe, we hope, and where we are met with cynicism, and doubt, and those who tell us that we can't, we will respond with that timeless creed that sums up the spirit of a people:

Yes We Can. Thank you, God bless you, and may God bless the United States of America.

⇥ BARACK OBAMA'S INAUGURAL ADDRESS, 2009 ⇤

My fellow citizens: I stand here today humbled by the task before us, grateful for the trust you've bestowed, mindful of the sacrifices borne by our ancestors.

I thank President Bush for his service to our nation— (applause)—as well as the generosity and cooperation he has shown throughout this transition.

Forty-four Americans have now taken the presidential oath. The words have been spoken during rising tides of prosperity and the still waters of peace. Yet, every so often, the oath is taken amidst gathering clouds and raging storms. At these moments, America has carried on not simply because of the skill or vision of those in high office, but because we, the people, have remained faithful to the ideals of our forebears and true to our founding documents.

So it has been; so it must be with this generation of Americans.

That we are in the midst of crisis is now well understood. Our nation is at war against a far-reaching network of violence and hatred. Our economy is badly weakened, a consequence of greed and irresponsibility on the part of some, but also our collective failure to make hard choices and prepare the nation for a new age. Homes have been lost, jobs shed, businesses shuttered. Our health care is too costly, our schools fail too many—and each day brings further evidence that the ways we use energy strengthen our adversaries and threaten our planet.

These are the indicators of crisis, subject to data and statistics. Less measurable, but no less profound, is a sapping of confidence across our land; a nagging fear that America's decline is inevitable, that the next generation must lower its sights.

Today I say to you that the challenges we face are real. They are serious and they are many. They will not be met easily or in a short span of time. But know this America: They will be met. [*Applause.*]

On this day, we gather because we have chosen hope over fear, unity of purpose over conflict and discord. On this day, we come to proclaim an end to the petty grievances and false promises, the recriminations and worn-out dogmas that for far too long have strangled our politics. We remain a young nation. But in the words of Scripture, the time has come to set aside childish things. The time has come to reaffirm our enduring spirit; to choose our better history; to carry forward that precious gift, that noble idea passed on from generation to generation: the God-given promise that all are equal, all are free, and all deserve a chance to pursue their full measure of happiness. [*Applause.*]

In reaffirming the greatness of our nation we understand that greatness is never a given. It must be earned. Our journey has never been one of short-cuts or settling for less. It has not been the path for the faint-hearted, for those that prefer leisure over work, or seek only the pleasures of riches and fame. Rather, it has been the risk-takers, the doers, the makers of things—some celebrated, but more often men and women obscure in their labor—who have carried us up the long rugged path towards prosperity and freedom.

For us, they packed up their few worldly possessions and traveled across oceans in search of a new life. For us, they toiled in sweatshops, and settled the West, endured the lash of the whip, and plowed the hard earth. For us, they fought and died in places like Concord and Gettysburg, Normandy and Khe Sahn.

Time and again these men and women struggled and sacrificed and worked till their hands were raw so that we might live a better life. They saw America as bigger than the sum of our individual ambitions, greater than all the differences of birth or wealth or faction.

This is the journey we continue today. We remain the most prosperous, powerful nation on Earth. Our workers are no less productive than when this crisis began. Our minds are no less inventive, our goods and services no less needed than they were last week, or last month, or last year. Our capacity remains undiminished. But our time of standing pat, of protecting narrow interests and putting off unpleasant decisions—that time has surely passed. Starting today, we must pick ourselves up, dust ourselves off, and begin again the work of remaking America. [*Applause.*]

For everywhere we look, there is work to be done. The state of our economy calls for action, bold and swift. And we will act, not only to create new jobs, but to lay a new foundation for growth. We will build the roads and bridges, the electric grids and digital lines that feed our commerce and bind us together. We'll restore science to its rightful place, and wield technology's wonders to raise health care's quality and lower its cost. We will harness the sun and the winds and the soil to fuel our cars and run our factories. And we will transform our schools and colleges and universities to meet the demands of a new age. All this we can do. All this we will do.

Now, there are some who question the scale of our ambitions, who suggest that our system cannot tolerate too many big plans. Their memories are short, for they have forgotten what this country has already done, what free men and women can achieve when imagination is joined to common purpose, and necessity to courage. What the cynics fail to understand is that the ground has shifted beneath them, that the stale political arguments that have consumed us for so long no longer apply.

The question we ask today is not whether our government is too big or too small, but whether it works—whether it helps families find jobs at a decent wage, care they can afford, a retirement that is dignified. Where the answer is yes, we intend to move forward. Where the answer is no, programs will end. And those of us who manage the public's dollars will be held to account, to spend wisely, reform bad habits, and do our business in the light of day, because only then can we restore the vital trust between a people and their government.

Nor is the question before us whether the market is a force for good or ill. Its power to generate wealth and expand freedom is unmatched. But this crisis has reminded us that without a watchful eye, the market can spin out of control. The nation cannot prosper long when it favors only the prosperous. The success of our economy has always depended not just on the size of our gross domestic product, but on the reach of our prosperity, on the ability to extend opportunity to every willing heart—not out of charity, but because it is the surest route to our common good. [*Applause.*]

As for our common defense, we reject as false the choice between our safety and our ideals. Our Founding Fathers— [*applause*]—our Founding Fathers, faced with perils that we can scarcely imagine, drafted a charter to assure the rule of law and the rights of man—a charter expanded by the blood of generations. Those ideals still light the world, and we will not give them up for expedience sake. [*Applause.*]

And so, to all the other peoples and governments who are watching today, from the grandest capitals to the small village where my father was born, know that America is a friend of each nation, and every man, woman and child who seeks a future of peace and dignity. And we are ready to lead once more. [*Applause.*]

Recall that earlier generations faced down fascism and communism not just with missiles and tanks, but with the sturdy alliances and enduring convictions. They understood that our power alone cannot protect us, nor does it entitle us to do as we please. Instead they knew that our power grows through its prudent use; our security emanates from the justness of our cause, the force of our example, the tempering qualities of humility and restraint.

We are the keepers of this legacy. Guided by these principles once more we can meet those new threats that demand even greater effort, even greater cooperation and understanding between nations. We will begin to responsibly leave Iraq to its people and forge a hard-earned peace in Afghanistan. With old friends and former foes, we'll work tirelessly to lessen the nuclear threat, and roll back the specter of a warming planet.

We will not apologize for our way of life, nor will we waver in its defense. And for those who seek to advance their aims by inducing terror and slaughtering innocents, we say to you now that our spirit is stronger and cannot be broken—you cannot outlast us, and we will defeat you. [*Applause.*]

For we know that our patchwork heritage is a strength, not a weakness. We are a nation of Christians and Muslims, Jews and Hindus, and non-believers. We are shaped by every language and culture, drawn from every end of this Earth; and because we have tasted the bitter swill of civil war and segregation, and emerged from that dark chapter stronger and more united, we cannot help but believe that the old hatreds shall someday pass; that the lines of tribe shall soon dissolve; that as the world grows smaller, our common humanity shall reveal itself; and that America must play its role in ushering in a new era of peace.

To the Muslim world, we seek a new way forward, based on mutual interest and mutual respect. To those leaders around the globe who seek to sow conflict, or blame their society's ills on the West, know that your people will judge you on what you can build, not what you destroy. [*Applause.*]

To those who cling to power through corruption and deceit and the silencing of dissent, know that you are on the wrong side of history, but that we will extend a hand if you are willing to unclench your fist. [*Applause.*]

To the people of poor nations, we pledge to work alongside you to make your farms flourish and let clean waters flow; to nourish starved bodies and feed hungry minds. And to those nations like ours that enjoy relative plenty, we say we can no longer afford indifference to the suffering outside our borders, nor can we consume the world's resources without regard to effect. For the world has changed, and we must change with it.

As we consider the role that unfolds before us, we remember with humble gratitude those brave Americans who at this very hour patrol far-off deserts and distant mountains. They have something to tell us, just as the fallen heroes who lie in Arlington whisper through the ages.

We honor them not only because they are the guardians of our liberty, but because they embody the spirit of service—a willingness to find meaning in something greater than themselves.

And yet at this moment, a moment that will define a generation, it is precisely this spirit that must inhabit us all. For as much as government can do, and must do, it is ultimately the faith and determination of the American people upon which this nation relies. It is the kindness to take in a stranger when the levees break, the selflessness of workers who would rather cut their hours than see a friend lose their job which sees us through our darkest hours. It is the firefighter's courage to storm a stairway filled with smoke, but also a parent's willingness to nurture a child that finally decides our fate.

Our challenges may be new. The instruments with which we meet them may be new. But those values upon which our success depends—honesty and hard work, courage and fair play, tolerance and curiosity, loyalty and patriotism—these things are old. These things are true. They have been the quiet force of progress throughout our history.

What is demanded, then, is a return to these truths. What is required of us now is a new era of responsibility—a recognition on the part of every American that we have duties to ourselves, our nation and the world; duties that we do not grudgingly accept, but rather seize gladly, firm in the knowledge that there is nothing so satisfying to the spirit, so defining of our character than giving our all to a difficult task.

This is the price and the promise of citizenship. This is the source of our confidence—the knowledge that God calls on us to shape an uncertain destiny. This is the meaning of our liberty and our creed, why men and women and children of every race and every faith can join in celebration across this magnificent mall; and why a man whose father less than 60 years ago might not have been served in a local restaurant can now stand before you to take a most sacred oath. [*Applause.*]

So let us mark this day with remembrance of who we are and how far we have traveled. In the year of America's birth, in the coldest of months, a small band of patriots huddled by dying campfires on the shores of an icy river. The capital was abandoned. The enemy was advancing. The snow was stained with blood. At the moment when the outcome of our revolution was most in doubt, the father of our nation ordered these words to be read to the people:

"Let it be told to the future world . . . that in the depth of winter, when nothing but hope and virtue could survive . . . that the city and the country, alarmed at one common danger, came forth to meet [it]."

America: In the face of our common dangers, in this winter of our hardship, let us remember these timeless words. With hope and virtue, let us brave once more the icy currents, and endure what storms may come. Let it be said by our children's children that when we were tested we refused to let this journey end, that we did not turn back nor did we falter; and with eyes fixed on the horizon and God's grace upon us, we carried forth that great gift of freedom and delivered it safely to future generations.

Thank you. God bless you. And God bless the United States of America. [*Applause.*]

⇥ MIDDLE EAST SPEECH, "ON A ⇤ NEW BEGINNING," JUNE 4, 2009

PRESIDENT OBAMA: Thank you very much. Good afternoon. I am honored to be in the timeless city of Cairo, and to be hosted by two remarkable institutions. For over a thousand years, Al-Azhar has stood as a beacon of Islamic learning; and for over a century, Cairo University has been a source of Egypt's advancement. And together, you represent the harmony between tradition and progress. I'm grateful for your hospitality, and the hospitality of the people of Egypt. And I'm also proud to carry with me the goodwill of the American people, and a greeting of peace from Muslim communities in my country: Assalaamu alaykum. [*Applause.*]

We meet at a time of great tension between the United States and Muslims around the world—tension rooted in historical forces that go beyond any current policy debate. The relationship between Islam and the West includes centuries of coexistence and cooperation, but also conflict and religious wars. More recently, tension has been fed by colonialism that denied rights and opportunities to many Muslims, and a Cold War in which Muslim-majority countries were too often treated as proxies without regard to their own aspirations. Moreover, the sweeping change brought by modernity and globalization led many Muslims to view the West as hostile to the traditions of Islam.

Violent extremists have exploited these tensions in a small but potent minority of Muslims. The attacks of September 11, 2001, and the continued efforts of these extremists to engage in violence against civilians has led some in my country to view Islam as inevitably hostile not only to America and Western countries, but also to human rights. All this has bred more fear and more mistrust.

So long as our relationship is defined by our differences, we will empower those who sow hatred rather than peace, those who promote conflict rather than the cooperation that can help all of our people achieve justice and prosperity. And this cycle of suspicion and discord must end.

I've come here to Cairo to seek a new beginning between the United States and Muslims around the world, one based on mutual interest and mutual respect, and one based upon the truth that America and Islam are not exclusive and need not be in competition. Instead, they overlap, and share common principles—principles of justice and progress; tolerance and the dignity of all human beings.

I do so recognizing that change cannot happen overnight. I know there's been a lot of publicity about this speech, but no single speech can eradicate years of mistrust, nor can I answer in the time that I have this afternoon all the complex questions that brought us to this point. But I am convinced that in order to move forward, we must say openly to each other the things we hold in our hearts and that too often are said only behind closed doors. There must be a sustained effort to listen to each other; to learn from each other; to respect one another; and to seek common ground. As the Holy Koran tells us, "Be conscious of God and speak always the truth." [*Applause.*] That is what I will try to do today—to speak the truth as best I can, humbled by the task before us, and firm in my belief that the interests we share as human beings are far more powerful than the forces that drive us apart.

Now part of this conviction is rooted in my own experience. I'm a Christian, but my father came from a Kenyan family that includes generations of Muslims. As a boy, I spent several years in Indonesia and heard the call of the azaan at the break of dawn and at the fall of dusk. As a young man, I worked in Chicago communities where many found dignity and peace in their Muslim faith.

As a student of history, I also know civilization's debt to Islam. It was Islam—at places like Al-Azhar—that carried the light of learning through so many centuries, paving the way for Europe's Renaissance and Enlightenment. It was innovation in Muslim communities—[*applause*] —it was innovation in Muslim communities that developed the order of algebra; our magnetic compass and tools of navigation; our mastery of pens and printing; our understanding of how disease spreads and how it can be healed. Islamic culture has given us majestic arches and soaring spires; timeless poetry and cherished music; elegant calligraphy and places of peaceful contemplation. And throughout history, Islam has demonstrated through words and deeds the possibilities of religious tolerance and racial equality. [*Applause.*]

I also know that Islam has always been a part of America's story. The first nation to recognize my country was Morocco. In signing the Treaty of Tripoli in 1796, our second President, John Adams, wrote, "The United States has in itself no character of enmity against the laws, religion or tranquility of Muslims." And since our founding, American Muslims have enriched the United States. They have fought in our wars, they have served in our government, they have stood for civil rights, they have started businesses, they have taught at our universities, they've excelled in our sports arenas, they've won Nobel Prizes, built our tallest building, and lit the Olympic Torch. And when the first Muslim American was recently elected to Congress, he took the oath to defend our Constitution using the same Holy Koran that one of our Founding Fathers—Thomas Jefferson—kept in his personal library. [*Applause.*]

So I have known Islam on three continents before coming to the region where it was first revealed. That experience guides my conviction that partnership between America and Islam must be based on what Islam is, not what it isn't. And I consider it part of my responsibility as President of the United States to fight against negative stereotypes of Islam wherever they appear. [*Applause.*]

But that same principle must apply to Muslim perceptions of America. [*Applause.*] Just as Muslims do not fit a crude stereotype, America is not the crude stereotype of a self-interested empire. The United States has been one of the greatest sources of progress that the world has ever known. We were born out of revolution against an empire. We were founded upon the ideal that all are created equal, and we have shed blood and struggled for centuries to give meaning to those words—within our borders, and around the world. We are shaped by every culture, drawn from every end of the Earth, and dedicated to a simple concept: E pluribus unum—"Out of many, one."

Now, much has been made of the fact that an African American with the name Barack Hussein Obama could be elected President. [*Applause.*] But my personal story is not so unique. The dream of opportunity for all people has not come true for everyone in America, but its promise exists for all who come to our shores—and that includes nearly 7 million American Muslims in our country today who, by the way, enjoy incomes and educational levels that are higher than the American average. [*Applause.*]

Moreover, freedom in America is indivisible from the freedom to practice one's religion. That is why there is a mosque in every state in our union, and over 1,200 mosques within our borders. That's why the United States government has gone to court to protect the right of women and girls to wear the hijab and to punish those who would deny it. [*Applause.*]

So let there be no doubt: Islam is a part of America. And I believe that America holds within her the truth that regardless of race, religion, or station in life, all of us share common aspirations—to live in peace and security; to get an education and to work with dignity; to love our families, our communities, and our God. These things we share. This is the hope of all humanity.

Of course, recognizing our common humanity is only the beginning of our task. Words alone cannot meet the needs of our people. These needs will be met only if we act boldly in the years ahead; and if we understand that the challenges we face are shared, and our failure to meet them will hurt us all.

For we have learned from recent experience that when a financial system weakens in one country, prosperity is hurt everywhere. When a new flu infects one human being, all are at risk. When one nation pursues a nuclear weapon, the risk of nuclear attack rises for all nations. When violent extremists operate in one stretch of mountains, people are endangered across an ocean. When innocents in Bosnia and Darfur are slaughtered, that is a stain on our collective conscience. [*Applause.*] That is what it means to share this world in the 21st century. That is the responsibility we have to one another as human beings.

And this is a difficult responsibility to embrace. For human history has often been a record of nations and tribes—and, yes, religions—subjugating one another in pursuit of their own interests. Yet in this new age, such attitudes are self-defeating. Given our interdependence, any world order that elevates one nation or group of people over another will inevitably fail. So whatever we think of the past, we must not be prisoners to it. Our problems must be dealt with through partnership; our progress must be shared. [*Applause.*]

Now, that does not mean we should ignore sources of tension. Indeed, it suggests the opposite: We must face these tensions squarely. And so in that spirit, let me speak as clearly and as plainly as I can about some specific issues that I believe we must finally confront together.

The first issue that we have to confront is violent extremism in all of its forms.

In Ankara, I made clear that America is not—and never will be—at war with Islam. [*Applause.*] We will, however, relentlessly confront violent extremists who pose a grave threat to our security—because we reject the same thing that people of all faiths reject: the killing of innocent men, women, and children. And it is my first duty as President to protect the American people.

The situation in Afghanistan demonstrates America's goals, and our need to work together. Over seven years ago, the United States pursued al Qaeda and the Taliban with broad international support. We did not go by choice; we went because of necessity. I'm aware that there's still some who would question or even justify the events of 9/11. But let us be clear: Al Qaeda killed nearly 3,000 people on that day. The victims were innocent men, women and children from America and many other nations who had done nothing to harm anybody. And yet al Qaeda chose to ruthlessly murder these people, claimed credit for the attack, and even now states their determination to kill on a massive scale. They have affiliates in many countries and are trying to expand their reach. These are not opinions to be debated; these are facts to be dealt with.

Now, make no mistake: We do not want to keep our troops in Afghanistan. We see no military—we seek no military bases there. It is agonizing for America to lose our young men and women. It is costly and politically difficult to continue this conflict. We would gladly bring every single one of our troops home if we could be confident that there were not violent extremists in Afghanistan and now Pakistan determined to kill as many Americans as they possibly can. But that is not yet the case.

And that's why we're partnering with a coalition of 46 countries. And despite the costs involved, America's commitment will not weaken. Indeed, none of us should tolerate these extremists. They have killed in many countries. They have killed people of different faiths—but more than any other, they have killed Muslims. Their actions are irreconcilable with the rights of human beings, the progress of nations, and with Islam. The Holy Koran teaches that whoever kills an innocent is as—it is as if he has killed all mankind. [*Applause.*] And the Holy Koran also says whoever saves a person, it is as if he has saved all mankind. [*Applause.*] The enduring faith of over a billion people is so much bigger than the narrow hatred of a few. Islam is not part of the problem in combating violent extremism—it is an important part of promoting peace.

Now, we also know that military power alone is not going to solve the problems in Afghanistan and Pakistan. That's why we plan to invest $1.5 billion each year over the next five years to partner with Pakistanis to build schools and hospitals, roads and businesses, and hundreds of millions to help those who've been displaced. That's why we are providing more than $2.8 billion to help Afghans develop their economy and deliver services that people depend on.

Let me also address the issue of Iraq. Unlike Afghanistan, Iraq was a war of choice that provoked strong differences in my country and around the world. Although I believe that the Iraqi people are ultimately better off without the tyranny of Saddam Hussein, I also believe that events in Iraq have reminded America of the need to use diplomacy and build international consensus to resolve our problems whenever possible. [*Applause.*] Indeed, we can recall the words of Thomas Jefferson, who said: "I hope that our wisdom will grow with our power, and teach us that the less we use our power the greater it will be."

Today, America has a dual responsibility: to help Iraq forge a better future—and to leave Iraq to Iraqis. And I have made it clear to the Iraqi people—[*applause*]—I have made it clear to the Iraqi people that we pursue no bases, and no claim on their territory or resources. Iraq's sovereignty is its own. And that's why I ordered the removal of our combat brigades by next August. That is why we will honor our agreement with Iraq's democratically elected government to remove combat troops from Iraqi cities by July, and to remove all of our troops from Iraq by 2012. [*Applause.*] We will help Iraq train its security forces and develop its economy. But we will support a secure and united Iraq as a partner, and never as a patron.

And finally, just as America can never tolerate violence by extremists, we must never alter or forget our principles. Nine-eleven was an enormous trauma to our country. The fear and anger that it provoked was understandable, but in some cases, it led us to act contrary to our traditions and our ideals. We are taking concrete actions to change course. I have unequivocally prohibited the use of torture by the United States, and I have ordered the prison at Guantanamo Bay closed by early next year. [*Applause.*]

So America will defend itself, respectful of the sovereignty of nations and the rule of law. And we will do so in partnership with Muslim communities which are also threatened. The sooner the extremists are isolated and unwelcome in Muslim communities, the sooner we will all be safer.

The second major source of tension that we need to discuss is the situation between Israelis, Palestinians and the Arab world.

America's strong bonds with Israel are well known. This bond is unbreakable. It is based upon cultural and historical ties, and the recognition that the aspiration for a Jewish homeland is rooted in a tragic history that cannot be denied.

Around the world, the Jewish people were persecuted for centuries, and anti-Semitism in Europe culminated in an unprecedented Holocaust. Tomorrow, I will visit Buchenwald, which was part of a network of camps where Jews were enslaved, tortured, shot and gassed to death by the Third Reich. Six million Jews were killed—more than the entire Jewish population of Israel today. Denying that fact is baseless, it is ignorant, and it is hateful. Threatening Israel with destruction—or repeating vile stereotypes about Jews—is deeply wrong, and only serves to evoke in the minds of Israelis this most painful of memories while preventing the peace that the people of this region deserve.

On the other hand, it is also undeniable that the Palestinian people—Muslims and Christians—have suffered in pursuit of a homeland. For more than 60 years they've endured the pain of dislocation. Many wait in refugee camps in the West Bank, Gaza, and neighboring lands for a life of peace and security that they have never been able to lead. They endure the daily humiliations—large and small—that come with occupation. So let there be no doubt: The situation for the Palestinian people is intolerable. And America will not turn our backs on the legitimate Palestinian aspiration for dignity, opportunity, and a state of their own. [*Applause.*]

For decades then, there has been a stalemate: two peoples with legitimate aspirations, each with a painful history that makes compromise elusive. It's easy to point fingers—for Palestinians to point to the displacement brought about by Israel's founding, and for Israelis to point to the constant hostility and attacks throughout its history from within its borders as well as beyond. But if we see this conflict only from one side or the other, then we will be blind to the truth: The only resolution is for the aspirations of both sides to be met through two states, where Israelis and Palestinians each live in peace and security. [*Applause.*]

That is in Israel's interest, Palestine's interest, America's interest, and the world's interest. And that is why I intend to personally pursue this outcome with all the patience and dedication that the task requires. [*Applause.*] The obligations—the obligations that the parties have agreed to under the road map are clear. For peace to come, it is time for them—and all of us—to live up to our responsibilities.

Palestinians must abandon violence. Resistance through violence and killing is wrong and it does not succeed. For centuries, black people in America suffered the lash of the whip as slaves and the humiliation of segregation. But it was not violence that won full and equal rights. It was a peaceful and determined insistence upon the ideals at the center of America's founding. This same story can be told by people from South Africa to South Asia; from Eastern Europe to Indonesia. It's a story with a simple truth: that violence is a dead end. It is a sign neither of courage nor power to shoot rockets at sleeping children, or to blow up old women on a bus. That's not how moral authority is claimed; that's how it is surrendered.

Now is the time for Palestinians to focus on what they can build. The Palestinian Authority must develop its capacity to govern, with institutions that serve the needs of its people. Hamas does have support among some Palestinians, but they also have to recognize they have responsibilities. To play a role in fulfilling Palestinian aspirations, to unify the Palestinian people, Hamas must put an end to violence, recognize past agreements, recognize Israel's right to exist.

At the same time, Israelis must acknowledge that just as Israel's right to exist cannot be denied, neither can Palestine's. The United States does not accept the legitimacy of continued Israeli settlements. [*Applause.*] This construction violates previous agreements and undermines efforts to achieve peace. It is time for these settlements to stop. [*Applause.*]

And Israel must also live up to its obligation to ensure that Palestinians can live and work and develop their society. Just as it devastates Palestinian families, the continuing humanitarian crisis in Gaza does not serve Israel's security; neither does the continuing lack of opportunity in the West Bank. Progress in the daily lives of the Palestinian people must be a critical part of a road to peace, and Israel must take concrete steps to enable such progress.

And finally, the Arab states must recognize that the Arab Peace Initiative was an important beginning, but not the end of their responsibilities. The Arab-Israeli conflict should no longer be used to distract the people of Arab nations from other problems. Instead, it must be a cause for action to help the Palestinian people develop the institutions that will sustain their state, to recognize Israel's legitimacy, and to choose progress over a self-defeating focus on the past.

America will align our policies with those who pursue peace, and we will say in public what we say in private to Israelis and Palestinians and Arabs. [*Applause.*] We cannot impose peace. But privately, many Muslims recognize that Israel will not go away. Likewise, many Israelis recognize the need for a Palestinian state. It is time for us to act on what everyone knows to be true.

Too many tears have been shed. Too much blood has been shed. All of us have a responsibility to work for the day when the mothers of Israelis and Palestinians can see their children grow up without fear; when the Holy Land of the three great faiths is the place of peace that God intended it to be; when Jerusalem is a secure and lasting home for Jews and Christians and Muslims, and a place for all of the children of Abraham to mingle peacefully together as in the story of Isra—[*applause*]— as in the story of Isra, when Moses, Jesus, and Mohammed, peace be upon them, joined in prayer. [*Applause.*]

The third source of tension is our shared interest in the rights and responsibilities of nations on nuclear weapons.

This issue has been a source of tension between the United States and the Islamic Republic of Iran. For many years, Iran has defined itself in part by its opposition to my country, and there is in fact a tumultuous history between us. In the middle of the Cold War, the United States played a role in the overthrow of a democratically elected Iranian government. Since the Islamic Revolution, Iran has played a role in acts of hostage-taking and violence against U.S. troops and civilians. This history is well known. Rather than remain trapped in the past, I've made it clear to Iran's leaders and people that my country is prepared to move forward. The question now is not what Iran is against, but rather what future it wants to build.

I recognize it will be hard to overcome decades of mistrust, but we will proceed with courage, rectitude, and resolve. There will be many issues to discuss between our two countries, and we are willing to move forward without preconditions on the basis of mutual respect. But it is clear to all concerned that when it comes to nuclear weapons, we have reached a decisive point. This is not simply about America's interests. It's about preventing a nuclear arms race in the Middle East that could lead this region and the world down a hugely dangerous path.

I understand those who protest that some countries have weapons that others do not. No single nation should pick and choose which nation holds nuclear weapons. And that's why I strongly reaffirmed America's commitment to seek a world in which no nations hold nuclear weapons. [*Applause.*] And any nation—including Iran—should have the right to access peaceful nuclear power if it complies with its responsibilities under the nuclear Non-Proliferation Treaty. That commitment is at the core of the treaty, and it must be kept for all who fully abide by it. And I'm hopeful that all countries in the region can share in this goal.

The fourth issue that I will address is democracy. [*Applause.*]

I know—I know there has been controversy about the promotion of democracy in recent years, and much of this controversy is connected to the war in Iraq. So let me be clear: No system of government can or should be imposed by one nation by any other.

That does not lessen my commitment, however, to governments that reflect the will of the people. Each nation gives life to this principle in its own way, grounded in the traditions of its own people. America does not presume to know what is best for everyone, just as we would not presume to pick the outcome of a peaceful election. But I do have an unyielding belief that all people yearn for certain things: the ability to speak your mind and have a say in how you are governed; confidence in the rule of law and the equal administration of justice; government that is transparent and doesn't steal from the people; the freedom to live as you choose. These are not just American ideas; they are human rights. And that is why we will support them everywhere. [*Applause.*]

Now, there is no straight line to realize this promise. But this much is clear: Governments that protect these rights are ultimately more stable, successful and secure. Suppressing ideas never succeeds in making them go away. America respects the right of all peaceful and law-abiding voices to be heard around the world, even if we disagree with them. And we will welcome all elected, peaceful governments—provided they govern with respect for all their people.

This last point is important because there are some who advocate for democracy only when they're out of power; once in power, they are ruthless in suppressing the rights of others. [*Applause.*] So no matter where it takes hold, government of the people and by the people sets a single standard for all who would hold power: You must maintain your power through consent, not coercion; you must respect the rights of minorities, and participate with a spirit of tolerance and compromise; you must place the interests of your people and the legitimate workings of the political process above your party. Without these ingredients, elections alone do not make true democracy.

AUDIENCE MEMBER: Barack Obama, we love you!

PRESIDENT OBAMA: Thank you. [*Applause.*] The fifth issue that we must address together is religious freedom.

Islam has a proud tradition of tolerance. We see it in the history of Andalusia and Cordoba during the Inquisition. I saw it firsthand as a child in Indonesia, where devout Christians worshiped freely in an overwhelmingly Muslim country. That is the spirit we need today. People in every country should be free to choose and live their faith based upon the persuasion of the mind and the heart and the soul. This tolerance is essential for religion to thrive, but it's being challenged in many different ways.

Among some Muslims, there's a disturbing tendency to measure one's own faith by the rejection of somebody else's faith. The richness of religious diversity must be upheld—whether it is for Maronites in Lebanon or the Copts in Egypt. [*Applause.*] And if we are being honest, fault lines must be closed among Muslims, as well, as the divisions between Sunni and Shia have led to tragic violence, particularly in Iraq.

Freedom of religion is central to the ability of peoples to live together. We must always examine the ways in which we protect it. For instance, in the United States, rules on charitable giving have made it harder for Muslims to fulfill their religious obligation. That's why I'm committed to working with American Muslims to ensure that they can fulfill zakat.

Likewise, it is important for Western countries to avoid impeding Muslim citizens from practicing religion as they see fit—for instance, by dictating what clothes a Muslim woman should wear. We can't disguise hostility towards any religion behind the pretence of liberalism.

In fact, faith should bring us together. And that's why we're forging service projects in America to bring together Christians, Muslims, and Jews. That's why we welcome efforts like Saudi Arabian King Abdullah's interfaith dialogue and Turkey's leadership in the Alliance of Civilizations. Around the world, we can turn dialogue into interfaith service, so bridges between peoples lead to action—whether it is combating malaria in Africa, or providing relief after a natural disaster.

The sixth issue—the sixth issue that I want to address is women's rights. [*Applause.*] I know—I know—and you can tell from this audience, that there is a healthy debate about this issue. I reject the view of some in the West that a woman who chooses to cover her hair is somehow less equal, but I do believe that a woman who is denied an education is denied equality. [*Applause.*] And it is no coincidence that countries where women are well educated are far more likely to be prosperous.

Now, let me be clear: Issues of women's equality are by no means simply an issue for Islam. In Turkey, Pakistan, Bangladesh, Indonesia, we've seen Muslim-majority countries elect a woman to lead. Meanwhile, the struggle for women's equality continues in many aspects of American life, and in countries around the world.

I am convinced that our daughters can contribute just as much to society as our sons. [*Applause.*] Our common prosperity will be advanced by allowing all humanity—men and women—to reach their full potential. I do not believe that women must make the same choices as men in order to be equal, and I respect those women who choose to live their lives in traditional roles. But it should be their choice. And that is why the United States will partner with any Muslim-majority country to support expanded literacy for girls, and to help young women pursue employment through micro-financing that helps people live their dreams. [Applause.]

Finally, I want to discuss economic development and opportunity.

I know that for many, the face of globalization is contradictory. The Internet and television can bring knowledge and information, but also offensive sexuality and mindless violence into the home. Trade can bring new wealth and opportunities, but also huge disruptions and change in communities. In all nations—including America—this change can bring fear. Fear that because of modernity we lose control over our economic choices, our politics, and most importantly our identities—those things we most cherish about our communities, our families, our traditions, and our faith.

But I also know that human progress cannot be denied. There need not be contradictions between development and tradition. Countries like Japan and South Korea grew their economies enormously while maintaining distinct cultures. The same is true for the astonishing progress within Muslim-majority countries from Kuala Lumpur to Dubai. In ancient times and in our times, Muslim communities have been at the forefront of innovation and education.

And this is important because no development strategy can be based only upon what comes out of the ground, nor can it be sustained while young people are out of work. Many Gulf states have enjoyed great wealth as a consequence of oil, and some are beginning to focus it on broader development. But all of us must recognize that education and innovation will be the currency of the 21st century—[*applause*]—and in too many Muslim communities, there remains underinvestment in these areas. I'm emphasizing such investment within my own country. And while America in the past has focused on oil and gas when it comes to this part of the world, we now seek a broader engagement.

On education, we will expand exchange programs, and increase scholarships, like the one that brought my father to America. [*Applause.*] At the same time, we will encourage more Americans to study in Muslim communities. And we will match promising Muslim students with internships in America; invest in online learning for teachers and children around the world; and create a new online network, so a young person in Kansas can communicate instantly with a young person in Cairo.

On economic development, we will create a new corps of business volunteers to partner with counterparts in Muslim-majority countries. And I will host a Summit on Entrepreneurship this year to identify how we can deepen ties between business leaders, foundations and social entrepreneurs in the United States and Muslim communities around the world.

On science and technology, we will launch a new fund to support technological development in Muslim-majority countries, and to help transfer ideas to the marketplace so they can create more jobs. We'll open centers of scientific excellence in Africa, the Middle East and Southeast Asia, and appoint new science envoys to collaborate on programs that develop new sources of energy, create green jobs, digitize records, clean water, grow new crops. Today I'm announcing a new global effort with the Organization of the Islamic Conference to eradicate polio. And we will also expand partnerships with Muslim communities to promote child and maternal health.

All these things must be done in partnership. Americans are ready to join with citizens and governments; community organizations, religious leaders, and businesses in Muslim communities around the world to help our people pursue a better life.

The issues that I have described will not be easy to address. But we have a responsibility to join together on behalf of the world that we seek—a world where extremists no longer threaten our people, and American troops have come home; a world where Israelis and Palestinians are each secure in a state of their own, and nuclear energy is used for peaceful purposes; a world where governments serve their citizens, and the rights of all God's children are respected. Those are mutual interests. That is the world we seek. But we can only achieve it together.

I know there are many—Muslim and non-Muslim—who question whether we can forge this new beginning. Some are eager to stoke the flames of division, and to stand in the way of progress. Some suggest that it isn't worth the effort—that we are fated to disagree, and civilizations are doomed to clash. Many more are simply skeptical that real change can occur. There's so much fear, so much mistrust that has built up over the years. But if we choose to be bound by the past, we will never move forward. And I want to particularly say this to young people of every faith, in every country—you, more than anyone, have the ability to reimagine the world, to remake this world.

All of us share this world for but a brief moment in time. The question is whether we spend that time focused on what pushes us apart, or whether we commit ourselves to an effort— a sustained effort—to find common ground, to focus on the future we seek for our children, and to respect the dignity of all human beings.

It's easier to start wars than to end them. It's easier to blame others than to look inward. It's easier to see what is different about someone than to find the things we share. But we should choose the right path, not just the easy path. There's one rule that lies at the heart of every religion—that we do unto others as we would have them do unto us. [*Applause.*] This truth transcends nations and peoples—a belief that isn't new; that isn't black or white or brown; that isn't Christian or Muslim or Jew. It's a belief that pulsed in the cradle of civilization, and that still beats in the hearts of billions around the world. It's a faith in other people, and it's what brought me here today.

We have the power to make the world we seek, but only if we have the courage to make a new beginning, keeping in mind what has been written.

The Holy Koran tells us: "O mankind! We have created you male and a female; and we have made you into nations and tribes so that you may know one another."

The Talmud tells us: "The whole of the Torah is for the purpose of promoting peace."

The Holy Bible tells us: "Blessed are the peacemakers, for they shall be called sons of God." [*Applause.*]

The people of the world can live together in peace. We know that is God's vision. Now that must be our work here on Earth.

Thank you. And may God's peace be upon you. Thank you very much. Thank you. [*Applause.*]

⇥ REMARKS ON FINANCIAL RESCUE ⇤
AND REFORM,
SEPTEMBER 14, 2009

THE PRESIDENT: Thank you very much. It is wonderful to be back in New York after having just been here last week. It is a beautiful day and we have some extraordinary guests here in the Hall today. I just want to mention a few.

First of all from my economic team, somebody who I think has done extraordinary work on behalf of all Americans and has helped to strengthen our financial system immeasurably, Secretary Tim Geithner—please give him a big round of applause. [*Applause.*] Somebody who is continually guiding me and keeping me straight on the numbers, the chair of the Council of Economic Advisers, Christina Romer is here. [*Applause.*] We have an extraordinary economic recovery board and as chairman somebody who knows more about the financial markets and the economy generally than just about anybody in this country, Paul Volcker. Thank you, Paul. [*Applause.*] The outstanding mayor of the city of New York, Mr. Michael Bloomberg. [*Applause.*] We have Assembly Speaker Sheldon Silver is here, as well; thank you. [*Applause.*]

We have a host of members of Congress, but there's one that I have to single out because he is going to be helping to shape the agenda going forward to make sure that we have one of the strongest, most dynamic, and most innovative financial markets in the world for many years to come, and that's my good friend, Barney Frank. [*Applause.*] I also want to thank our hosts from the National Park Service here at Federal Hall and all the other outstanding public officials who are here.

Thanks for being here. Thank you for your warm welcome. It's a privilege to be in historic Federal Hall. It was here more than two centuries ago that our first Congress served and our first President was inaugurated. And I just had a chance to glance at the Bible upon which George Washington took his oath. It was here, in the early days of the Republic, that

Hamilton and Jefferson debated how best to administer a young economy and ensure that our nation rewarded the talents and drive of its people. And two centuries later, we still grapple with these questions—questions made more acute in moments of crisis.

It was one year ago today that we experienced just such a crisis. As investors and pension-holders watched with dread and dismay, and after a series of emergency meetings often conducted in the dead of the night, several of the world's largest and oldest financial institutions had fallen, either bankrupt, bought, or bailed out: Lehman Brothers, Merrill Lynch, AIG, Washington Mutual, Wachovia. A week before this began, Fannie Mae and Freddie Mac had been taken over by the government. Other large firms teetered on the brink of insolvency. Credit markets froze as banks refused to lend not only to families and businesses, but to one another. Five trillion dollars of Americans' household wealth evaporated in the span of just three months. That was just one year ago.

Congress and the previous administration took difficult but necessary action in the days and months that followed. Nonetheless, when this administration walked through the door in January, the situation remained urgent. The markets had fallen sharply; credit was not flowing. It was feared that the largest banks—those that remained standing—had too little capital and far too much exposure to risky loans. And the consequences had spread far beyond the streets of lower Manhattan. This was no longer just a financial crisis; it had become a full-blown economic crisis, with home prices sinking and businesses struggling to access affordable credit, and the economy shedding an average of 700,000 jobs every single month.

We could not separate what was happening in the corridors of our financial institutions from what was happening on the factory floors and around the kitchen tables. Home foreclosures linked those who took out home loans and those who repackaged those loans as securities. A lack of access to affordable credit threatened the health of large firms and small businesses, as well as all those whose jobs depended on them. And a weakened financial system weakened the broader economy, which in turn further weakened the financial system.

So the only way to address successfully any of these challenges was to address them together. And this administration, under the outstanding leadership of Tim Geithner and Christy Romer and Larry Summers and others, moved quickly on all fronts, initializing a financial—a financial stability plan to rescue the system from the crisis and restart lending for all those affected by the crisis. By opening and examining the books of large financial firms, we helped restore the availability of two things that had been in short supply: capital and confidence. By taking aggressive and innovative steps in credit markets, we spurred lending not just to banks, but to folks looking to buy homes or cars, take out student loans, or finance small businesses. Our home ownership plan has helped responsible homeowners refinance to stem the tide of lost homes and lost home values.

And the recovery plan is providing help to the unemployed and tax relief for working families, all the while spurring consumer spending. It's prevented layoffs of tens of thousands of teachers and police officers and other essential public servants. And thousands of recovery projects are underway all across America, including right here in New York City, putting people to work building wind turbines and solar panels, renovating schools and hospitals, repairing our nation's roads and bridges.

Eight months later, the work of recovery continues. And though I will never be satisfied while people are out of work and our financial system is weakened, we can be confident that the storms of the past two years are beginning to break. In fact, while there continues to be a need for government involvement to stabilize the financial system, that necessity is waning. After months in which public dollars were flowing into our financial system, we're finally beginning to see money flowing back to taxpayers. This doesn't mean taxpayers will escape the worst financial crisis in decades entirely unscathed. But banks have repaid more than $70 billion, and in those cases where the government's stakes have been sold completely, taxpayers have actually earned a 17 percent return on their investment. Just a few months ago, many experts from across the ideological spectrum feared that ensuring financial stability would require even more tax dollars. Instead, we've been able to eliminate a $250 billion reserve included in our budget because that fear has not been realized.

While full recovery of the financial system will take a great deal more time and work, the growing stability resulting from these interventions means we're beginning to return to normalcy. But here's what I want to emphasize today: Normalcy cannot lead to complacency.

Unfortunately, there are some in the financial industry who are misreading this moment. Instead of learning the lessons of Lehman and the crisis from which we're still recovering, they're choosing to ignore those lessons. I'm convinced they do so not just at their own peril, but at our nation's. So I want everybody here to hear my words: We will not go back to the days of reckless behavior and unchecked excess that was at the heart of this crisis, where too many were motivated only by the appetite for quick kills and bloated bonuses. Those on Wall Street cannot resume taking risks without regard for consequences, and expect that next time, American taxpayers will be there to break their fall.

And that's why we need strong rules of the road to guard against the kind of systemic risks that we've seen. And we have a responsibility to write and enforce these rules to protect consumers of financial products, to protect taxpayers, and to protect our economy as a whole. Yes, there must—these rules must be developed in a way that doesn't stifle innovation and enterprise. And I want to say very clearly here today, we want to work with the financial industry to achieve that end. But the old ways that led to this crisis cannot stand. And to the extent that some have so readily returned to them underscores the need for change and change now. History cannot be allowed to repeat itself.

So what we're calling for is for the financial industry to join us in a constructive effort to update the rules and regulatory structure to meet the challenges of this new century. That is what my administration seeks to do. We've sought ideas and input from industry leaders and policy experts, academics, consumer advocates, and the broader public. And we've worked closely with leaders in the Senate and the House, including not only Barney, but also Senators Chris Dodd and Richard Shelby, and Barney is already working with his counterpart, Sheldon [sic] Bachus. And we intend to pass regulatory reform through Congress.

And taken together, we're proposing the most ambitious overhaul of the financial regulatory system since the Great Depression. But I want to emphasize that these reforms are rooted in a simple principle: We ought to set clear rules of the road that promote transparency and accountability. That's how we'll make certain that markets foster responsibility, not recklessness. That's how we'll make certain that markets reward those who compete honestly and vigorously within the system, instead of those who are trying to game the system.

So let me outline specifically what we're talking about. First, we're proposing new rules to protect consumers and a new Consumer Financial Protection Agency to enforce those rules. [*Applause.*] This crisis was not just the result of decisions made by the mightiest of financial firms. It was also the result of decisions made by ordinary Americans to open credit cards and take on mortgages. And while there were many who took out loans they knew they couldn't afford, there were also millions of Americans who signed contracts they didn't fully understand offered by lenders who didn't always tell the truth.

This is in part because there is no single agency charged with making sure that doesn't happen. That's what we intend to change. The Consumer Financial Protection Agency will have the power to make certain that consumers get information that is clear and concise, and to prevent the worst kinds of abuses. Consumers shouldn't have to worry about loan contracts designed to be unintelligible, hidden fees attached to their mortgage, and financial penalties—whether through a credit card or a debit card—that appear without warning on their statements. And responsible lenders, including community banks, doing the right thing shouldn't have to worry about ruinous competition from unregulated competitors.

Now there are those who are suggesting that somehow this will restrict the choices available to consumers. Nothing could be further from the truth. The lack of clear rules in the past meant we had the wrong kind of innovation: The firm that could make its products look the best by doing the best job of hiding the real costs ended up getting the business. For example, we had "teaser" rates on credit cards and mortgages that lured people in and then surprised them with big rate increases. By setting ground rules, we'll increase the kind of competition that actually provides people better and greater choices, as companies compete to offer the best products, not the ones that are most complex or the most confusing.

Second, we've got to close the loopholes that were at the heart of the crisis. Where there were gaps in the rules, regulators lacked the authority to take action. Where there were overlaps, regulators often lacked accountability for inaction. These weaknesses in oversight engendered systematic, and systemic, abuse.

Under existing rules, some companies can actually shop for the regulator of their choice—and others, like hedge funds, can operate outside of the regulatory system altogether. We've seen the development of financial instruments—like derivatives and credit default swaps—without anyone examining the risks, or regulating all of the players. And we've seen lenders profit by providing loans to borrowers who they knew would never repay, because the lender offloaded the loan and the consequences to somebody else. Those who refused to game the system are at a disadvantage.

Now, one of the main reasons this crisis could take place is that many agencies and regulators were responsible for oversight of individual financial firms and their subsidiaries, but no one was responsible for protecting the system as the whole—as a whole. In other words, regulators were charged with seeing the trees, but not the forest. And even then, some firms that posed a "systemic risk" were not regulated as strongly as others, exploiting loopholes in the system to take on greater risk with less scrutiny. As a result, the failure of one firm threatened the viability of many others. We were facing one of the largest financial crises in history, and those responsible for oversight were caught off guard and without the authority to act.

And that's why we'll create clear accountability and responsibility for regulating large financial firms that pose a systemic risk. While holding the Federal Reserve fully accountable for regulation of the largest, most interconnected firms, we'll create an oversight council to bring together regulators from across markets to share information, to identify gaps in regulation, and to tackle issues that don't fit neatly into an organizational chart. We'll also require these financial firms to meet stronger capital and liquidity requirements and observe greater constraints on their risky behavior. That's one of the lessons of the past year. The only way to avoid a crisis of this magnitude is to ensure that large firms can't take risks that threaten our entire financial system, and to make sure that they have the resources to weather even the worst of economic storms.

Even as we've proposed safeguards to make the failure of large and interconnected firms less likely, we've also created—proposed creating what's called "resolution authority" in the event that such a failure happens and poses a threat to the stability of the financial system. This is intended to put an end to the idea that some firms are "too big to fail." For a market to function, those who invest and lend in that market must believe that their money is actually at risk. And the system as a whole isn't safe until it is safe from the failure of any individual institution.

If a bank approaches insolvency, we have a process through the FDIC that protects depositors and maintains confidence in the banking system. This process was created during the Great Depression when the failure of one bank led to runs on other banks, which in turn threatened the banking system as a whole. That system works. But we don't have any kind of process in place to contain the failure of a Lehman Brothers or AIG or any of the largest and most interconnected financial firms in our country.

And that's why, when this crisis began, crucial decisions about what would happen to some of the world's biggest companies—companies employing tens of thousands of people and holding trillions of dollars of assets—took place in hurried discussions in the middle of the night. That's why we've had to rely on taxpayer dollars. The only resolution authority we currently have that would prevent a financial meltdown involved tapping the Federal Reserve or the federal treasury. With so much at stake, we should not be forced to choose between allowing a company to fail into a rapid and chaotic dissolution that threatens the economy and innocent people, or, alternatively, forcing taxpayers to foot the bill. So our plan would put the cost of a firm's failures on those who own its stock and loaned it money. And if taxpayers ever have to step in again to prevent a second Great Depression, the financial industry will have to pay the taxpayer back—every cent.

Finally, we need to close the gaps that exist not just within this country but among countries. The United States is leading a coordinated response to promote recovery and to restore prosperity among both the world's largest economies and the world's fastest growing economies. At a summit in London in April, leaders agreed to work together in an unprecedented way to spur global demand but also to address the underlying problems that caused such a deep and lasting global recession. And this work will continue next week in Pittsburgh when I convene the G20, which has proven to be an effective forum for coordinating policies among key developed and emerging economies and one that I see taking on an important role in the future.

Essential to this effort is reforming what's broken in the global financial system—a system that links economies and spreads both rewards and risks. For we know that abuses in financial markets anywhere can have an impact everywhere; and just as gaps in domestic regulation lead to a race to the bottom, so do gaps in regulation around the world. What we need instead is a global race to the top, including stronger capital standards, as I've called for today. As the United States is aggressively reforming our regulatory system, we're going to be working to ensure that the rest of the world does the same.

And this is something that Secretary Geithner has already been actively meeting with finance ministers around the world to discuss.

A healthy economy in the 21st century also depends on our ability to buy and sell goods in markets across the globe. And make no mistake, this administration is committed to pursuing expanded trade and new trade agreements. It is absolutely essential to our economic future. And each time that we have met—at the G20 and the G8—we have reaffirmed the need to fight against protectionism. But no trading system will work if we fail to enforce our trade agreements, those that have already been signed. So when—as happened this weekend—we invoke provisions of existing agreements, we do so not to be provocative or to promote self-defeating protectionism, we do so because enforcing trade agreements is part and parcel of maintaining an open and free trading system.

And just as we have to live up to our responsibilities on trade, we have to live up to our responsibilities on financial reform as well. I have urged leaders in Congress to pass regulatory reform this year and both Congressman Frank and Senator Dodd, who are leading this effort, have made it clear that that's what they intend to do. Now there will be those who defend the status quo—there always are. There will be those who argue we should do less or nothing at all. There will be those who engage in revisionist history or have selective memories, and don't seem to recall what we just went through last year. But to them I'd say only this: Do you really believe that the absence of sound regulation one year ago was good for the financial system? Do you believe the resulting decline in markets and wealth and unemployment, the wrenching hardship that families are going through all across the country, was somehow good for our economy? Was that good for the American people?

I have always been a strong believer in the power of the free market. I believe that jobs are best created not by government, but by businesses and entrepreneurs willing to take a risk on a good idea. I believe that the role of the government is not to disparage wealth, but to expand its reach; not to stifle markets, but to provide the ground rules and level playing field that helps to make those markets more vibrant—and that will allow us to better tap the creative and innovative potential of our people. For we know that it is the dynamism of our people that has been the source of America's progress and prosperity.

So I promise you, I did not run for President to bail out banks or intervene in capital markets. But it is important to note that the very absence of common-sense regulations able to keep up with a fast-paced financial sector is what created the need for that extraordinary intervention—not just with our administration, but the previous administration. The lack of sensible rules of the road, so often opposed by those who claim to speak for the free market, ironically led to a rescue far more intrusive than anything any of us—Democratic or Republican, progressive or conservative—would have ever proposed or predicted.

At the same time, we have to recognize that what's needed now goes beyond just the reforms that I've mentioned. For what took place one year ago was not merely a failure of regulation or legislation; it wasn't just a failure of oversight or foresight. It was also a failure of responsibility—it was fundamentally a failure of responsibility—that allowed Washington to become a place where problems—including structural problems in our financial system—were ignored rather than solved. It was a failure of responsibility that led homebuyers and derivative traders alike to take reckless risks that they couldn't afford to take. It was a collective failure of responsibility in Washington, on Wall Street, and across America that led to the near-collapse of our financial system one year ago.

So restoring a willingness to take responsibility—even when it's hard to do—is at the heart of what we must do. Here on Wall Street, you have a responsibility. The reforms I've laid out will pass and these changes will become law. But one of the most important ways to rebuild the system stronger than it was before is to rebuild trust stronger than before—and you don't have to wait for a new law to do that. You don't have to wait to use plain language in your dealings with consumers. You don't have to wait for legislation to put the 2009 bonuses of your senior executives up for a shareholder vote. You don't have to wait for a law to overhaul your pay system so that folks are rewarded for long-term performance instead of short-term gains.

The fact is, many of the firms that are now returning to prosperity owe a debt to the American people. They were not the cause of this crisis, and yet American taxpayers, through their government, had to take extraordinary action to stabilize the financial industry. They shouldered the burden of the bailout and they are still bearing the burden of the fallout—in lost jobs and lost homes and lost opportunities. It is neither right nor responsible after you've recovered with the help of your government to shirk your obligation to the goal of wider recovery, a more stable system, and a more broadly shared prosperity.

So I want to urge you to demonstrate that you take this obligation to heart. To put greater effort into helping families who need their mortgages modified under my administration's homeownership plan. To help small business owners who desperately need loans and who are bearing the brunt of the decline in available credit. To help communities that would benefit from the financing you could provide, or the community development institutions you could support. To come up with creative approaches to improve financial education and to bring banking to those who live and work entirely outside of the banking system. And, of course, to embrace serious financial reform, not resist it.

Just as we are asking the private sector to think about the long term, I recognize that Washington has to do so as well. When my administration came through the door, we not only faced a financial crisis and costly recession, we also found waiting a trillion dollar deficit. So yes, we have to take extraordinary action in the wake of an extraordinary economic crisis. But I am absolutely committed to putting this nation on a sound and secure fiscal footing. That's why we're pushing to restore pay-as-you-go rules in Congress, because I will not go along with the old Washington ways which said it was okay to pass spending bills and tax cuts without a plan to pay for it.

That's why we're cutting programs that don't work or are out of date. That's why I've insisted that health insurance reform—as important as it is—not add a dime to the deficit, now or in the future.

There are those who would suggest that we must choose between markets unfettered by even the most modest of regulations, and markets weighed down by onerous regulations that suppress the spirit of enterprise and innovation. If there is one lesson we can learn from last year, it is that this is a false choice. Common-sense rules of the road don't hinder the market, they make the market stronger. Indeed, they are essential to ensuring that our markets function fairly and freely.

One year ago, we saw in stark relief how markets can spin out of control; how a lack of common-sense rules can lead to excess and abuse; how close we can come to the brink. One year later, it is incumbent upon us to put in place those reforms that will prevent this kind of crisis from ever happening again, reflecting painful but important lessons that we've learned, and that will help us move from a period of reckless irresponsibility, a period of crisis, to one of responsibility and prosperity. That's what we must do. And I'm confident that's what we will do.

Thank you very much, everybody. [*Applause.*]

⇥ REMARKS TO THE UNITED NATIONS ⇤ GENERAL ASSEMBLY, SEPTEMBER 23, 2009

THE PRESIDENT: Good morning. Mr. President, Mr. Secretary General, fellow delegates, ladies and gentlemen, it is my honor to address you for the first time as the 44th President of the United States. [*Applause.*] I come before you humbled by the responsibility that the American people have placed upon me, mindful of the enormous challenges of our moment in history, and determined to act boldly and collectively on behalf of justice and prosperity at home and abroad.

I have been in office for just nine months—though some days it seems a lot longer. I am well aware of the expectations that accompany my presidency around the world. These expectations are not about me. Rather, they are rooted, I believe, in a discontent with a status quo that has allowed us to be increasingly defined by our differences, and outpaced by our problems. But they are also rooted in hope—the hope that real change is possible, and the hope that America will be a leader in bringing about such change.

I took office at a time when many around the world had come to view America with skepticism and distrust. Part of this was due to misperceptions and misinformation about my country. Part of this was due to opposition to specific policies, and a belief that on certain critical issues, America has acted unilaterally, without regard for the interests of others. And this has fed an almost reflexive anti-Americanism, which too often has served as an excuse for collective inaction.

Now, like all of you, my responsibility is to act in the interest of my nation and my people, and I will never apologize for defending those interests. But it is my deeply held belief that in the year 2009—more than at any point in human history—the interests of nations and peoples are shared. The religious convictions that we hold in our hearts can forge new bonds among people, or they can tear us apart. The technology we harness can light the path to peace, or forever darken it. The energy we use can sustain our planet, or destroy it. What happens to the hope of a single child—anywhere—can enrich our world, or impoverish it.

In this hall, we come from many places, but we share a common future. No longer do we have the luxury of indulging our differences to the exclusion of the work that we must do together. I have carried this message from London to Ankara; from Port of Spain to Moscow; from Accra to Cairo; and it is what I will speak about today—because the time has come for the world to move in a new direction. We must embrace a new era of engagement based on mutual interest and mutual respect, and our work must begin now.

We know the future will be forged by deeds and not simply words. Speeches alone will not solve our problems—it will take persistent action. For those who question the character and cause of my nation, I ask you to look at the concrete actions we have taken in just nine months.

On my first day in office, I prohibited—without exception or equivocation—the use of torture by the United States of America. [*Applause.*] I ordered the prison at Guantanamo Bay closed, and we are doing the hard work of forging a framework to combat extremism within the rule of law. Every nation must know: America will live its values, and we will lead by example.

We have set a clear and focused goal: to work with all members of this body to disrupt, dismantle, and defeat al Qaeda and its extremist allies—a network that has killed thousands of people of many faiths and nations, and that plotted to blow up this very building. In Afghanistan and Pakistan, we and many nations here are helping these governments develop the capacity to take the lead in this effort, while working to advance opportunity and security for their people.

In Iraq, we are responsibly ending a war. We have removed American combat brigades from Iraqi cities, and set a deadline of next August to remove all our combat brigades from Iraqi territory. And I have made clear that we will help Iraqis transition to full responsibility for their future, and keep our commitment to remove all American troops by the end of 2011.

I have outlined a comprehensive agenda to seek the goal of a world without nuclear weapons. In Moscow, the United States and Russia announced that we would pursue substantial reductions in our strategic warheads and launchers. At the Conference on Disarmament, we agreed on a work plan to negotiate an end to the production of fissile materials for nuclear weapons. And this week, my Secretary of State will become the first senior American representative to the annual Members Conference of the Comprehensive Test Ban Treaty.

Upon taking office, I appointed a Special Envoy for Middle East Peace, and America has worked steadily and aggressively to advance the cause of two states—Israel and Palestine—in which peace and security take root, and the rights of both Israelis and Palestinians are respected.

To confront climate change, we have invested $80 billion in clean energy. We have substantially increased our fuel-efficiency standards. We have provided new incentives for conservation, launched an energy partnership across the Americas, and moved from a bystander to a leader in international climate negotiations.

To overcome an economic crisis that touches every corner of the world, we worked with the G20 nations to forge a coordinated international response of over $2 trillion in stimulus to bring the global economy back from the brink. We mobilized resources that helped prevent the crisis from spreading further to developing countries. And we joined with others to launch a $20 billion global food security initiative that will lend a hand to those who need it most, and help them build their own capacity.

We've also re-engaged the United Nations. We have paid our bills. We have joined the Human Rights Council. [*Applause.*] We have signed the Convention of the Rights of Persons with Disabilities. We have fully embraced the Millennium Development Goals. And we address our priorities here, in this institution—for instance, through the Security Council meeting that I will chair tomorrow on nuclear non-proliferation and disarmament, and through the issues that I will discuss today.

This is what we have already done. But this is just a beginning. Some of our actions have yielded progress. Some have laid the groundwork for progress in the future. But make no mistake: This cannot solely be America's endeavor. Those who used to chastise America for acting alone in the world cannot now stand by and wait for America to solve the world's problems alone. We have sought—in word and deed—a new era of engagement with the world. And now is the time for all of us to take our share of responsibility for a global response to global challenges.

Now, if we are honest with ourselves, we need to admit that we are not living up to that responsibility. Consider the course that we're on if we fail to confront the status quo: Extremists sowing terror in pockets of the world; protracted conflicts that grind on and on; genocide; mass atrocities; more nations with nuclear weapons; melting ice caps and ravaged populations; persistent poverty and pandemic disease. I say this not to sow fear, but to state a fact: The magnitude of our challenges has yet to be met by the measure of our actions.

This body was founded on the belief that the nations of the world could solve their problems together. Franklin Roosevelt, who died before he could see his vision for this institution become a reality, put it this way—and I quote: "The structure of world peace cannot be the work of one man, or one party, or one nation. . . . It cannot be a peace of large nations—or of small nations. It must be a peace which rests on the cooperative effort of the whole world."

The cooperative effort of the whole world. Those words ring even more true today, when it is not simply peace, but our very health and prosperity that we hold in common. Yet we also know that this body is made up of sovereign states. And sadly, but not surprisingly, this body has often become a forum for sowing discord instead of forging common ground; a venue for playing politics and exploiting grievances rather than solving problems. After all, it is easy to walk up to this podium and point figures—point fingers and stoke divisions. Nothing is easier than blaming others for our troubles, and absolving ourselves of responsibility for our choices and our actions. Anybody can do that. Responsibility and leadership in the 21st century demand more.

In an era when our destiny is shared, power is no longer a zero-sum game. No one nation can or should try to dominate another nation. No world order that elevates one nation or group of people over another will succeed. No balance of power among nations will hold. The traditional divisions between nations of the South and the North make no sense in an interconnected world; nor do alignments of nations rooted in the cleavages of a long-gone Cold War.

The time has come to realize that the old habits, the old arguments, are irrelevant to the challenges faced by our people. They lead nations to act in opposition to the very goals that they claim to pursue—and to vote, often in this body, against the interests of their own people. They build up walls between us and the future that our people seek, and the time has come for those walls to come down. Together, we must build new coalitions that bridge old divides—coalitions of different faiths and creeds; of north and south, east, west, black, white, and brown.

The choice is ours. We can be remembered as a generation that chose to drag the arguments of the 20th century into the 21st; that put off hard choices, refused to look ahead, failed to keep pace because we defined ourselves by what we were against instead of what we were for. Or we can be a generation that chooses to see the shoreline beyond the rough waters ahead; that comes together to serve the common interests of human beings, and finally gives meaning to the promise embedded in the name given to this institution: the United Nations.

That is the future America wants—a future of peace and prosperity that we can only reach if we recognize that all nations have rights, but all nations have responsibilities as well. That is the bargain that makes this work. That must be the guiding principle of international cooperation.

Today, let me put forward four pillars that I believe are fundamental to the future that we want for our children: nonproliferation and disarmament; the promotion of peace and security; the preservation of our planet; and a global economy that advances opportunity for all people.

First, we must stop the spread of nuclear weapons, and seek the goal of a world without them.

This institution was founded at the dawn of the atomic age, in part because man's capacity to kill had to be contained. For decades, we averted disaster, even under the shadow of a superpower stand-off. But today, the threat of proliferation is growing in scope and complexity. If we fail to act, we will invite nuclear arms races in every region, and the prospect of wars and acts of terror on a scale that we can hardly imagine.

A fragile consensus stands in the way of this frightening outcome, and that is the basic bargain that shapes the Nuclear Non-Proliferation Treaty. It says that all nations have the right to peaceful nuclear energy; that nations with nuclear weapons have a responsibility to move toward disarmament; and those without them have the responsibility to forsake them. The next 12 months could be pivotal in determining whether this compact will be strengthened or will slowly dissolve.

America intends to keep our end of the bargain. We will pursue a new agreement with Russia to substantially reduce our strategic warheads and launchers. We will move forward with ratification of the Test Ban Treaty, and work with others to bring the treaty into force so that nuclear testing is permanently prohibited. We will complete a Nuclear Posture Review that opens the door to deeper cuts and reduces the role of nuclear weapons. And we will call upon countries to begin negotiations in January on a treaty to end the production of fissile material for weapons.

I will also host a summit next April that reaffirms each nation's responsibility to secure nuclear material on its territory, and to help those who can't—because we must never allow a single nuclear device to fall into the hands of a violent extremist. And we will work to strengthen the institutions and initiatives that combat nuclear smuggling and theft.

All of this must support efforts to strengthen the NPT. Those nations that refuse to live up to their obligations must face consequences. Let me be clear, this is not about singling out individual nations—it is about standing up for the rights of all nations that do live up to their responsibilities. Because a world in which IAEA inspections are avoided and the United Nation's demands are ignored will leave all people less safe, and all nations less secure.

In their actions to date, the governments of North Korea and Iran threaten to take us down this dangerous slope. We respect their rights as members of the community of nations. I've said before and I will repeat, I am committed to diplomacy that opens a path to greater prosperity and more secure peace for both nations if they live up to their obligations.

But if the governments of Iran and North Korea choose to ignore international standards; if they put the pursuit of nuclear weapons ahead of regional stability and the security and opportunity of their own people; if they are oblivious to the dangers of escalating nuclear arms races in both East Asia and the Middle East—then they must be held accountable. The world must stand together to demonstrate that international law is not an empty promise, and that treaties will be enforced. We must insist that the future does not belong to fear.

That brings me to the second pillar for our future: the pursuit of peace.

The United Nations was born of the belief that the people of the world can live their lives, raise their families, and resolve their differences peacefully. And yet we know that in too many parts of the world, this ideal remains an abstraction—a distant dream. We can either accept that outcome as inevitable, and tolerate constant and crippling conflict, or we can recognize that the yearning for peace is universal, and reassert our resolve to end conflicts around the world.

That effort must begin with an unshakeable determination that the murder of innocent men, women and children will never be tolerated. On this, no one can be—there can be no dispute. The violent extremists who promote conflict by distorting faith have discredited and isolated themselves. They offer nothing but hatred and destruction. In confronting them, America will forge lasting partnerships to target terrorists, share intelligence, and coordinate law enforcement and protect our people. We will permit no safe haven for al Qaeda to launch attacks from Afghanistan or any other nation. We will stand by our friends on the front lines, as we and many nations will do in pledging support for the Pakistani people tomorrow. And we will pursue positive engagement that builds bridges among faiths, and new partnerships for opportunity.

Our efforts to promote peace, however, cannot be limited to defeating violent extremists. For the most powerful weapon in our arsenal is the hope of human beings—the belief that the future belongs to those who would build and not destroy; the confidence that conflicts can end and a new day can begin.

And that is why we will support—we will strengthen our support for effective peacekeeping, while energizing our efforts to prevent conflicts before they take hold. We will pursue a lasting peace in Sudan through support for the people of Darfur and the implementation of the Comprehensive Peace Agreement, so that we secure the peace that the Sudanese people deserve. [*Applause.*] And in countries ravaged by violence—from Haiti to Congo to East Timor—we will work with the U.N. and other partners to support an enduring peace.

I will also continue to seek a just and lasting peace between Israel, Palestine, and the Arab world. [*Applause.*] We will continue to work on that issue. Yesterday, I had a constructive meeting with Prime Minister Netanyahu and President Abbas. We have made some progress. Palestinians have strengthened their efforts on security. Israelis have facilitated greater freedom of movement for the Palestinians. As a result of these efforts on both sides, the economy in the West Bank has begun to grow. But more progress is needed. We continue to call on Palestinians to end incitement against Israel, and we continue to emphasize that America does not accept the legitimacy of continued Israeli settlements. [*Applause.*]

The time has come—the time has come to re-launch negotiations without preconditions that address the permanent status issues: security for Israelis and Palestinians, borders, refugees, and Jerusalem. And the goal is clear: Two states living side by side in peace and security—a Jewish state of Israel, with true security for all Israelis; and a viable, independent Palestinian state with contiguous territory that ends the occupation that began in 1967, and realizes the potential of the Palestinian people. [*Applause.*]

As we pursue this goal, we will also pursue peace between Israel and Lebanon, Israel and Syria, and a broader peace between Israel and its many neighbors. In pursuit of that goal, we will develop regional initiatives with multilateral participation, alongside bilateral negotiations.

Now, I am not naïve. I know this will be difficult. But all of us—not just the Israelis and the Palestinians, but all of us—must decide whether we are serious about peace, or whether we will only lend it lip service. To break the old patterns, to break the cycle of insecurity and despair, all of us must say publicly what we would acknowledge in private. The United States does Israel no favors when we fail to couple an unwavering commitment to its security with an insistence that Israel respect the legitimate claims and rights of the Palestinians. [*Applause.*] And—and nations within this body do the Palestinians no favors when they choose vitriolic attacks against Israel over constructive willingness to recognize Israel's legitimacy and its right to exist in peace and security. [*Applause.*]

We must remember that the greatest price of this conflict is not paid by us. It's not paid by politicians. It's paid by the Israeli girl in Sderot who closes her eyes in fear that a rocket will take her life in the middle of the night. It's paid for by the Palestinian boy in Gaza who has no clean water and no country to call his own. These are all God's children. And after all the politics and all the posturing, this is about the right of every human being to live with dignity and security. That is a lesson embedded in the three great faiths that call one small slice of Earth the Holy Land. And that is why, even though there will be setbacks and false starts and tough days, I will not waver in my pursuit of peace. [*Applause.*]

Third, we must recognize that in the 21st century, there will be no peace unless we take responsibility for the preservation of our planet. And I thank the Secretary General for hosting the subject of climate change yesterday.

The danger posed by climate change cannot be denied. Our responsibility to meet it must not be deferred. If we continue down our current course, every member of this Assembly will see irreversible changes within their borders. Our efforts to end conflicts will be eclipsed by wars over refugees and resources. Development will be devastated by drought and famine. Land that human beings have lived on for millennia will disappear. Future generations will look back and wonder why we refused to act; why we failed to pass on—why we failed to pass on an environment that was worthy of our inheritance.

And that is why the days when America dragged its feet on this issue are over. We will move forward with investments to transform our energy economy, while providing incentives to make clean energy the profitable kind of energy. We will press ahead with deep cuts in emissions to reach the goals that we set for 2020, and eventually 2050. We will continue to promote renewable energy and efficiency, and share new technologies with countries around the world. And we will seize every opportunity for progress to address this threat in a cooperative effort with the entire world.

And those wealthy nations that did so much damage to the environment in the 20th century must accept our obligation to lead. But responsibility does not end there. While we must acknowledge the need for differentiated responses, any effort to curb carbon emissions must include the fast-growing carbon emitters who can do more to reduce their air pollution without inhibiting growth. And any effort that fails to help the poorest nations both adapt to the problems that climate change have already wrought and help them travel a path of clean development simply will not work.

It's hard to change something as fundamental as how we use energy. I know that. It's even harder to do so in the midst of a global recession. Certainly, it will be tempting to sit back and wait for others to move first. But we cannot make this journey unless we all move forward together. As we head into Copenhagen, let us resolve to focus on what each of us can do for the sake of our common future.

And this leads me to the final pillar that must fortify our future: a global economy that advances opportunity for all people.

The world is still recovering from the worst economic crisis since the Great Depression. In America, we see the engine of growth beginning to churn, and yet many still struggle to find a job or pay their bills. Across the globe, we find promising signs, but little certainty about what lies ahead. And far too many people in far too many places live through the daily crises that challenge our humanity—the despair of an empty stomach; the thirst brought on by dwindling water supplies; the injustice of a child dying from a treatable disease; or a mother losing her life as she gives birth.

In Pittsburgh, we will work with the world's largest economies to chart a course for growth that is balanced and sustained. That means vigilance to ensure that we do not let up until our people are back to work. That means taking steps to rekindle demand so that global recovery can be sustained. And that means setting new rules of the road and strengthening regulation for all financial centers, so that we put an end to the greed and the excess and the abuse that led us into this disaster, and prevent a crisis like this from ever happening again.

At a time of such interdependence, we have a moral and pragmatic interest, however, in broader questions of development—the questions of development that existed even before this crisis happened. And so America will continue our historic effort to help people feed themselves. We have set aside $63 billion to carry forward the fight against HIV/AIDS, to end deaths from tuberculosis and malaria, to eradicate polio, and to strengthen public health systems. We are joining with other countries to contribute H1N1 vaccines to the World Health Organization. We will integrate more economies into a system of global trade. We will support the Millennium Development Goals, and approach next year's summit with a global plan to make them a reality. And we will set our sights on the eradication of extreme poverty in our time.

Now is the time for all of us to do our part. Growth will not be sustained or shared unless all nations embrace their responsibilities. And that means that wealthy nations must open their markets to more goods and extend a hand to those with less, while reforming international institutions to give more nations a greater voice. And developing nations must root out the corruption that is an obstacle to progress—for opportunity cannot thrive where individuals are oppressed and business have to pay bribes. That is why we support honest police and independent judges; civil society and a vibrant private sector. Our goal is simple: a global economy in which growth is sustained, and opportunity is available to all.

Now, the changes that I've spoken about today will not be easy to make. And they will not be realized simply by leaders like us coming together in forums like this, as useful as that may be. For as in any assembly of members, real change can only come through the people we represent. That is why we must do the hard work to lay the groundwork for progress in our own capitals. That's where we will build the consensus to end conflicts and to harness technology for peaceful purposes, to change the way we use energy, and to promote growth that can be sustained and shared.

I believe that the people of the world want this future for their children. And that is why we must champion those principles which ensure that governments reflect the will of the people. These principles cannot be afterthoughts—democracy and human rights are essential to achieving each of the goals that I've discussed today, because governments of the people and by the people are more likely to act in the broader interests of their own people, rather than narrow interests of those in power.

The test of our leadership will not be the degree to which we feed the fears and old hatreds of our people. True leadership will not be measured by the ability to muzzle dissent, or to intimidate and harass political opponents at home. The people of the world want change. They will not long tolerate those who are on the wrong side of history.

This Assembly's Charter commits each of us—and I quote—"to reaffirm faith in fundamental human rights, in the dignity and worth of the human person, in the equal rights of men and women." Among those rights is the freedom to speak your mind and worship as you please; the promise of equality of the races, and the opportunity for women and girls to pursue their own potential; the ability of citizens to have a say in how you are governed, and to have confidence in the administration of justice. For just as no nation should be forced to accept the tyranny of another nation, no individual should be forced to accept the tyranny of their own people. [*Applause.*]

As an African American, I will never forget that I would not be here today without the steady pursuit of a more perfect union in my country. And that guides my belief that no matter how dark the day may seem, transformative change can be forged by those who choose to side with justice. And I pledge that America will always stand with those who stand up for their dignity and their rights—for the student who seeks to learn; the voter who demands to be heard; the innocent who longs to be free; the oppressed who yearns to be equal.

Democracy cannot be imposed on any nation from the outside. Each society must search for its own path, and no path is perfect. Each country will pursue a path rooted in the culture of its people and in its past traditions. And I admit that America has too often been selective in its promotion of democracy. But that does not weaken our commitment; it only reinforces it. There are basic principles that are universal; there are certain truths which are self-evident—and the United States of America will never waver in our efforts to stand up for the right of people everywhere to determine their own destiny. [*Applause.*]

Sixty-five years ago, a weary Franklin Roosevelt spoke to the American people in his fourth and final inaugural address. After years of war, he sought to sum up the lessons that could be drawn from the terrible suffering, the enormous sacrifice that had taken place. "We have learned," he said, "to be citizens of the world, members of the human community."

The United Nations was built by men and women like Roosevelt from every corner of the world—from Africa and Asia, from Europe to the Americas. These architects of international cooperation had an idealism that was anything but naïve—it was rooted in the hard-earned lessons of war; rooted in the wisdom that nations could advance their interests by acting together instead of splitting apart.

Now it falls to us—for this institution will be what we make of it. The United Nations does extraordinary good around the world—feeding the hungry, caring for the sick, mending places that have been broken. But it also struggles to enforce its will, and to live up to the ideals of its founding.

I believe that those imperfections are not a reason to walk away from this institution—they are a calling to redouble our efforts. The United Nations can either be a place where we bicker about outdated grievances, or forge common ground; a place where we focus on what drives us apart, or what brings us together; a place where we indulge tyranny, or a source of moral authority. In short, the United Nations can be an institution that is disconnected from what matters in the lives of our citizens, or it can be an indispensable factor in advancing the interests of the people we serve.

We have reached a pivotal moment. The United States stands ready to begin a new chapter of international cooperation—one that recognizes the rights and responsibilities of all nations. And so, with confidence in our cause, and with a commitment to our values, we call on all nations to join us in building the future that our people so richly deserve.

Thank you very much, everybody. [*Applause.*]

⇥ REMARKS ON THE DEATH OF ⇤ OSAMA BIN LADEN, MAY 2, 2011

THE PRESIDENT: Good evening. Tonight, I can report to the American people and to the world that the United States has conducted an operation that killed Osama bin Laden, the leader of al Qaeda, and a terrorist who's responsible for the murder of thousands of innocent men, women, and children.

It was nearly 10 years ago that a bright September day was darkened by the worst attack on the American people in our history. The images of 9/11 are seared into our national memory—hijacked planes cutting through a cloudless September sky; the Twin Towers collapsing to the ground; black smoke billowing up from the Pentagon; the wreckage of Flight 93 in Shanksville, Pennsylvania, where the actions of heroic citizens saved even more heartbreak and destruction.

And yet we know that the worst images are those that were unseen to the world. The empty seat at the dinner table. Children who were forced to grow up without their mother or their father. Parents who would never know the feeling of their child's embrace. Nearly 3,000 citizens taken from us, leaving a gaping hole in our hearts.

On September 11, 2001, in our time of grief, the American people came together. We offered our neighbors a hand, and we offered the wounded our blood. We reaffirmed our ties to each other, and our love of community and country. On that day, no matter where we came from, what God we prayed to, or what race or ethnicity we were, we were united as one American family.

We were also united in our resolve to protect our nation and to bring those who committed this vicious attack to justice. We quickly learned that the 9/11 attacks were carried out by al Qaeda—an organization headed by Osama bin Laden, which had openly declared war on the United States and was committed to killing innocents in our country and around the globe. And so we went to war against al Qaeda to protect our citizens, our friends, and our allies.

Over the last 10 years, thanks to the tireless and heroic work of our military and our counterterrorism professionals, we've made great strides in that effort. We've disrupted terrorist attacks and strengthened our homeland defense. In Afghanistan, we removed the Taliban government, which had given bin Laden and al Qaeda safe haven and support. And around the globe, we worked with our friends and allies to capture or kill scores of al Qaeda terrorists, including several who were a part of the 9/11 plot.

Yet Osama bin Laden avoided capture and escaped across the Afghan border into Pakistan. Meanwhile, al Qaeda continued to operate from along that border and operate through its affiliates across the world.

And so shortly after taking office, I directed Leon Panetta, the director of the CIA, to make the killing or capture of bin Laden the top priority of our war against al Qaeda, even as we continued our broader efforts to disrupt, dismantle, and defeat his network.

Then, last August, after years of painstaking work by our intelligence community, I was briefed on a possible lead to bin Laden. It was far from certain, and it took many months to run this thread to ground. I met repeatedly with my national security team as we developed more information about the possibility that we had located bin Laden hiding within a compound deep inside of Pakistan. And finally, last week, I determined that we had enough intelligence to take action, and authorized an operation to get Osama bin Laden and bring him to justice.

Today, at my direction, the United States launched a targeted operation against that compound in Abbottabad, Pakistan. A small team of Americans carried out the operation with extraordinary courage and capability. No Americans were harmed. They took care to avoid civilian casualties. After a firefight, they killed Osama bin Laden and took custody of his body.

For over two decades, bin Laden has been al Qaeda's leader and symbol, and has continued to plot attacks against our country and our friends and allies. The death of bin Laden marks the most significant achievement to date in our nation's effort to defeat al Qaeda.

Yet his death does not mark the end of our effort. There's no doubt that al Qaeda will continue to pursue attacks against us. We must—and we will—remain vigilant at home and abroad.

As we do, we must also reaffirm that the United States is not—and never will be—at war with Islam. I've made clear, just as President Bush did shortly after 9/11, that our war is not against Islam. Bin Laden was not a Muslim leader; he was a mass murderer of Muslims. Indeed, al Qaeda has slaughtered scores of Muslims in many countries, including our own. So his demise should be welcomed by all who believe in peace and human dignity.

Over the years, I've repeatedly made clear that we would take action within Pakistan if we knew where bin Laden was. That is what we've done. But it's important to note that our counterterrorism cooperation with Pakistan helped lead us to bin Laden and the compound where he was hiding. Indeed, bin Laden had declared war against Pakistan as well, and ordered attacks against the Pakistani people.

Tonight, I called President Zardari, and my team has also spoken with their Pakistani counterparts. They agree that this is a good and historic day for both of our nations. And going forward, it is essential that Pakistan continue to join us in the fight against al Qaeda and its affiliates.

The American people did not choose this fight. It came to our shores, and started with the senseless slaughter of our citizens. After nearly 10 years of service, struggle, and sacrifice, we know well the costs of war. These efforts weigh on me every time I, as Commander-in-Chief, have to sign a letter to a family that has lost a loved one, or look into the eyes of a service member who's been gravely wounded.

So Americans understand the costs of war. Yet as a country, we will never tolerate our security being threatened, nor stand idly by when our people have been killed. We will be relentless in defense of our citizens and our friends and allies. We will be true to the values that make us who we are. And on nights like this one, we can say to those families who have lost loved ones to al Qaeda's terror: Justice has been done.

Tonight, we give thanks to the countless intelligence and counterterrorism professionals who've worked tirelessly to achieve this outcome. The American people do not see their work, nor know their names. But tonight, they feel the satisfaction of their work and the result of their pursuit of justice.

We give thanks for the men who carried out this operation, for they exemplify the professionalism, patriotism, and unparalleled courage of those who serve our country. And they are part of a generation that has borne the heaviest share of the burden since that September day.

Finally, let me say to the families who lost loved ones on 9/11 that we have never forgotten your loss, nor wavered in our commitment to see that we do whatever it takes to prevent another attack on our shores.

And tonight, let us think back to the sense of unity that prevailed on 9/11. I know that it has, at times, frayed. Yet today's achievement is a testament to the greatness of our country and the determination of the American people.

The cause of securing our country is not complete. But tonight, we are once again reminded that America can do whatever we set our mind to. That is the story of our history, whether it's the pursuit of prosperity for our people, or the struggle for equality for all our citizens; our commitment to stand up for our values abroad, and our sacrifices to make the world a safer place.

Let us remember that we can do these things not just because of wealth or power, but because of who we are: one nation, under God, indivisible, with liberty and justice for all.

Thank you. May God bless you. And may God bless the United States of America.

⇥ 2012 STATE OF THE UNION ADDRESS, ⇤ JANUARY 24, 2012

THE PRESIDENT: Mr. Speaker, Mr. Vice President, members of Congress, distinguished guests, and fellow Americans:

Last month, I went to Andrews Air Force Base and welcomed home some of our last troops to serve in Iraq. Together, we offered a final, proud salute to the colors under which more than a million of our fellow citizens fought—and several thousand gave their lives.

We gather tonight knowing that this generation of heroes has made the United States safer and more respected around the world. [*Applause.*] For the first time in nine years, there are no Americans fighting in Iraq. [*Applause.*] For the first time in two decades, Osama bin Laden is not a threat to this country. [*Applause.*] Most of al Qaeda's top lieutenants have been defeated. The Taliban's momentum has been broken, and some troops in Afghanistan have begun to come home.

These achievements are a testament to the courage, self-lessness and teamwork of America's Armed Forces. At a time when too many of our institutions have let us down, they exceed all expectations. They're not consumed with personal ambition. They don't obsess over their differences. They focus on the mission at hand. They work together.

Imagine what we could accomplish if we followed their example. [*Applause.*] Think about the America within our reach: A country that leads the world in educating its people. An America that attracts a new generation of high-tech manu-facturing and high-paying jobs. A future where we're in control of our own energy, and our security and prosperity aren't so tied to unstable parts of the world. An economy built to last, where hard work pays off, and responsibility is rewarded.

We can do this. I know we can, because we've done it before. At the end of World War II, when another generation of heroes returned home from combat, they built the strongest economy and middle class the world has ever known. [*Applause.*] My grandfather, a veteran of Patton's Army, got the chance to go to college on the GI Bill. My grandmother, who worked on a bomber assembly line, was part of a workforce that turned out the best products on Earth.

The two of them shared the optimism of a nation that had triumphed over a depression and fascism. They understood they were part of something larger; that they were contributing to a story of success that every American had a chance to share—the basic American promise that if you worked hard, you could do well enough to raise a family, own a home, send your kids to college, and put a little away for retirement.

The defining issue of our time is how to keep that promise alive. No challenge is more urgent. No debate is more important. We can either settle for a country where a shrinking number of people do really well while a growing number of Americans barely get by, or we can restore an economy where everyone gets a fair shot, and everyone does their fair share, and everyone plays by the same set of rules. [*Applause.*] What's at stake aren't Democratic values or Republican values, but American values. And we have to reclaim them.

Let's remember how we got here. Long before the recession, jobs and manufacturing began leaving our shores. Technology made businesses more efficient, but also made some jobs obsolete. Folks at the top saw their incomes rise like never before, but most hardworking Americans struggled with costs that were growing, paychecks that weren't, and personal debt that kept piling up.

In 2008, the house of cards collapsed. We learned that mortgages had been sold to people who couldn't afford or understand them. Banks had made huge bets and bonuses with other people's money. Regulators had looked the other way, or didn't have the authority to stop the bad behavior.

It was wrong. It was irresponsible. And it plunged our economy into a crisis that put millions out of work, saddled us with more debt, and left innocent, hardworking Americans holding the bag. In the six months before I took office, we lost nearly 4 million jobs. And we lost another 4 million before our policies were in full effect.

Those are the facts. But so are these: In the last 22 months, businesses have created more than 3 million jobs. [*Applause.*]

Last year, they created the most jobs since 2005. American manufacturers are hiring again, creating jobs for the first time since the late 1990s. Together, we've agreed to cut the deficit by more than $2 trillion. And we've put in place new rules to hold Wall Street accountable, so a crisis like this never happens again. [*Applause.*]

The state of our Union is getting stronger. And we've come too far to turn back now. As long as I'm President, I will work with anyone in this chamber to build on this momentum. But I intend to fight obstruction with action, and I will oppose any effort to return to the very same policies that brought on this economic crisis in the first place. [*Applause.*]

No, we will not go back to an economy weakened by outsourcing, bad debt, and phony financial profits. Tonight, I want to speak about how we move forward, and lay out a blueprint for an economy that's built to last—an economy built on American manufacturing, American energy, skills for American workers, and a renewal of American values.

Now, this blueprint begins with American manufacturing.

On the day I took office, our auto industry was on the verge of collapse. Some even said we should let it die. With a million jobs at stake, I refused to let that happen. In exchange for help, we demanded responsibility. We got workers and automakers to settle their differences. We got the industry to retool and restructure. Today, General Motors is back on top as the world's number-one automaker. [*Applause.*] Chrysler has grown faster in the U.S. than any major car company. Ford is investing billions in U.S. plants and factories. And together, the entire industry added nearly 160,000 jobs.

We bet on American workers. We bet on American ingenuity. And tonight, the American auto industry is back. [*Applause.*]

What's happening in Detroit can happen in other industries. It can happen in Cleveland and Pittsburgh and Raleigh. We can't bring every job back that's left our shore. But right now, it's getting more expensive to do business in places like China. Meanwhile, America is more productive. A few weeks ago, the CEO of Master Lock told me that it now makes business sense for him to bring jobs back home. [*Applause.*] Today, for the first time in 15 years, Master Lock's unionized plant in Milwaukee is running at full capacity. [*Applause.*]

So we have a huge opportunity, at this moment, to bring manufacturing back. But we have to seize it. Tonight, my message to business leaders is simple: Ask yourselves what you can do to bring jobs back to your country, and your country will do everything we can to help you succeed. [*Applause.*]

We should start with our tax code. Right now, companies get tax breaks for moving jobs and profits overseas. Meanwhile, companies that choose to stay in America get hit with one of the highest tax rates in the world. It makes no sense, and everyone knows it. So let's change it.

First, if you're a business that wants to outsource jobs, you shouldn't get a tax deduction for doing it. [*Applause.*] That money should be used to cover moving expenses for companies like Master Lock that decide to bring jobs home. [*Applause.*]

Second, no American company should be able to avoid paying its fair share of taxes by moving jobs and profits overseas. [*Applause.*] From now on, every multinational company should have to pay a basic minimum tax. And every penny should go towards lowering taxes for companies that choose to stay here and hire here in America. [*Applause.*]

Third, if you're an American manufacturer, you should get a bigger tax cut. If you're a high-tech manufacturer, we should double the tax deduction you get for making your products here. And if you want to relocate in a community that was hit hard when a factory left town, you should get help financing a new plant, equipment, or training for new workers. [*Applause.*]

So my message is simple. It is time to stop rewarding businesses that ship jobs overseas, and start rewarding companies that create jobs right here in America. Send me these tax reforms, and I will sign them right away. [*Applause.*]

We're also making it easier for American businesses to sell products all over the world. Two years ago, I set a goal of doubling U.S. exports over five years. With the bipartisan trade agreements we signed into law, we're on track to meet that goal ahead of schedule. [*Applause.*] And soon, there will be millions of new customers for American goods in Panama, Colombia, and South Korea. Soon, there will be new cars on the streets of Seoul imported from Detroit, and Toledo, and Chicago. [*Applause.*]

I will go anywhere in the world to open new markets for American products. And I will not stand by when our competitors don't play by the rules. We've brought trade cases against China at nearly twice the rate as the last administration—and it's made a difference. [*Applause.*] Over a thousand Americans are working today because we stopped a surge in Chinese tires. But we need to do more. It's not right when another country lets our movies, music, and software be pirated. It's not fair when foreign manufacturers have a leg up on ours only because they're heavily subsidized.

Tonight, I'm announcing the creation of a Trade Enforcement Unit that will be charged with investigating unfair trading practices in countries like China. [*Applause.*] There will be more inspections to prevent counterfeit or unsafe goods from crossing our borders. And this Congress should make sure that no foreign company has an advantage over American manufacturing when it comes to accessing financing or new markets like Russia. Our workers are the most productive on Earth, and if the playing field is level, I promise you—America will always win. [*Applause.*]

I also hear from many business leaders who want to hire in the United States but can't find workers with the right skills. Growing industries in science and technology have twice as many openings as we have workers who can do the job. Think about—openings at a time when millions of Americans are looking for work. It's inexcusable. And we know how to fix it.

Jackie Bray is a single mom from North Carolina who was laid off from her job as a mechanic. Then Siemens opened a gas turbine factory in Charlotte, and formed a partnershipwith Central Piedmont Community College. The company helped the college design courses in laser and robotics training. It paid Jackie's tuition, then hired her to help operate their plant.

I want every American looking for work to have the same opportunity as Jackie did. Join me in a national commitment to train 2 million Americans with skills that will lead directly to a job. [*Applause.*] My administration has already lined up more companies that want to help. Model partnerships between businesses like Siemens and community colleges in places like Charlotte, and Orlando, and Louisville are up and running. Now you need to give more community colleges the resources they need to become community career centers—places that teach people skills that businesses are looking for right now, from data management to high-tech manufacturing.

And I want to cut through the maze of confusing training programs, so that from now on, people like Jackie have one program, one website, and one place to go for all the information and help that they need. It is time to turn our unemployment system into a reemployment system that puts people to work. [*Applause.*]

These reforms will help people get jobs that are open today. But to prepare for the jobs of tomorrow, our commitment to skills and education has to start earlier.

For less than 1 percent of what our nation spends on education each year, we've convinced nearly every state in the country to raise their standards for teaching and learning—the first time that's happened in a generation.

But challenges remain. And we know how to solve them.

At a time when other countries are doubling down on education, tight budgets have forced states to lay off thousands of teachers. We know a good teacher can increase the lifetime income of a classroom by over $250,000. A great teacher can offer an escape from poverty to the child who dreams beyond his circumstance. Every person in this chamber can point to a teacher who changed the trajectory of their lives. Most teachers work tirelessly, with modest pay, sometimes digging into their own pocket for school supplies—just to make a difference.

Teachers matter. So instead of bashing them, or defending the status quo, let's offer schools a deal. Give them the resources to keep good teachers on the job, and reward the best ones. [*Applause.*] And in return, grant schools flexibility: to teach with creativity and passion; to stop teaching to the test; and to replace teachers who just aren't helping kids learn. That's a bargain worth making. [*Applause.*]

We also know that when students don't walk away from their education, more of them walk the stage to get their diploma. When students are not allowed to drop out, they do better. So tonight, I am proposing that every state—every state—requires that all students stay in high school until they graduate or turn 18. [*Applause.*]

When kids do graduate, the most daunting challenge can be the cost of college. At a time when Americans owe more in tuition debt than credit card debt, this Congress needs to stop the interest rates on student loans from doubling in July. [*Applause.*]

Extend the tuition tax credit we started that saves millions of middle-class families thousands of dollars, and give more young people the chance to earn their way through college by doubling the number of work-study jobs in the next five years. [*Applause.*]

Of course, it's not enough for us to increase student aid. We can't just keep subsidizing skyrocketing tuition; we'll run out of money. States also need to do their part, by making higher education a higher priority in their budgets. And colleges and universities have to do their part by working to keep costs down.

Recently, I spoke with a group of college presidents who've done just that. Some schools redesign courses to help students finish more quickly. Some use better technology. The point is, it's possible. So let me put colleges and universities on notice: If you can't stop tuition from going up, the funding you get from taxpayers will go down. [*Applause.*] Higher education can't be a luxury—it is an economic imperative that every family in America should be able to afford.

Let's also remember that hundreds of thousands of talented, hardworking students in this country face another challenge: the fact that they aren't yet American citizens. Many were brought here as small children, are American through and through, yet they live every day with the threat of deportation. Others came more recently, to study business and science and engineering, but as soon as they get their degree, we send them home to invent new products and create new jobs somewhere else.

That doesn't make sense.

I believe as strongly as ever that we should take on illegal immigration. That's why my administration has put more boots on the border than ever before. That's why there are fewer illegal crossings than when I took office. The opponents of action are out of excuses. We should be working on comprehensive immigration reform right now. [*Applause.*]

But if election-year politics keeps Congress from acting on a comprehensive plan, let's at least agree to stop expelling responsible young people who want to staff our labs, start new businesses, defend this country. Send me a law that gives them the chance to earn their citizenship. I will sign it right away. [*Applause.*]

You see, an economy built to last is one where we encourage the talent and ingenuity of every person in this country. That means women should earn equal pay for equal work. [*Applause.*] It means we should support everyone who's willing to work, and every risk-taker and entrepreneur who aspires to become the next Steve Jobs.

After all, innovation is what America has always been about. Most new jobs are created in start-ups and small businesses. So let's pass an agenda that helps them succeed. Tear down regulations that prevent aspiring entrepreneurs from getting the financing to grow. [*Applause.*] Expand tax relief to small businesses that are raising wages and creating good jobs. Both parties agree on these ideas. So put them in a bill, and get it on my desk this year. [*Applause.*]

Innovation also demands basic research. Today, the discoveries taking place in our federally financed labs and universities could lead to new treatments that kill cancer cells but leave healthy ones untouched. New lightweight vests for cops and soldiers that can stop any bullet. Don't gut these investments in our budget. Don't let other countries win the race for the future. Support the same kind of research and innovation that led to the computer chip and the Internet; to new American jobs and new American industries.

And nowhere is the promise of innovation greater than in American-made energy. Over the last three years, we've opened millions of new acres for oil and gas exploration, and tonight, I'm directing my administration to open more than 75 percent of our potential offshore oil and gas resources. [*Applause.*] Right now—right now—American oil production is the highest that it's been in eight years. That's right—eight years. Not only that—last year, we relied less on foreign oil than in any of the past 16 years. [*Applause.*]

But with only 2 percent of the world's oil reserves, oil isn't enough. This country needs an all-out, all-of-the-above strategy that develops every available source of American energy. [*Applause.*] A strategy that's cleaner, cheaper, and full of new jobs.

We have a supply of natural gas that can last America nearly 100 years. [*Applause.*] And my administration will take every possible action to safely develop this energy. Experts believe this will support more than 600,000 jobs by the end of the decade. And I'm requiring all companies that drill for gas on public lands to disclose the chemicals they use. [*Applause.*] Because America will develop this resource without putting the health and safety of our citizens at risk.

The development of natural gas will create jobs and power trucks and factories that are cleaner and cheaper, proving that we don't have to choose between our environment and our economy. [*Applause.*] And by the way, it was public research dollars, over the course of 30 years, that helped develop the technologies to extract all this natural gas out of shale rock—reminding us that government support is critical in helping businesses get new energy ideas off the ground. [*Applause.*]

Now, what's true for natural gas is just as true for clean energy. In three years, our partnership with the private sector has already positioned America to be the world's leading manufacturer of high-tech batteries. Because of federal investments, renewable energy use has nearly doubled, and thousands of Americans have jobs because of it.

When Bryan Ritterby was laid off from his job making furniture, he said he worried that at 55, no one would give him a second chance. But he found work at Energetx, a wind turbine manufacturer in Michigan. Before the recession, the factory only made luxury yachts. Today, it's hiring workers like Bryan, who said, "I'm proud to be working in the industry of the future."

Our experience with shale gas, our experience with natural gas, shows us that the payoffs on these public investments don't always come right away. Some technologies don't pan out; some companies fail. But I will not walk away from the promise of clean energy. I will not walk away from workers like Bryan. [*Applause.*] I will not cede the wind or solar or battery industry to China or Germany because we refuse to make the same commitment here.

We've subsidized oil companies for a century. That's long enough. [*Applause.*] It's time to end the taxpayer giveaways to an industry that rarely has been more profitable, and double-down on a clean energy industry that never has been more promising. Pass clean energy tax credits. Create these jobs. [*Applause.*]

We can also spur energy innovation with new incentives. The differences in this chamber may be too deep right now to pass a comprehensive plan to fight climate change. But there's no reason why Congress shouldn't at least set a clean energy standard that creates a market for innovation. So far, you haven't acted. Well, tonight, I will. I'm directing my administration to allow the development of clean energy on enough public land to power 3 million homes. And I'm proud to announce that the Department of Defense, working with us, the world's largest consumer of energy, will make one of the largest commitments to clean energy in history—with the Navy purchasing enough capacity to power a quarter of a million homes a year. [*Applause.*]

Of course, the easiest way to save money is to waste less energy. So here's a proposal: Help manufacturers eliminate energy waste in their factories and give businesses incentives to upgrade their buildings. Their energy bills will be $100 billion lower over the next decade, and America will have less pollution, more manufacturing, more jobs for construction workers who need them. Send me a bill that creates these jobs. [*Applause.*]

Building this new energy future should be just one part of a broader agenda to repair America's infrastructure. So much of

America needs to be rebuilt. We've got crumbling roads and bridges; a power grid that wastes too much energy; an incomplete high-speed broadband network that prevents a small business owner in rural America from selling her products all over the world.

During the Great Depression, America built the Hoover Dam and the Golden Gate Bridge. After World War II, we connected our states with a system of highways. Democratic and Republican administrations invested in great projects that benefited everybody, from the workers who built them to the businesses that still use them today.

In the next few weeks, I will sign an executive order clearing away the red tape that slows down too many construction projects. But you need to fund these projects. Take the money we're no longer spending at war, use half of it to pay down our debt, and use the rest to do some nation-building right here at home. [*Applause.*]

There's never been a better time to build, especially since the construction industry was one of the hardest hit when the housing bubble burst. Of course, construction workers weren't the only ones who were hurt. So were millions of innocent Americans who've seen their home values decline. And while government can't fix the problem on its own, responsible homeowners shouldn't have to sit and wait for the housing market to hit bottom to get some relief.

And that's why I'm sending this Congress a plan that gives every responsible homeowner the chance to save about $3,000 a year on their mortgage, by refinancing at historically low rates. [*Applause.*] No more red tape. No more runaround from the banks. A small fee on the largest financial institutions will ensure that it won't add to the deficit and will give those banks that were rescued by taxpayers a chance to repay a deficit of trust. [*Applause.*]

Let's never forget: Millions of Americans who work hard and play by the rules every day deserve a government and a financial system that do the same. It's time to apply the same rules from top to bottom. No bailouts, no handouts, and no copouts. An America built to last insists on responsibility from everybody.

We've all paid the price for lenders who sold mortgages to people who couldn't afford them, and buyers who knew they couldn't afford them. That's why we need smart regulations to prevent irresponsible behavior. [*Applause.*] Rules to prevent financial fraud or toxic dumping or faulty medical devices—these don't destroy the free market. They make the free market work better.

There's no question that some regulations are outdated, unnecessary, or too costly. In fact, I've approved fewer regulations in the first three years of my presidency than my Republican predecessor did in his. [*Applause.*] I've ordered every federal agency to eliminate rules that don't make sense. We've already announced over 500 reforms, and just a fraction of them will save business and citizens more than $10 billion over the next five years. We got rid of one rule from 40 years ago that could have forced some dairy farmers to spend $10,000 a year proving that they could contain a spill—because milk was somehow classified as an oil. With a rule like that, I guess it was worth crying over spilled milk. [*Laughter and applause.*]

Now, I'm confident a farmer can contain a milk spill without a federal agency looking over his shoulder. [*Applause.*] Absolutely. But I will not back down from making sure an oil company can contain the kind of oil spill we saw in the Gulf two years ago. [*Applause.*] I will not back down from protecting our kids from mercury poisoning, or making sure that our food is safe and our water is clean. I will not go back to the days when health insurance companies had unchecked power to cancel your policy, deny your coverage, or charge women differently than men. [*Applause.*]

And I will not go back to the days when Wall Street was allowed to play by its own set of rules. The new rules we passed restore what should be any financial system's core purpose: Getting funding to entrepreneurs with the best ideas, and getting loans to responsible families who want to buy a home, or start a business, or send their kids to college.

So if you are a big bank or financial institution, you're no longer allowed to make risky bets with your customers' deposits. You're required to write out a "living will" that details exactly how you'll pay the bills if you fail—because the rest of us are not bailing you out ever again. [*Applause.*] And if you're a mortgage lender or a payday lender or a credit card company, the days of signing people up for products they can't afford with confusing forms and deceptive practices—those days are over. Today, American consumers finally have a watchdog in Richard Cordray with one job: To look out for them. [*Applause.*]

We'll also establish a Financial Crimes Unit of highly trained investigators to crack down on large-scale fraud and protect people's investments. Some financial firms violate major anti-fraud laws because there's no real penalty for being a repeat offender. That's bad for consumers, and it's bad for the vast majority of bankers and financial service professionals who do the right thing. So pass legislation that makes the penalties for fraud count.

And tonight, I'm asking my Attorney General to create a special unit of federal prosecutors and leading state attorney general to expand our investigations into the abusive lending and packaging of risky mortgages that led to the housing crisis. [*Applause.*] This new unit will hold accountable those who broke the law, speed assistance to homeowners, and help turn the page on an era of recklessness that hurt so many Americans.

Now, a return to the American values of fair play and shared responsibility will help protect our people and our economy. But it should also guide us as we look to pay down our debt and invest in our future.

Right now, our most immediate priority is stopping a tax hike on 160 million working Americans while the recovery is still fragile. [*Applause.*] People cannot afford losing $40 out of each paycheck this year. There are plenty of ways to get this done. So let's agree right here, right now: No side issues. No drama. Pass the payroll tax cut without delay. Let's get it done. [*Applause.*]

When it comes to the deficit, we've already agreed to more than $2 trillion in cuts and savings. But we need to do more, and that means making choices. Right now, we're poised to spend nearly $1 trillion more on what was supposed to be a temporary tax break for the wealthiest 2 percent of Americans. Right now, because of loopholes and shelters in the tax code, a quarter of all millionaires pay lower tax rates than millions of middle-class households. Right now, Warren Buffett pays a lower tax rate than his secretary.

Do we want to keep these tax cuts for the wealthiest Americans? Or do we want to keep our investments in everything else—like education and medical research; a strong military and care for our veterans? Because if we're serious about paying down our debt, we can't do both.

The American people know what the right choice is. So do I. As I told the Speaker this summer, I'm prepared to make more reforms that rein in the long-term costs of Medicare and Medicaid, and strengthen Social Security, so long as those programs remain a guarantee of security for seniors.

But in return, we need to change our tax code so that people like me, and an awful lot of members of Congress, pay our fair share of taxes. [*Applause.*]

Tax reform should follow the Buffett Rule. If you make more than $1 million a year, you should not pay less than 30 percent in taxes. And my Republican friend Tom Coburn is right: Washington should stop subsidizing millionaires. In fact, if you're earning a million dollars a year, you shouldn't get special tax subsidies or deductions. On the other hand, if you make under $250,000 a year, like 98 percent of American families, your taxes shouldn't go up. [*Applause.*] You're the ones struggling with rising costs and stagnant wages. You're the ones who need relief.

Now, you can call this class warfare all you want. But asking a billionaire to pay at least as much as his secretary in taxes? Most Americans would call that common sense.

We don't begrudge financial success in this country. We admire it. When Americans talk about folks like me paying my fair share of taxes, it's not because they envy the rich. It's because they understand that when I get a tax break I don't need and the country can't afford, it either adds to the deficit, or somebody else has to make up the difference—like a senior on a fixed income, or a student trying to get through school, or a family trying to make ends meet. That's not right. Americans know that's not right. They know that this generation's success is only possible because past generations felt a responsibility to each other, and to the future of their country, and they know our way of life will only endure if we feel that same sense of shared responsibility. That's how we'll reduce our deficit. That's an America built to last. [*Applause.*]

Now, I recognize that people watching tonight have differing views about taxes and debt, energy and health care. But no matter what party they belong to, I bet most Americans are thinking the same thing right about now: Nothing will get done in Washington this year, or next year, or maybe even the year after that, because Washington is broken.

Can you blame them for feeling a little cynical?

The greatest blow to our confidence in our economy last year didn't come from events beyond our control. It came from a debate in Washington over whether the United States would pay its bills or not. Who benefited from that fiasco?

I've talked tonight about the deficit of trust between Main Street and Wall Street. But the divide between this city and the rest of the country is at least as bad—and it seems to get worse every year.

Some of this has to do with the corrosive influence of money in politics. So together, let's take some steps to fix that. Send me a bill that bans insider trading by members of Congress; I will sign it tomorrow. [*Applause.*] Let's limit any elected official from owning stocks in industries they impact. Let's make sure people who bundle campaign contributions for Congress can't lobby Congress, and vice versa—an idea that has bipartisan support, at least outside of Washington.

Some of what's broken has to do with the way Congress does its business these days. A simple majority is no longer enough to get anything—even routine business—passed through the Senate. [*Applause.*] Neither party has been blameless in these tactics. Now both parties should put an end to it. [*Applause.*] For starters, I ask the Senate to pass a simple rule that all judicial and public service nominations receive a simple up or down vote within 90 days. [*Applause.*]

The executive branch also needs to change. Too often, it's inefficient, outdated and remote. [*Applause.*] That's why I've asked this Congress to grant me the authority to consolidate the federal bureaucracy, so that our government is leaner, quicker, and more responsive to the needs of the American people. [*Applause.*]

Finally, none of this can happen unless we also lower the temperature in this town. We need to end the notion that the two parties must be locked in a perpetual campaign of mutual destruction; that politics is about clinging to rigid ideologies instead of building consensus around common-sense ideas.

I'm a Democrat. But I believe what Republican Abraham Lincoln believed: That government should do for people only what they cannot do better by themselves, and no more. [*Applause.*] That's why my education reform offers more competition, and more control for schools and states. That's why we're getting rid of regulations that don't work. That's why our health care law relies on a reformed private market, not a government program.

On the other hand, even my Republican friends who complain the most about government spending have supported federally financed roads, and clean energy projects, and federal offices for the folks back home.

The point is, we should all want a smarter, more effective government. And while we may not be able to bridge our biggest philosophical differences this year, we can make real progress. With or without this Congress, I will keep taking actions that help the economy grow. But I can do a whole lot more with your help. Because when we act together, there's nothing the United States of America can't achieve. [*Applause.*] That's the lesson we've learned from our actions abroad over the last few years.

Ending the Iraq war has allowed us to strike decisive blows against our enemies. From Pakistan to Yemen, the al Qaeda operatives who remain are scrambling, knowing that they can't escape the reach of the United States of America. [*Applause.*]

From this position of strength, we've begun to wind down the war in Afghanistan. Ten thousand of our troops have come home. Twenty-three thousand more will leave by the end of this summer. This transition to Afghan lead will continue, and we will build an enduring partnership with Afghanistan, so that it is never again a source of attacks against America. [*Applause.*]

As the tide of war recedes, a wave of change has washed across the Middle East and North Africa, from Tunis to Cairo; from Sana'a to Tripoli. A year ago, Qaddafi was one of the world's longest-serving dictators—a murderer with American blood on his hands. Today, he is gone. And in Syria, I have no doubt that the Assad regime will soon discover that the forces of change cannot be reversed, and that human dignity cannot be denied. [*Applause.*]

How this incredible transformation will end remains uncertain. But we have a huge stake in the outcome. And while it's ultimately up to the people of the region to decide their fate, we will advocate for those values that have served our own country so well. We will stand against violence and intimidation. We will stand for the rights and dignity of all human beings—men and women; Christians, Muslims and Jews. We will support policies that lead to strong and stable democracies and open markets, because tyranny is no match for liberty.

And we will safeguard America's own security against those who threaten our citizens, our friends, and our interests. Look at Iran. Through the power of our diplomacy, a world that was once divided about how to deal with Iran's nuclear program now stands as one. The regime is more isolated than ever before; its leaders are faced with crippling sanctions, and as long as they shirk their responsibilities, this pressure will not relent.

Let there be no doubt: America is determined to prevent Iran from getting a nuclear weapon, and I will take no options off the table to achieve that goal. [*Applause.*]

But a peaceful resolution of this issue is still possible, and far better, and if Iran changes course and meets its obligations, it can rejoin the community of nations.

The renewal of American leadership can be felt across the globe. Our oldest alliances in Europe and Asia are stronger than ever. Our ties to the Americas are deeper. Our ironclad commitment—and I mean ironclad—to Israel's security has meant the closest military cooperation between our two countries in history. [*Applause.*]

We've made it clear that America is a Pacific power, and a new beginning in Burma has lit a new hope. From the coalitions we've built to secure nuclear materials, to the missions we've led against hunger and disease; from the blows we've dealt to our enemies, to the enduring power of our moral example, America is back.

Anyone who tells you otherwise, anyone who tells you that America is in decline or that our influence has waned, doesn't know what they're talking about. [*Applause.*]

That's not the message we get from leaders around the world who are eager to work with us. That's not how people feel from Tokyo to Berlin, from Cape Town to Rio, where opinions of America are higher than they've been in years. Yes, the world is changing. No, we can't control every event. But America remains the one indispensable nation in world affairs—and as long as I'm President, I intend to keep it that way. [*Applause.*]

That's why, working with our military leaders, I've proposed a new defense strategy that ensures we maintain the finest military in the world, while saving nearly half a trillion dollars in our budget. To stay one step ahead of our adversaries, I've already sent this Congress legislation that will secure our country from the growing dangers of cyber-threats. [*Applause.*]

Above all, our freedom endures because of the men and women in uniform who defend it. [*Applause.*] As they come home, we must serve them as well as they've served us. That includes giving them the care and the benefits they have earned—which is why we've increased annual VA spending every year I've been President. [*Applause.*] And it means enlisting our veterans in the work of rebuilding our nation.

With the bipartisan support of this Congress, we're providing new tax credits to companies that hire vets. Michelle and Jill Biden have worked with American businesses to secure a pledge of 135,000 jobs for veterans and their families. And tonight, I'm proposing a Veterans Jobs Corps that will help our communities hire veterans as cops and firefighters, so that America is as strong as those who defend her. [*Applause.*]

Which brings me back to where I began. Those of us who've been sent here to serve can learn a thing or two from the service of our troops. When you put on that uniform, it doesn't matter if you're black or white; Asian, Latino, Native American; conservative, liberal; rich, poor; gay, straight. When you're marching into battle, you look out for the person next to you, or the mission fails. When you're in the thick of the fight, you rise or fall as one unit, serving one nation, leaving no one behind.

One of my proudest possessions is the flag that the SEAL Team took with them on the mission to get bin Laden. On it are each of their names. Some may be Democrats. Some may be Republicans. But that doesn't matter. Just like it didn't matter that day in the Situation Room, when I sat next to Bob Gates—a man who was George Bush's defense secretary—and Hillary Clinton—a woman who ran against me for president.

All that mattered that day was the mission. No one thought about politics. No one thought about themselves. One of the young men involved in the raid later told me that he didn't deserve credit for the mission. It only succeeded, he said, because every single member of that unit did their job—the pilot who landed the helicopter that spun out of control; the translator who kept others from entering the compound; the troops who separated the women and children from the fight; the SEALs who charged up the stairs. More than that, the mission only succeeded because every member of that unit trusted each other—because you can't charge up those stairs, into darkness and danger, unless you know that there's somebody behind you, watching your back.

So it is with America. Each time I look at that flag, I'm reminded that our destiny is stitched together like those 50 stars and those 13 stripes. No one built this country on their own. This nation is great because we built it together. This nation is great because we worked as a team. This nation is great because we get each other's backs. And if we hold fast to that truth, in this moment of trial, there is no challenge too great; no mission too hard. As long as we are joined in common purpose, as long as we maintain our common resolve, our journey moves forward, and our future is hopeful, and the state of our Union will always be strong.

Thank you, God bless you, and God bless the United States of America. [*Applause.*]

For Dr. Shel's analysis of other outstanding speeches, visit www.askdrshel.com.

ENDNOTES

INTRODUCTION

1. Tom Baldwin, "Europe Shows Love for Barack Obama—Unfortunately It Has No Vote," *Times Online*, June 7, 2008.

2. Jonathan Freedland, *The Guardian*, "Barack Obama in Cairo: The Speech No Other President Could Make," June 4, 2009.

3. Such as in May 2008 at a Portland, Oregon, rally.

4. Caroline Kennedy, *New York Times*, "A President Like My Father," January 27, 2008.

5. Interview on ABC News, *This Week with George Stephanopoulos*, August 10, 2008.

CHAPTER 2

1. Full text of Senator Barack Obama's announcement for president, Springfield, IL, February 10, 2007.

2. Remarks of Senator Barack Obama: primary night, Raleigh, NC, May 6, 2008.

3. Remarks of Senator Barack Obama: Pennsylvania primary night, Evansville, IN, April 22, 2008.

4. Full text of Senator Barack Obama's announcement for president, Springfield, IL, February 10, 2007.

5. Remarks of Senator Barack Obama: final primary night, St. Paul, MN, June 3, 2008.

CHAPTER 3

1. Jesse Jackson, CNN interview, July 10, 2008.

2. Remarks of Senator Barack Obama: Virginia Jefferson-Jackson dinner, Richmond, VA, February 9, 2008.

3. CNN Interview immediately following the Democratic National Convention keynote address, July 27, 2004.

4. Monica Davey, *New York Times*, "As Quickly as Overnight, a Democratic Star Is Born," March 18, 2004.

5. *New York Times*, "The Democrats; The Convention in Boston—The Illinois Candidate; Day After, Keynote Speaker Finds Admirers Everywhere," July 29, 2004.

6. Remarks of Senator Barack Obama: Kennedy endorsement event, Washington, DC, January 28, 2008.

7. Davey, Monica. *New York Times*, "As Quickly as Overnight, a Democratic Star Is Born," March 18, 2004.

8. Remarks of Senator Barack Obama: AP annual luncheon, Washington, DC, April 14, 2008.

9. Remarks of Senator Barack Obama: primary night, Raleigh, NC, May 6, 2008.

10. Comments of Jamal Simmons, CNN, June 3, 2008.

11. Remarks of President Barack Obama on the death of Osama bin Laden, May 2, 2011.

12. Remarks of Senator Barack Obama: "A More Perfect Union," Philadelphia, PA, March 18, 2008.

13. Remarks of Senator Barack Obama: Kennedy endorsement event, Washington, DC, January 28, 2008.

14. Remarks of Senator Barack Obama: Kennedy endorsement event, Washington, DC, January 28, 2008.

15. State of the Union address, U.S. Capitol, Washington, DC, January 25, 2011.

16. Remarks of President Barack Obama: "On a New Beginning," Cairo, Egypt, June 4, 2009.

17. Remarks of President Barack Obama to the Joint Session of the Indian Parliament, New Delhi, India, November 8, 2010.

18. Remarks of Senator Barack Obama: discussion with working women, Albuquerque, NM, June 23, 2008.

19. Remarks of Senator Barack Obama: "A Metropolitan Strategy for America's Future," Miami, FL, June 21, 2008.

20. Remarks of President Barack Obama: "On a New Beginning," Cairo, Egypt, June 4, 2009.

21. Keynote address at the 2004 Democratic National Convention, July 27, 2004.

22. Remarks of Senator Barack Obama: "A More Perfect Union," Philadelphia, PA, March 18, 2008.

23. Remarks of Senator Barack Obama: "The Great Need of the Hour," Atlanta, GA, January 20, 2008.

24. Remarks of Senator Barack Obama: "Remembering Dr. Martin Luther King Jr.," Fort Wayne, IN, April 04, 2008.

25. State of the Union address, U.S. Capitol, Washington, DC, January 25, 2011.

CHAPTER 4

1. Remarks of Senator Barack Obama: "Our Moment Is Now," Des Moines, IA, December 27, 2007.

2. Remarks of Senator Barack Obama: South Carolina victory speech, Columbia, SC, January 26, 2008.

3. Remarks of Senator Barack Obama: "Our Moment Is Now," Des Moines, IA, December 27, 2007.

4. Remarks of Senator Barack Obama: "Our Kids, Our Future," Manchester, NH, November 20, 2007.

5. Remarks of President Barack Obama at the National Governors Association Meeting, Washington, DC, February 27, 2012.

6. Remarks of Senator Barack Obama: "A Call to Serve," Mt. Vernon, IA, December 5, 2007.

7. Remarks of President Barack Obama on American energy, Nashua, NH, March 1, 2012.

8. Remarks of Senator Barack Obama: final primary night, St. Paul, MN, June 3, 2008.

9. Remarks of Senator Barack Obama: "Our Moment Is Now," Des Moines, IA, December 27, 2007.

CHAPTER 5

1. Jessica Curry, "Obama Under the Lights," *Chicago Life Magazine*, August 1, 2004.

2. Remarks of Barack Obama at the Robert F. Kennedy Human Rights Award Ceremony, November 16, 2005.

3. Remarks of Barack Obama: final primary night, St. Paul, MN, June 3, 2008.

4. Remarks of Senator Barack Obama: Iowa caucus night, Des Moines, IA, January 3, 2008.

5. Remarks of President Barack Obama on the death of Osama bin Laden, May 2, 2011.

6. Remarks of President Barack Obama to the Joint Session of the Indian Parliament, New Delhi, India, November 8, 2010.

7. Remarks of President Barack Obama at AIPAC Policy Conference, Washington, DC, March 4, 2012.

8. Remarks of Barack Obama: Kennedy endorsement event, Washington, DC, January 28, 2008.

9. Also known as fictio.

10. Keynote address at the 2004 Democratic National Convention, July 27, 2004.

11. Remarks of Barack Obama: Iowa caucus night, Des Moines, IA, January 3, 2008.

12. Remarks of Barack Obama: "The Great Need of the Hour," Atlanta, GA, January 20, 2008.

13. Remarks of Barack Obama: "A More Perfect Union," Philadelphia, PA, March 18, 2008.

14. Remarks of President Barack Obama at the National Governors Association Meeting, Washington, DC, February 27, 2012.

15. State of the Union address, U.S. Capitol, Washington, DC, January 25, 2011.

CHAPTER 6

1. Remarks of President Barack Obama on American energy, Nashua, NH, March 1, 2012.

2. Remarks of President Barack Obama at AIPAC Policy Conference, Washington, DC, March 4, 2012.

3. Remarks of Barack Obama: final primary night, St. Paul, MN, June 3, 2008.

4. Remarks of Barack Obama: Virginia Jefferson-Jackson dinner, Richmond, VA, February 9, 2008.

5. Barack Obama's announcement for president, Springfield, IL, February 10, 2007.

6. Remarks of President Barack Obama at AIPAC Policy Conference, Washington, DC, March 4, 2012.

7. Remarks of President Barack Obama on the resignation of General Stanley McChrystal, Rose Garden, Washington, DC, June 23, 2010.

8. Remarks of President Barack Obama to the Joint Session of the Indian Parliament, New Delhi, India, November 8, 2010.

9. Remarks of President Barack Obama on the resignation of General Stanley McChrystal, Rose Garden, Washington, DC, June 23, 2010.

10. Remarks of President Barack Obama on the death of Osama bin Laden, May 2, 2011.

11. Remarks of President Barack Obama on the S&P downgrade, August 8, 2011.

12. Abraham Lincoln, Gettysburg Address.

13. State of the Union address, U.S. Capitol, Washington, DC, January 25, 2011.

14. Remarks of President Barack Obama on the S&P downgrade, August 8, 2011.

15. Remarks of President Barack Obama at AIPAC policy conference, Washington, DC, March 4, 2012.

16. Remarks of Barack Obama: Iowa caucus night, Des Moines, IA, January 3, 2008.

17. Remarks of President Barack Obama on American energy, Nashua, NH, March 1, 2012.

18. State of the Union address, U.S. Capitol, Washington, DC, January 25, 2011.

19. Full text of Senator Barack Obama's announcement for president, Springfield, IL, February 10, 2007.

20. Remarks of Barack Obama: "Our Moment Is Now," Des Moines, IA, December 27, 2007.

21. Remarks of Barack Obama: "Our Moment Is Now," Des Moines, IA, December 27, 2007.

22. Remarks of Barack Obama: New Hampshire primary, Nashua, NH, January 8, 2008.

23. Remarks of Barack Obama: South Carolina victory speech, Columbia, SC, January 26, 2008.

CHAPTER 7

1. Remarks of President Barack Obama on the resignation of General Stanley McChrystal, Rose Garden, Washington, DC, June 23, 2010.

2. Remarks of President Barack Obama at AIPAC policy conference, Washington, DC, March 4, 2012.

3. Remarks of Barack Obama: "Our Moment Is Now," Des Moines, IA, December 27, 2007.

4. Remarks of President Barack Obama on American energy, Nashua, NH, March 1, 2012.

5. Remarks of President Barack Obama to the Joint Session of the Indian Parliament, New Delhi, India, November 8, 2010.

6. Remarks of Barack Obama: Virginia Jefferson-Jackson dinner, Richmond, VA, February 9, 2008.

7. Remarks of President Barack Obama on the resignation of General Stanley McChrystal, Rose Garden, Washington, DC, June 23, 2010.

8. Remarks of President Barack Obama on the death of Osama bin Laden, May 2, 2011.

9. State of the Union address, U.S. Capitol, Washington, DC, January 25, 2011.

10. Remarks of Barack Obama: Pennsylvania primary night, Evansville, IN, April 22, 2008.

11. Remarks of Senator Barack Obama: final primary night, St. Paul, MN, June 3, 2008.

12. Remarks of Senator Barack Obama: "The Great Need of the Hour," Atlanta, GA, January 20, 2008.

CHAPTER 8

1. Remarks of Barack Obama: AP annual luncheon, Washington, DC, April 14, 2008.

CHAPTER 9

1. Remarks of Barack Obama: primary night, Raleigh, NC, May 6, 2008.

2. Remarks of Barack Obama: "A Call to Serve," Mt. Vernon, IA, December 5, 2007.

3. Remarks of Barack Obama: "Our Moment Is Now," Des Moines, IA, December 27, 2007.

4. Remarks of Barack Obama: "Our Moment Is Now," Des Moines, IA, December 27, 2007.

5. Remarks of Barack Obama: Virginia Jefferson-Jackson dinner, Richmond, VA, February 9, 2008.

6. Remarks of Barack Obama: New Hampshire primary, Nashua, NH, January 8, 2008.

7. Remarks of Barack Obama: "The Great Need of the Hour," Atlanta, GA, January 20, 2008.

8. Remarks of Barack Obama: final primary night, St. Paul, MN, June 3, 2008.

9. Remarks of Barack Obama: New Hampshire primary, Nashua, NH, January 8, 2008.

10. Barack Obama's announcement for president, Springfield, IL, February 10, 2007.

11. Remarks of Barack Obama: "Our Moment Is Now," Des Moines, IA, December 27, 2007.

Dr. Shel Leanne, a graduate of Harvard and Oxford, is the president of Regent Crest, a leadership development firm. "Dr. Shel" conducts leadership workshops and provides executive coaching for high-potential leaders. Her insights have been cited in *Newsweek* (Japan), the *Wall Street Journal*, Businessweek.com, and FastCompany.com. Her books are published in 14 languages. She worked previously for McKinsey & Company and as a Harvard faculty member. She can be contacted at www.askdrshel.com.